Catalepsy, Memory, and Suggestion in Psychological Automatism

IØI3Ø468

Pierre Janet's *L'Automatisme Psychologique*, originally published in 1889, is one of the earliest and most important books written on the study of trauma and dissociation. Here it is made available, in two volumes, in English for the first time, with a new preface by Giuseppe Craparo and Onno van der Hart.

Catalepsy, Memory, and Suggestion in Psychological Automatism, the first volume, examines three aspects of trauma and dissociation. Janet first explores catalepsy and analogous states, including comparing catalepsy to somnambulism, then discusses somnambulism, memory, and forgetting. Finally, Janet considers suggestion, amnesia, and distraction, as well as considering characteristics of suggestible individuals. Janet's work is an unsurpassed experimental study of human actions in their simplest and most rudimentary forms, and a fundamental contribution to our understanding of trauma-related dissociation.

This seminal work will be of great interest to researchers and students of psychoanalysis, philosophy, and modernism, as well as psychotherapists and psychoanalysts working with clients who have experienced trauma. It is accompanied by *Subconscious Acts, Anesthesias, and Psychological Disaggregation in Psychological Automatism: Partial Automatism*.

Pierre Janet (1859–1947) is regarded as one of the most seminal researchers, clinicians, and thinkers of the last two centuries. His work spanned the fields of psychotherapy, psychology, and philosophy.

Giuseppe Craparo, PhD, is a psychologist, psychoanalyst, and Associate Professor of clinical psychology at the Kore University of Enna, Italy.

Onno van der Hart, PhD, is a psychologist, former psychotherapist, and Emeritus Professor at Utrecht University, the Netherlands.

Catalepsy, Memory, and Suggestion in Psychological Automatism

Total Automatism

Pierre Janet

Edited by Giuseppe Craparo and Onno van der Hart

Translated by Adam Crabtree and Sarah Osei-Bonsu

Routledge
Taylor & Francis Group

LONDON AND NEW YORK

First published in English 2022
by Routledge
2 Park Square, Milton Park, Abingdon, Oxon OX14 4RN

and by Routledge
605 Third Avenue, New York, NY 10158

Routledge is an imprint of the Taylor & Francis Group, an informa business

© 2022 Giuseppe Craparo and Onno van der Hart

The right of Giuseppe Craparo and Onno van der Hart to be identified as editors of this work has been asserted by them in accordance with sections 77 and 78 of the Copyright, Designs and Patents Act 1988.

All rights reserved. No part of this book may be reprinted or reproduced or utilised in any form or by any electronic, mechanical, or other means, now known or hereafter invented, including photocopying and recording, or in any information storage or retrieval system, without permission in writing from the publishers.

Trademark notice: Product or corporate names may be trademarks or registered trademarks, and are used only for identification and explanation without intent to infringe.

L'automatisme Psychologique: Essai de Psychologie Expérimentale sur les Formes Inférieures de L'activité Humaine published in French by LIBRARIE FÉLIX ALCAN, Paris, 1889.

British Library Cataloguing-in-Publication Data
A catalogue record for this book is available from the British Library

Library of Congress Cataloging-in-Publication Data
A catalog record has been requested for this book

ISBN: 978-0-367-25416-2 (hbk)
ISBN: 978-0-367-25411-7 (pbk)
ISBN: 978-0-429-28767-1 (ebk)

DOI: 10.4324/9780429287671

Typeset in Times New Roman
by Deanta Global Publishing Services, Chennai, India

Contents

Preface to the English edition

Giuseppe Craparo and Onno van der Hart

In 1889 the great French philosopher, psychiatrist and psychologist, Pierre Janet published his master work, that is, his doctoral thesis in philosophy, *L'Automatisme Psychologique: Essai de Psychologie Expérimentale Sur Les Formes Inférieures de l'Activité Humaine*. Over time, several unsuccessful attempts have been made to translate this still often-cited book into English. Finally, one hundred and thirty-two years after the publication of *L'Automatisme Psychologique*, and eight years after the publishing of the Italian edition (2013; Francesca Ortu, transl.), the English edition (divided, for editorial reasons, into two volumes titled respectively *Catalepsy, Memory, and Suggestion in Psychological Automatism. Total Automatism* and *Subconscious Acts, Anesthesias, and Psychological Disaggregation in Psychological Automatism. Partial Automatism*), has materialized: this is an essential feat that now allows not only readers of the French and Italian languages, but a much wider audience to benefit from Janet's paramount study on hysteria and dissociation, "hailed from the start as a classic of the psychological sciences" (Ellenberger, 1970, p. 361). With ten reprints by 1929, it played a major role in the psychopathology literature during the late nineteenth and early twentieth centuries: with the rediscovery of trauma-related dissociation in psychiatry and psychology in the fourth quarter of the last century, many scientists and clinicians felt increasingly called upon to refer to the original French edition. During its centenary, John C. Nemiah, M.D. expressed this praise when, in his Editorial for the *American Journal of Psychiatry*, he stated that "the French may yet take unalloyed pride in having produced one of the most seminal psychiatric clinicians and thinkers of the last two centuries" (1989, p. 1527). Nemiah concluded his *laudatio* by claiming that "[t]he advances in psychiatric knowledge during the 100 years since [*L'Automatisme Psychologique*] was written have not improved on Janet's scientific method and vision" (p. 1529).

This book contains the fruits of experimental research performed by Janet between 1882 and 1888 in the psychiatric hospital of Le Havre – which eventually honored him by taking on his name. In these studies, he observed the "lower forms of human activity" in detail. In line with philosophers such as Maine de Biran, Henri Bergson, Hippolyte Taine, his uncle Paul Janet, and psychiatrists and psychologists such as Jacques-Joseph Moreau de Tours and

Théodule-Armand Ribot, Janet considered the concept of "activity" to lie at the core of psychic life, in relation to a hierarchical interpretation of the human mind as comprising different levels of consciousness; the higher levels include the function of reality ("the ability to act upon exterior objects and to change reality"; Ellenberger, 1970, p. 376), as well as presentification (experiencing the present as most real, as the center of one's history and expected future; cf., Janet, 1928), social and experimental actions, while the lowest level is the domain of automatism and reflexes.

For Janet, consciousness could not exist without action, nor could there be action without consciousness. Accordingly, Janet seemed to propose the construct of activity as lying at the intersection between mind, brain, and body, de facto overtaking the cartesian dualism (Descartes, 1637) separating *res cogitans* (thinking thing) from *res extensa* (extended thing): in this regard, Janet was in agreement with Spinoza (1670), for whom "The object of the idea consulting the human mind is the body" (Part II, Proposition XIII). With his mind/body model, Janet anticipated the current neuroscientific and psychological researches on embodied cognition.

This premise is necessary to understand the psychodynamic processes of his patients suffering from hysteria, such as Rose, Lucie, Marie, and Léonie, the main subjects in this book. In these and other patients, Janet regarded hypnosis, possession states, catalepsy, somnambulism, successive existences, distractions, anesthesia, paralysis, and contractures as examples of what he called psychological automatisms: automatisms because they were regular and predetermined, and psychological because they were accompanied by sensibility and consciousness (Van der Hart & Friedman, 2019).

Contrary to the psychiatrist Prosper Despine (1880), who thought that psychological automatism consisted only of mechanical acts, Janet argued that it was determined by elementary forms of consciousness. He stated:

> The term automatic refers to a movement with two characteristics. First, it should have something spontaneous about it, at least in appearance, having its source in the object itself, which moves itself and does not need an impulse from without. A mechanical doll that walks by itself would be called an automaton; a pump which one operates from the outside would not be. Next, it is necessary that the movement remains very regular, operating under a rigorous determinism, without variations or caprice. Now the principle exertions of human activity possess precisely these two characteristics: they are induced and are not created by an outside force; they originate from the subject himself, and yet they are so regular that there can be no question here of free will, which higher faculties require. But there is also another meaning we often apply to the word *automatic*, one not so easily accepted. For some authors an automatic activity is not only a regular and rigorously determined one, but also one that is purely mechanical, without consciousness.
>
> (Janet, 1889/2021, p. 1)

Regarding automatisms, Janet distinguishes total automatism and partial automatism: in total automatism, the patient's consciousness is completely dominated by a reproduction of past experience, while in partial automatism only a dissociative part of the personality is occupied by it. For instance, his patient Lucie manifested as the dominant existence or part of her personality anesthesia, while another existence or part, Adrienne, felt pain when her arm was pinched.

Both "total automatism" and "partial automatism" involve a *désagrégation* or dissociation of the personality, which accompanies a "narrowing of the field of consciousness". Together, these phenomena stem from a "decrease of the personal synthesis" (lowering of the integrative capacity). As Janet stated, in psychopathologies such as hysteria, "*the power of psychic synthesis is weakened and lets escape, apart from personal perception, quite a considerable number of psychological phenomena: it is the state of disaggregation*" (p. 77, vol. II). He contrasted this "state of psychological misery" with a state of psychological health, including a high power of mental synthesis (integrative capacity); one in which "*all psychological phenomena, whatever their origin, are united in the same personal perception*" (p. 76, vol. II). In short, Janet regarded the fundamental character of hysteria and related disorders as consisting of two interrelated aspects, that is, a "psychological désagrégation" – not a repression of unconscious sexual drives – and a narrowing of the field of consciousness. It should be noted that, while Janet used in *L'Automatisme Psychologique* the notion of disaggregation, in his previous and subsequent publications he mostly used the term dissociation, that is, in the sense of a structural dissociation of the personality, instead.

Moreover, it is important to underline that in Janet's view, *disaggregation* or dissociation *is not an active defensive mechanism* of the self. It is rather a *passive* falling away of higher mental functions ("psychological misery") consequent to vehement emotions evoked in situations, often of a threatening nature such as traumatizing events, with which the individual is unable to cope. As Janet stated in his Autobiography,

> These events, which had established a violent emotion and a destruction of the psychological system, had left traces. The remembrance of these events, the mental work involved in their recall and settlement, persisted in the form of lower and more or less conscious psychological processes, absorbed a great deal of strength, and played a part in the persistent weakening. Here still, if I am not mistaken, this notion has been fruitful and has given rise to a whole theory of neurosis and psychosis by the subconscious persistence of an emotional traumatism...
>
> (1930, p. 128)

From Janet's clinical perspective, hysterical symptoms originate from vehement emotions ("*emotions véhémentes*" or "*émotions violentes*") inherent in traumatic experiences which have a disintegrating effect on one's personality. There exists some misunderstanding in the literature with regard to Janet's emphasis on lowered integrative capacity in patients suffering of hysteria, that is, dissociation of the personality. This misunderstanding may be attributed to Breuer and Freud (1895/1974), who highlighted Janet's view on a constitutional weakness in this regard, which they contrasted with their emphasis on the pathogenic role of traumatic experiences (while eventually also recognizing the role of constitutional factors). Indeed, Janet was clear in his view that people are differently endowed with regard to the integrative capacity. However, he did notice the pathogenic or dissolving role of traumatic experiences in lowering this capacity. Still, being the careful researcher that he was, he was reluctant to generalize too easily, and noticed that extreme exhaustion and serious illness could also have this effect. In fact, in his books published between 1889 and 1904, he determined traumatic experiences as an etiological factor in 257 cases out of 591 (the majority not suffering from hysteria but rather psychasthenia) (Crocq & De Verbizier, 1989).

Trauma-related disaggregation or dissociation of the personality manifested in dissociative "existences," which he also called "personalities," "parts of the personality," or "selves" – some of which he also labeled as subconscious "fixed ideas" (subsequently called "complexes" by, for instance, Jung). They remain isolated from personal consciousness and control of the presenting part of the personality, thus having a more or less autonomous life and development. In both total and partial automatism, these "fixed ideas" have their own, at least rudimentary "sense and idea of self" (*idée du moi*) and continue to exist at a subconscious level. From his patient Léonie, for example, Janet learned about her "successive existences" or, in modern parlance, alternating dissociative parts of her personality, and from Marie, that such a part was involved in her dissociative anesthesia. These "existences" all included their own subconscious memories. Thus, nowadays we would like to emphasize that the development of these "existences," "parts of the personality," etc., does not involve a mere falling apart of psychological elements but also a lower-order kind of integrative actions (Van der Hart & Rydberg, 2019): otherwise only chaos would remain.

It should be remembered that it was Janet (1910) who coined the term *subconscious* – not be confused with the notion of the Freudian unconscious. Indeed, unlike the Freudian unconscious, which is the seat of all drives, the Janetian subconsciousness has this fundamental characteristic: subconscious are all those mental functions and contents which exist outside the individual's personal consciousness. In traumatized individuals, these functions and contents outside their narrowed field of consciousness are dissociative in nature: they involve the existence of dissociative parts of the personality and their subconscious fixed ideas (cf. Bühler & Heim, 2009; Ellenberger, 1970).

We are delighted and immensely grateful that, finally, clinicians and researchers in the field of trauma and dissociation who are unfamiliar with the French language will be able to read this fundamental publication, written by Pierre Janet, the father of contemporary psychotraumatology, and be inspired by it.

References

Breuer, J., & Freud, S. (1895). Studies on hysteria. *S.E.*, 2, 19–305. London: Hogarth, 1975.

Bühler, K.-E., & Heim, G. (2009). Psychopathological approaches in Pierre Janet's conception of the subconscious. *Psychopathology*, 42(3), 190–200.

Crocq, L., & De Verbizier, J. (1989). Le traumatisme psychologique dans l'oeuvre de Pierre Janet. *Annales Médico-Psychologiuques*, 147, 983–987.

Descartes, R. (1637). *Meditations on first philosophy*. Cambridge: Cambridge University Press, 1986.

Ellenberger, H. F. (1970). *The discovery of the unconscious: The history and evolution of dynamic psychiatry*. New York: Basic Books.

Janet, P. (1910). Le subconscient. *Scientia*, 4(7), 64–79.

Janet, P. (1928). *L'évolution de la mémoire et de la notion du temps*. Paris: A. Chahine.

Janet, P. (1930). Pierre Janet autobiography. In: C. Murchison (Ed.), *History of psychology in autobiography* (Vol. 1, pp. 123–133). Worchester, MA: Clark University Press.

Nemiah, J. C. (1989). Janet redivivus: The centenary of *L'automatisme Psychologique*. *American Journal of Psychiatry*, 146(12), 1527–1529.

Spinoza, B. (1670). *Tractatus theologicus politicus*. Hamburg: Heinrich Künrath.

Van der Hart, O., & Friedman, B. (2019). A reader's guide to Pierre Janet: A neglected intellectual heritage. In: G. Craparo, F. Ortu, O. van der Hart (Eds.), *Rediscovering Pierre Janet: Trauma, dissociation, and a new context for psychoanalysis* (pp. 4–27). London and New York: Routledge.

Acknowledgments

We are very much indebted to Sarah Osei-Bonsu and Adam Crabtree for their hard work and dedication to do as much justice as possible to the original text in their superb translation. Where others before them gave up in their translation attempts at some point, Sarah and Adam succeeded and hopefully have experienced what Janet called acts of triumph.

The realization of the English-language edition of this book is made possible by generous donations of the European Society for Trauma and Dissociation, International Society for the Study of Trauma and Dissociation, the Association Française Pierre Janet (AFPJ), the Institut Européen de Thérapies Somato-Psychiques (represented by its cofounders, Bernard Mayer and Françoise Pasqualin, President of AFPJ) and the following colleagues: Orit Badouk Epstein, Suzette Boon, Danny Brom, Martin Dorahy, Alessandro Lombardo, Elizabeth Howell, Sheldon Itzkowitz, Bessel van der Kolk, Andreas Laddis, Harriet Mall, Dolores Mosquera, Ellert Nijenhuis, Pat Ogden, Roger Solomon, and Kathy Steele – to whom we express our deep gratitude.

We wish to thank Gerhard Heim, Andrew Moskowitz, Francesca Ortu, Jenny Ann Rydberg, and Isabelle Saillot for their precious advice and comments. We are also very grateful for the support, including precious editorial work, we received from Jayanthi Chander and Susannah Frearson at Routledge during the production process.

Introduction

It is nearly always the more lofty forms of human activity – will, resoluteness, free choice – that are studied by philosophers. Naturally, we are interested in the manifestations of the activity that has been most useful for helping us understand the conduct of humanity, their responsibility, and the moral value of their actions. But although this way of approaching the question may perhaps be the most natural, it is also the most difficult and dangerous, since the most elevated and most important phenomena are far from being the simplest. On the contrary, they present modifications and accessory developments that prevent their true nature from being well understood. Today, in psychology and the other sciences, we prefer to study the most elementary facts, because we know that this more easily attainable knowledge will greatly clarify the more complex forms. It is *human activity in its simplest and most rudimentary forms* that will be the object of this study.

This elementary activity, whether noted in animals or studied in subjects by psychiatrists, has been designated by a name that is important to maintain – that of *automatic activity*. This name, even according to its etymological sense (αὐτὸς, self, μάτος, effort, from which μάομαι or μχίομχι, to try, to make an effort, Littré) appears to apply just as much to the individuals who undertake these actions. The term automatic refers to a movement with two characteristics. First, it should have something spontaneous about it, at least in appearance, having its source in the object itself, which moves itself and does not need an impulse from without. A mechanical doll that walks by itself would be called an automaton; a pump which one operates from the outside would not be. Next, it is necessary that the movement remain very regular, operating under a rigorous determinism, without variations or caprice. Now the principle exertions of human activity possess precisely these two characteristics: they are induced and are not created by an outside force; they originate from the subject themselves, and yet they are so regular that there can be no question here of free will, which higher faculties require. But there is also another meaning we often apply to the word *automatic*, one not so easily accepted. For some authors an automatic activity is not only a regular and rigorously determined one, but also one that is purely mechanical, without consciousness. This signification has been the origin of numerous confusions, and many philosophers refuse to recognize an

DOI: 10.4324/9780429287671-101

automatism in the human mind, which is real and without which many phenomena are inexplicable, because they believe that to admit automatism is to suppress consciousness and reduce man to a pure mechanism of extended, feelingless elements. We believe that one can accept both automatism and consciousness at the same time, and thereby give satisfaction to those who recognize that there is an elementary form of activity in man that is as completely determined as an automaton, and to those who want to retain consciousness and sensibility for man even in his simplest actions. In other words, it does not seem to us that the exterior manifestations of a living being in movement can be separated from some kind of intelligence and an associated consciousness accompanying that activity from within, and *our goal is to not only to demonstrate that there is a human activity that merits the name "automatic," but also that it is legitimate to call it a psychological automatism.*

Those philosophers who have considered activity as a psychological phenomenon, but who have examined it only in its most perfect manifestations, have very clearly separated it from other phenomena of the mind and have considered it as a peculiar faculty distinct from intelligence and sensibility. Without doubt, complicated phenomena that, as they develop, acquire a host of precise characteristics, do clearly separate themselves from each other, and it is certainly not legitimate to confuse abstract reasoning with practical accomplishment. But do not these faculties, so different when they manifest, come together in their origin? Do they not arise from a lower form of life and consciousness where activity, sensibility, and intelligence are totally fused? This is what we believe we can establish, and *for us the study of the elementary forms of activity will be, at one and the same time, the study of the elementary forms of sensation and consciousness.*

Another characteristic always attributed to higher activity is that of unity: the power of will which appears to be as single and indivisible as the person that manifests it. It is impossible to comprehend human actions if one tries to represent all activities within this model. Unity and systematization seem to us to be the end, not the point of departure, of thought. The automatism we are studying often manifests through sentiments and multiple actions that are independent of each other, before giving way to a single, personal will. From this starting point, we can set forth the general divisions of our work. *We will first study automatism in its simplest form, when it is complete* and occupies the whole mind; that is to say, when we note only one thought and one single automatic action in the mind of a person. But it will then be necessary for us to admit that in many cases automatism can be partial and only occupy a part of the mind, when many elementary activities can develop simultaneously in the same thought.

Finally, human activity sometimes presents itself in abnormal forms, incoherent and convulsive movements, unconscious acts which are unknown even to the very one who carries them out, and impulsive desires which are contrary to the will and which the subject cannot resist. These irregularities are incomprehensible if one only knows the theory of the will as free and unitary. Will they become more intelligible through the examination of lower forms of activity? The study of these abnormal activities will permit us to complete and verify the solutions that will be given to the preceding problems.

The method we have tried to use, without claiming to have succeeded, is the method of the natural sciences. Without bringing preconceived ideas to this problem, we have collected the facts, that is, the simple actions we wanted to study, through observation. We have only formulated those hypotheses that are necessary to account for well-observed facts, and, insofar as possible, we have verified the consequences of these hypotheses through experimentation. An investigation of this kind cannot be carried out by means of personal observations of events as they occur in one's own consciousness. Indeed, it is difficult to make the phenomena that present themselves to us the object of regular experimentation. They are much too complicated and they occur in a milieu of circumstances that are numerous and difficult to delineate. In addition, and above all, they are always incomplete. Consciousness does not give us knowledge of all the psychological phenomena that take place in us, and we hope to reconfirm this indisputable truth. It is because of this that psychologists encounter grave difficulties when they attempt to confine themselves to personal observation of consciousness. When one wants to show that there are "uniformities of succession among states of mind," when, in a word, one wants to make psychology a science analogous to the other sciences, one is stopped by this difficulty: "that in a series of associations one continually runs into unconscious representations."[1] Since for many authors an unconscious phenomenon is uniquely physiological, they continually appeal to physiology and its laws to explain the phenomena of mind. Although this appeal may often be useful, it seems to us that it is sometimes premature, because then, on the one hand, psychology gives up trying to discover the true laws of mental phenomena, and, on the other hand, physiology simply notes coincidences between mental and physical facts and does not really explain the laws of consciousness. Stuart Mill, when he supported the legitimacy of a scientific psychology[2] against Auguste Comte, responded in a confused way to this difficulty. In fact, the difficulty is insoluble if we only accept as legitimate phenomena of consciousness the incomplete facts furnished by personal consciousness. In order to have simple, precise, and complete phenomena, it is necessary to observe them in others and appeal to objective psychology. It is true that we know psychological phenomena in others only indirectly and psychology cannot begin this way. But we can infer their existence from acts, gestures, and language, just as the chemist determines the elements of the stars from the rays of the spectrum, and the certainty of one set of operations is as great as the other. Our study of automatism, therefore, will be an essay in experimental and objective psychology.

One of the great advantages that observation of others has over personal observation is that we can choose the subjects we wish to study and take precisely those who show the phenomena we want to examine most closely. But individuals who present a phenomenon or characteristic hardly ever found in normal persons to such an exceptional degree are inevitably going to be ill. This is, I believe, not at all inconvenient. It is necessary to accept in mental matters that great principle universally accepted by physicists since Claude Bernard, that the laws of the ill are the same as those of the healthy, and that in the ill one finds only an exaggeration or diminution of certain phenomena that are already found in the healthy. If one knows the mentally ill well, there will be no difficulty studying normal psychology. Moreover, from another point of view, "man is known only by half if he is only observed in health. The state of illness constitutes as important a part of his mental existence as of his physical existence."[3] It is not a bad thing that psychology goes into the details of various mental perturbations, instead of always staying with generalities that are too abstract to be of any practical use. That is why an experimental psychology will necessarily be, from many points of view, an abnormal psychology.

All experimentation supposes that one varies the phenomena and the conditions in which they present themselves. The illness produces some of the modifications for us, but in a manner too slow and in conditions that are not very precise. One can only create genuine psychological experiments if one artificially changes the state of consciousness of a person in a manner that is determined and calculated beforehand. Moreau (de Tours), a very philosophical psychiatrist, claimed that he obtained this result by means of hashish intoxication. "This was," he says, "an excellent means of experimenting with the origin of madness."[4] Although I entirely share the enthusiasm for psychological experimentation which Moreau (de Tours) was among the first to voice, I do not agree with the method he used. Having assisted (but once, it is true) with an intoxication produced by hashish, I found that the physical disturbance caused by this substance was too grave and destructive to justify the small psychological gain. Besides, the mental modifications obtained in this way were not under the control of the experimenter and could not be directed by him. Also, this method of psychological experimentation is in reality hardly practical.

By contrast, there is a state that is easy to bring about and not at all dangerous in which mental modifications are obtained very easily, and which Moreau would have preferred to all others if he had known of it – the state of artificial somnambulism. Already Maine de Biran, one of the precursors of scientific psychology, in his novel investigations of sleep, dreams and somnambulism, was insistent on the advantages to be obtained from the study of these phenomena. He interested himself in the experiments of the magnetizers of his time, and he followed their séances and frequently spoke about them.

Later, Taine also pointed out the uses of somnambulism in psychology.[5] Moreover, we know the work of Jouffroy de Maury and many other psychologists on the subject. The magnetizers were insistent on the advantages of their procedures: "In giving us the means to functionally separate the diverse inner workings of thought, to reduce its exercise to its elementary operations..., also, in teaching us *to bring forward* an entire class of modes of being of the faculties of the soul, Braidism provided an experimental basis for psychology which has since become a positive science and taken its place in the broadened framework of animal physiology."[6] Nevertheless, unjustifiable prejudices and the fear of the label of charlatanism, which has become associated with the operations of animal magnetism, have for a long time hampered following this advice. It has taken all the works and all the discoveries of the contemporary scientists whose names are well known to put beyond doubt the existence of nervous sleep and the advantages that science can derive from its study. We will not discuss here the genuineness of somnambulism nor the danger of simulation; this discussion would be long and especially trite, since one can find that already done very well elsewhere. Moreover, we believe, as does Dr. Despine, who has studied somnambulism in depth, that, "to hold the facile opinion that these things are fraudulent is an easy way to dispense oneself from studying what one does not comprehend." It suffices to set up certain precautions, which each experimenter should be able to take according to circumstances, in order to guard against attempts at deception, which, in my opinion, are rarer than generally believed. Also, without insisting on this point, we are speaking only about those conditions we have used ourselves in our investigation of hypnotic sleep.

The subjects on whom these studies have been conducted were almost all, except where we indicate otherwise, women suffering from nervous illnesses which were more or less serious, particularly from the multifaceted illness that goes under the name of hysteria. These neuroses – having as their principal characteristic a great mental instability – offer us, both by the natural opportunities that they provide and by the predisposition for somnambulism they engender, most favourable ground for psychological experimentation and especially for the study of automatism. However, the study of subjects of this kind presents special difficulties. They are extremely changeable, and without even speaking about their tendency to deceive (which has been ascribed to them with some exaggeration), they are not always in the same physical and mental state. It is necessary to stay with them for a long time and, with great concentration, "to study them not for a moment, but in all phases of their illness"[7] in order to know exactly in what circumstances and under what conditions one is experimenting. Then too, because of their plasticity, they easily submit to all external influences and change themselves very rapidly according to the books one gives them to read or the words one imprudently speaks in their presence. Because of this characteristic, it is impossible to do an experiment with them that has any value if one studies them on one occasion only, at random, without knowing exactly their state of illness, their character, their preconceived ideas, etc. It is equally impossible to establish any natural fact if one questions them in public or if one makes known to persons present what experiment one is doing or the outcome one expects. It is necessary to study them often and to always experiment alone or with competent persons who are acquainted with the questions in advance and who are familiar with the indispensable precautions that must be used.

These are the conditions we have tried to fulfill in the investigations we are going to present. They were carried out on fourteen hysterical and hypnotizable women, on five men suffering from the same illness, and on eight other individuals who suffer from insanity or epilepsy. The number of subjects could easily have been increased had we not wanted to experiment only on closely observed subjects whose physical and mental state could be completely ascertained.Moreover, it was not necessary to cite separately the experiments done on all these subjects. Since many of them were identical to each other, we did not learn anything new, and giving their names and characteristics would uselessly complicate our presentation. It seemed to us that it was preferable to repeat, when possible, the greater part of the experiences of a small number of subjects who, once they are well known, would be cited in preference to the others. That is why, apart from some particular cases, most of the facts referred to describe four principal subjects designated by first names rather than letters: Léonie, Lucie, Rose and Marie.[8] These four persons, more than the rest, seem to us to fulfill the conditions of a useful psychological experiment. Since they have been studied over a long period of time, the details of their illness and character are well known. Having been examined with care and only by competent persons, they have been least affected by examples they might imitate or by imprudent words.

None of our precautions could have been taken and none of our studies would have been possible had we not been sustained in our work by persons very capable of handling this kind of undertaking. Studies of the mental individual are really not possible for philosophers today without the help of those devoted to the study of the physical individual. The psychologist cannot grapple with the experimental study of the phenomena of consciousness without the physician, who shows him which subjects are suffering from the particular illness that he needs to observe, and who forewarns him about possible mishaps and constantly gives him the benefit of his experience. Although this association of physicians and psychologists today might be quite common, I cannot refrain from mentioning how much help and encouragement was given me by the physicians of Le Havre. I would especially like to express my thanks and affection to Dr. Gilbert and Dr. Powilewicz who, notwithstanding the difficulties and anxieties such research can cause, were willing to take part in my work. If the observations reported in this book, perhaps more than the theories proposed here, are of some value or interest, it is to them that the principle credit should be given.

Le Havre
December 1888

Notes

1 Lange, *Histoire du Matérialisme.* Trans., 1877, II, 42.
2 Mill, *Logique.* Trans., 1880, II, 433.
3 Broussais, *De l'Irritation et de la Folie*, 26.
4 Moreau (de Tours), *Du Haschich et de l'Aliénation Mentale*, 1845, 30.
5 Taine, *De l'Intelligence*, 1878, 1, 5.

6 Dr. Philips (Durand de Gros), *Cours Théorique et Pratique de Braidisme ou Hypnotisme Nerveux*, 1860, 169.
7 Despine, *Du Somnambulisme Étudié au Point de Vue Scientifique*, 1880, 322.
8 In order not to hamper our psychological studies with accessory descriptions, we will put in an appendix some medical and biographical details which will be useful to know about the principal subjects we cite.

Chapter 1

Isolated psychological phenomena

Condillac, when he undertook to analyze the human mind, imagined an ingenious method to clarify and simplify some of the complex phenomena that present themselves to consciousness. He supposed an animated statue, capable of experiencing every emotion and understanding all thoughts, but having none at first, and, into this absolutely empty mind, he imagined introducing sensations, one after the other and in isolation. It was an excellent scientific approach. The multiplicity of phenomena that interact with each other in the universe prevents us from knowing their relationships and their dependencies. Now by the stroke of a magic wand, let us remove all these phenomena, and in this absolute emptiness, reproduce, in isolation, a single fact. As a result, nothing will be easier to see than the role and consequences of this phenomenon. They will show themselves to us without confusion. This is the ideal method of science, and Condillac hoped to apply it to the mind. Unfortunately, this method, theoretically so beautiful, was completely impracticable, for the philosopher did not possess the statue of which he spoke and did not know how to reduce a consciousness to its elementary phenomena. Also, he did his experiment in imagination, instead of questioning nature and paying attention to the answer. He himself made up the questions and the answers, and in place of the analysis he hoped to obtain, he substituted a completely artificial construction.

Fortunately, we are actually able to reproduce the very experience that Condillac dreamed of but could not bring about. We have available true living statues whose minds are empty of thoughts and we can introduce into this consciousness, one by one, the phenomena whose psychological development we desire to study. Thanks to a state of illness, long known by physicians but little examined by philosophers, we are in possession of this statue. It is the nervous disease most often referred to as *catalepsy* that will provide us with these abrupt and complete suppressions, and the consequent gradual restorations of awareness, that we want to have available for our experiments. "Catalepsy," says Saint-Bourdin (one of the first authors who made a precise study of this disease), "is a condition of the brain, intermittent, apyretic, characterized by the suspension of understanding and sensitivity, and the ability of the muscles to receive and maintain any degree of contraction given to them."[1] This definition, while not perfect, gives a fair general

DOI: 10.4324/9780429287671-1

idea of the maladaptive state that occurs naturally in some predisposed individuals following a shock or emotion, and can be artificially produced in some subjects by various well known methods. There is no need to become engaged, at least at the beginning of this work, in seeking the origin of this state. We can say of catalepsy what Ballet said about language disorders: "It does not matter to us whether this or that disorder of speech or writing is produced by a tumor, a softening of focus, or a toxic agent. 'The wheels of a watch,' says Buzzard, 'may as well be stopped by a hair as by a grain of sand; the disorder that arises remains the same, whatever the cause that produced it.'"[2] We can thus examine the psychological state produced by this disease, without worrying about its origin.

No doubt a person with catalepsy will not have the ideal simplicity of the statue of Condillac. The state will be more or less perfect, and its interpretation will always raise problems. But a real experiment, even if it presents some obscurity, is worth a hundred times more than a simple but imaginary theory. Let us begin, therefore, according to our method, by describing this state and its most general characteristics. We will then review the various interpretations that are possible and the hypothesis that seems most likely. Finally, returning to experience, we will verify the consequences of this hypothesis in the details and varieties that this maladaptive state can present. Thus, we will have described and interpreted a state where, as Condillac said, the phenomena of consciousness present themselves, as we believe, in an isolated state.

1.1 Description of phenomena evoked during the cataleptic state

It is unfortunate to begin our description of states where psychological automatism shows itself by describing a state that is quite rare and experiments which cannot easily be repeated. However, this should not surprise us. We want to study at first very simple phenomena, yet nature always presents complex things. Nothing is more complicated than a normal mind, and similarly nothing is more complicated than madness or a crisis of ordinary hysteria. We are forced to choose rare phenomena if we want them to be simple. Also, although we have ourselves observed a fairly large number of people affected by these nervous diseases in which the cataleptic state can occur, we have never witnessed a crisis of natural catalepsy that was absolutely complete. Those we have seen were only imperfect varieties. We have only collected the description of two natural crises; one was observed in Paris at the hospital of La Pitié by my brother Jules Janet, and the other was produced by a bolt of lightning on a subject that I knew, but I did not witness the event. I have been able to observe artificial catalepsies more frequently, but on three subjects only.

Catalepsy could sometimes be evoked in Lucie by suddenly showing her a bright magnesium light, or by slightly compressing her eyes during somnambulism. Catalepsy naturally occurred sometimes during the somnambulism of Rose or Léonie. It was also produced when they, emerging from somnambulism, opened their eyes to the light. All the other individuals I studied only presented varieties of the state called somnambulism, or catalepsies so transient that we would, as has often happened, disregard them. It is therefore necessary to describe this state from the few artificial catalepsies that we have been able to examine. Some citations will show that they do not differ in their essential traits from natural catalepsy.

So, whatever the means used to produce catalepsy, let us examine the features the subject presents; and let us choose, as an example, the catalepsy of Léonie, since hers is quite complete and comes closest to the classical description.[3] The first and most obvious characteristic is the absolute immobility of the subject. A normal person cannot remain for several minutes without any movement. Some movements of the hands, eyelids, lips, or some light skin tremors always manifest the activity of thought and feeling relating to external things. Léonie, on the contrary, in the state we describe, invariably preserves the attitude in which catalepsy overtook her, without the smallest tremor revealing consciousness and thought. The eyes themselves are wide open, without any blinking of the eyelids, remaining fixed in the same direction. In a nutshell, the movements of organic life, pulse beats and breathing, alone remain, and all the movements that depend on the life of relationship and which express consciousness are removed. If we do not intervene and especially if we abstain from touching the subject, this state persists without any modification for long periods of time. We have seen natural catalepsies last for days and artificial catalepsies continue for several hours. In the subjects that I study, this state never lasts long and does not extend more than a quarter hour; it naturally changes and stops presenting this character of absolute mental inertia.

As long as subjects remain cataleptic, we can perform various experiments with them which help us establish important characteristics. These characteristics, which are the consequence of the previously described inertia, can be reduced to four main ones; we will describe them briefly because they are all well known.

1. *The continuation or persistence of all the modifications* that can be produced in the state of the subject. If we touch the limbs, we realize that they are extremely mobile and, so to speak, light, that they offer no resistance, and that we can very easily move them. If we leave them in a new position, they do not fall back according to the laws of gravity; they remain absolutely motionless in the position where we left them. The arms, legs, head, and trunk of the subject can be put in any position, even the strangest, so that these subjects are naturally compared to painted mannequins that we can place in any pose. Even Léonie's face is susceptible to modification in this way. If one opens her mouth or raises or lowers her eyebrows, her form, like a mask of wax, lets itself be moulded and preserves the new expression. For others, the muscles of the abdomen themselves preserve the imprint of a hand.[4] There are many different studies of great importance dealing with these cataleptic attitudes. With precision devices, one can see that these postures

remain invariable. In contrast to the inevitable shaking that occurs very quickly in the extended arm of a normal individual, the limbs of these individuals stay in the air for a long time without moving. Instead of producing an acceleration and a change in the respiratory rhythm, as always happens in the normal person, this fatiguing position of the arm does not change the slow movement of the chest.[5] Only after a long time, one hour or more, according to some authors, twenty or twenty-five minutes according to others, does the arm begin to descend due to fatigue or muscle wear; but this descent is very slow and regular without the jolts and oscillations that we see in normal individuals. Since the catalepsy of Léonie did not last more than a quarter of an hour, I did not observe this descent, which would have probably started a little later.

These "poses" are among the best-known and most characteristic phenomena of natural catalepsy, as these few observations show. Here is a quotation extracted from a description of Laennec and Maisonneuve reported by Saint-Bourdin:[6] "He speaks to her, but she does not hear; he touches her, but she does not seem to feel it; he raises an arm, the arm remains in the position where he put it; the patient was trained to stand, neck bent, one leg lifted, and maintain the given position." Here is another by Saint-Bourdin:[7] "She kept the same attitude she had at the instant of the attack: if she was standing, she remained there; if she was going up the steps, she had a leg elevated to lift her; and during all the time of catalepsy she maintained the same attitude. During this state, raising one of her arms, turning her head, putting her on one foot with her arms extended, one could place her in any position, provided the body was in balance, she kept perfectly to the end the last attitude she had been given." It is true, however, that natural catalepsy does not always exhibit this flexibility, which is very nearly always present in artificial catalepsy. "In other patients, the body is in such a state of rigidity that, if pushed, they fall without changing their attitude."[8] We will have to return to this difference. Let us just notice that stiffness, apparent contracture of the members, still maintains here a characteristic aspect and is properly cataleptic. The contracture is not general, that is to say, it does not invade all the muscles in the same way and to the highest degree, because it would then arise as a special attitude always the same, as is well described in the tetanus attack or in some epileptic seizures: the body would be extended, curved back, the limbs extended, the wrists along the body and bent inwards, the fists closed, etc. Muscles, on the other hand, are contracted to different degrees, giving the body an expressive attitude, as in the case of Saint-Bourdin cited above, where the body stiffened in the attitude of prayer, knees bent and hands clasped, could be reversed without changing posture. This detail is important to distinguish catalepsy from a true general contracture.

Another modification that can be imposed on cataleptic members is movement. If, instead of placing the arm in a state of immobility, one makes it oscillate two or three times and lets go in the middle of the movement, the oscillation persists, whereas before, the position persisted. We can thus communicate to the arms, legs, or head of this manikin a movement that will not stop before the end of the attack. The same character is found again, although perhaps less often reported, in descriptions of natural catalepsy: "A five-year-old girl, having been deeply shocked one day that her sister had, in the course of the meal, removed the choice morsel she herself wanted, suddenly became stiff. She had extended her hand with her spoon in toward the dish and remained in this state. She looked at her sister with eyes of indignation. Although she was addressed loudly and excitedly, she did not hear; she moved neither mouth nor lips; *she walked when she was pushed and was led with the hand.*"[9]

We could also reference among cataleptics persistent sensations or even images. Léonie or Lucie will remain indefinitely with their eyes fixed on a light that has been shined on them. These phenomena are difficult to study in cataleptics and will become clearer as we proceed. What we have reported is sufficient to verify this first character of catalepsy: the continuation and persistence of all modifications imposed on the subject.

2. *Imitation or repetition.* Instead of touching the subject, let us place ourselves in front of the subject, in the direction of her gaze, and perform a movement ourselves instead of moving her members. Slowly Léonie will move and place her arm and then her whole body exactly in the position we took. This phenomenon is called *specular or mirror imitation*, because the subject ordinarily imitates with their left arm the movement we are performing with the right arm and looks like our own image in a mirror. The fact is however not absolutely general, because, if Léonie imitates in this way, Lucie, in these same imitations, does not reverse attitudes; and her catalepsy is much less complete. Instead of performing an action in the subject's view, we can affect her hearing, or at least this appears to be the case. We will not study this phenomenon in Léonie, who barely manifests it, but move on to Rose, where it is quite complete. If I speak loudly next to her while she's in a cataleptic state, she repeats my words exactly, with the same intonation. This fact has been called *echolalia* or *word echo*. It is very curious; the subject changes, so to speak, into a phonograph and repeats all the sounds that strike her ear, without seeming to be affected in the least by the meaning of the words. Normally the sounds are repeated with the mouth, but in one case, Dr. Powilewicz, then present, having clapped his hands, Rose repeated the noise, also clapping her hands: here echolalia is mixed with imitation.

3. *Generalization or expression of phenomena.* Most often changes imposed on the subject remain partial and affect only one member, but sometimes, when the cataleptic state is complete, they show a tendency to generalize and to affect the whole body. Jules Janet has observed a natural cataleptic who always repeated with his left arm what was done to his right arm and vice versa. This is the phenomenon of *synkinesis* that I only observed in Léonie and for certain acts only. If I close one fist, the other is closed in the same way. If I raise her hand in front of

her in the prayer position, the other hand takes the same position and rests against the first. Movements which complete each other in this way are, for her, acts that are familiar and usual.

These same habitual acts are likely to become much more widespread and to cause a change in the whole body of the subject. This is one of the best-known and most popular phenomena of catalepsy, if we can say so, because it always produces an extraordinary spectacle. We see the figure, the whole body, come alive, harmonize with the attitude of one of the members, and create a striking expression of reality. If I close one of Léonie's fists, the other also closes, the arms rise in the position of the attack, the body straightens, the expression changes; tight lips, clenched fists, and frowning express only anger. If I place my extended hand close to my lips, she also places her hand there and seems to send kisses. Her attitude suddenly changes and, instead of expressing fury, lips and eyes and everything smiles. We can change these attitudes indefinitely with these plastic poses and make the subject express love, prayer, terror, or mockery, always with equal perfection. To go from one attitude to another, it is enough to slightly modify one of the gestures of the body. With Léonie, it is even enough to touch the muscles of her face.[10] In the case of Léonie, her face is cataleptic like the rest of her body. It is enough to raise her eyebrows so that they stay as they have been placed, and they bring into the whole body the attitude of terror. The expression is no less violent because it is evoked by such an insignificant cause.

4. *Association of states with each other.* Until now, the subject has had nothing of her own and has never come out of the state in which she had been placed. We must now note cases in which the scene played out is much more complete and more developed. I put Léonie's hands in the attitude of prayer and her countenance takes an ecstatic expression. I leave her in this state because I want to wait to see how long the expression will be retained. I see her getting up from the seat where she is sitting and very slowly move two steps forward. At this moment, she bends her knees, but always with a marked slowness; she kneels and leans forward, with head bowed and eyes raised to heaven in a wonderfully ecstatic posture. Will she stay that way and, when the attitude is completed, maintain cataleptic immobility? No; next she rises without my touching her, drops her head further and puts her clasped hands in front of her mouth. She advances five or six steps, even more slowly than before. What is she doing? Here she performs a respectful greeting, kneels once more, and raises her head slightly and, with half-closed eyes, opens her lips. This gives one the impression that she is going to communion. Next, having made communion, she rises, performs another greeting, and, with her head completely inclined, returns to kneel in her original position. This whole scene, having lasted a quarter of an hour, then terminates with the end of the cataleptic state.

This is the most complicated act I have seen during catalepsy. We note that it consists of successive phenomena that evoke one another, instead of being, as before, merely the continuation of the same modification. It is important to compare this with other actions evoked through a particular meaning which have the character of being composed of successive actions that are distinguished one from the other. If joyful music is played in the presence of the subject, she laughs, then begins to dance. Sad music makes her cry. If you put a piece of thread in Léonie's hand, she performs the gesture of threading a needle and beginning to sew. If you put a pencil in her hand, she makes the gesture of writing, but only dashes, indefinitely. If you put an umbrella in her hand, she opens it and holds it over her head, etc. "A natural cataleptic, studied by Forestier, greedily ate (*vorabat*) everything placed in her mouth."[11] One finds, in works that deal with catalepsy, a great number of these complex and connected actions. I only want to briefly bring to mind those cataleptic phenomena that are well known, but which seem to me of great importance at the beginning of a study of automatism. As Charcot says,[12] "In true catalepsy there is absolute mental inertia…; the best method for studying hypnotic suggestion is to start from there."

1.2 The mechanical or physical interpretation of these phenomena

Can the phenomena that we have just described be of interest to psychology? That is the first question one ought to pose in considering cataleptics. Do these immobile women, statue-like, without resistance of any kind and without speech, nevertheless think? Do they have some kind of consciousness that connects them to us? One might very well doubt that and ask whether their organic life alone, which is the only thing that seems to be operating, is not enough to explain all the observed phenomena. This is the explanation found in Haidenhain's writings. He explains cataleptic movements as reflex actions of the lower centers of the brain, not touching on higher centers where consciousness develops. This is also the opinion of the English mental specialist Maudsley. Lastly, it is the doctrine put forward and defended in a far-ranging way in the works of Dr. Despine.[13] This author refuses to recognize any kind of consciousness not only during catalepsy, but even during somnambulism. For him all the actions performed during these abnormal states seem to be purely "organic," analogous to those that the heart and lungs perform ceaselessly without our knowledge. They are indeed automatic actions, but "automatic acts of the ganglia, of the bulb, of the hemispheres," because "we must not talk about unconscious and automatic activity of the mind; this is contradictory. Rather we must talk about unconscious activity of such and such a nerve center." "Carpenter," he adds, "was wrong to call these acts sensory-motor or ideo-motor because they involve neither sensation nor idea; there are no true automatic actions of the mind." Finally: "To ask psychology for an explanation of somnambulism would be to take a wrong road; only physiology can give an explanation."[14] Because our goal in this work, if we are not too ambitious, is to prove precisely the contrary, it is our duty to study thoroughly the opinions of Dr. Despine, who seems to halt our work at its very beginning. If one applies this thesis of absolute unconsciousness to somnambulists, as the author does, it is completely untenable. To claim that a person who speaks, resolves problems, spontaneously manifests sympathies and antipathies, acts in his own particular way, and often resists our commands is nothing more than a mechanical puppet is to go back to Descartes' celebrated theory of animal-machines, because the consciousness of a somnambulist is more obvious than the consciousness of a dog, and today no one doubts the consciousness of a dog. But applied to cataleptic states, this theory has no force, and, since it is necessary always to put the theories one wants to discuss in their best light, it is appropriate, in regard to this latter point of view, to study the thesis of Dr. Despine. We hope to show that, even in the latter case, his arguments are not completely convincing and leave the field open for other suppositions.

The arguments of Dr. Despine, put forward in the midst of a great number of works on somnambulism, which are all (it is interesting to note) psychological studies, can be arranged in two groups:

(1) *Most of the proofs are based on the fact of the forgetfulness* that characterizes the phenomenon of somnambulism and especially those of catalepsy: "By consciousness,"[15] says the author, "we mean the awareness, the perception by the self, by the being which is aware of existing, of what takes place in its personality, of its own actions, of itself; in this work there will be no question of this kind of consciousness." Given this kind of definition of consciousness, it follows that if there are actions that the self does not attribute to itself, that it is not aware of having done, these actions are not due to being conscious. "When it is a matter of a weighty action, capable of acting on the senses to a high degree, if the individual who has performed the action knows nothing about it, it would be against nature to attribute this not-knowing to forgetting. One can only explain it as a non-participation of the self, of personal consciousness, in this action, which is entirely due to unconscious psychic activity, that is to say, to automatic activity of the brain during a momentary suspension of the conscious activity of this organ."[16] Now, there is no state of which this forgetting would be more characteristic than the cataleptic state. Sometimes somnambulists retain part of the memory of their actions. But cataleptics awaken from their attack convinced that nothing abnormal has taken place. Furthermore, if, instead of completely awakening, the cataleptic subject simply passes into another abnormal state, similar in appearance, such as the state of somnambulism, she will not any longer have the memory of the preceding attitudes and movements. "This not-knowing can only be explained by the non-participation of the self in what the body has done, because the cerebral activity which characterizes the self, the conscious personality, has been paralyzed."[17]

This same characteristic is found among individuals who have inhaled ether or chloroform. The patient will use words that indicate that, "her self, her conscious being has not in any way participated in what has taken place, because the ill person would, immediately upon returning to herself, affirm that she has not experienced anything, but was completely unaware that she had been operated on or tended to, or that she had uttered words and carried out actions. Those violent reactions that one would speak about, those diverse phenomena are therefore purely automatic." Since the state of a cataleptic or somnambulistic individual resembles very much the state of an individual who has been chloroformed (the demonstration of this point forms one of the most interesting parts of Despine's work), one can be used to reach conclusions about the other. Chloroform suppresses sensation and consciousness, and that is precisely why it is employed. Since somnambulism presents the same characteristics, particularly the same forgetting, we are justified in believing that it brings the same kind of unconsciousness.

It suffices to go through these discussions and others of the same kind, where forgetting is always accepted as proof of unconsciousness, to become aware of the fragility of this position. It is therefore impossible that truly conscious acts could be forgotten? When it comes to somnambulists, says Despine, this kind of forgetting is impossible. Very well, we will need to search out the reasons for this forgetting, which will, perhaps, be difficult to find. But even though we may not always be able explain it, forgetting something that has truly been conscious is nonetheless possible and really does happen. If, as an English author says,[18] a reader of *The Times* were suddenly killed after reading, he would certainly not have a memory of reading. Would one then conclude that he had done his reading without consciousness? If that were true we would not be able to accept as real anyone's consciousness, even our own, for we can never be certain that tomorrow an accident or illness will not wipe out memory.

But admitting for a moment what seems inadmissible – that forgetting would be sufficient proof of absolute unconsciousness – would it not follow that there could be no memory of cataleptic phenomena? It is true that, at least for the subjects I have studied, there is no memory when they return to the state which conventionally is called the waking state or normal state. But a certain remembering does immediately manifest in catalepsies in which, through habit, the subject performs actions more and more perfectly through repetition. Finally – and this is most important – there exists for these same individuals certain psychological states, certain somnambulisms (since that is the conventional name), in which the subject has perfect memory of the catalepsy. "You placed my hands like this," Léonie says to me, "as if I were playing the flute; you had me close my fists, etc." It is true that this memory is found only in certain somnambulisms that are very deep and so difficult to obtain that they were for a long time unknown. We will discuss these somnambulisms later,[19] but it is good to know at this point that memory of catalepsy does exist. But, Despine will say, this memory only exists in another abnormal state, which is a state of unconsciousness. "If her conscious activity, being paralyzed, does not have knowledge of what happened during the attack, because it has not received the imprint of it, the automatic activity, which has participated in the actions have conserved their imprint, and the memory returns in another attack."[20]

Thus, if memory returns in the normal state, that would be a good proof of consciousness. But since it returns in another state, it is only a proof of physical automatism. This shows that memory is evidence neither for consciousness nor unconsciousness and that it is necessary to go beyond issues of memory to research the characteristics of the state of cataleptics.

(2) *The second group of proofs* which Dr. Despine uses to determine the absence of consciousness during somnambulism seems *to be drawn from analogies that this state presents with certain phenomena of insensibility.* Some very complicated acts are carried out under conditions such that they do not seem to be sensed by the person who does them. We are not going to insist on these questionable cases. "An apoplectic close to death, while still in the coma into which he had fallen, took his watch from the table at the head of his bed and, with an attitude of profound attention, made it strike the hour."[21] This observation does not prove very much, since on the one hand this individual, at the moment of performing the act, was not yet dead, and perhaps (no one can prove the contrary) had some remnant of consciousness, and on the other hand, since he died shortly after, he will never be able to say whether or not he was aware of what he did. In a very interesting chapter, the author lists the actions performed by a decapitated frog, by a new cut in half, by the stumps of a praying mantis, etc., to demonstrate that these actions, which perfectly resemble those which conscious intelligence commands in other cases, are now done without consciousness, because the organ necessary for consciousness has been removed. "This intelligent power manifested through the lower trunk could not derive from a self, from a being who is aware of existing. Otherwise there would be two separate beings in this animal: one for the upper trunk, which can act with intelligence, and another for the lower trunk. Now this is not admissible in the present state of this science."[22] We respond: why is it inadmissible? The absolute unity of the self is a metaphysical conclusion – true, perhaps, but one that should derive from the facts and not be imposed on them. The only proofs you have of the consciousness of an animal arise from the intelligent adaptation of its movements. It is necessary to see if this intelligent adaptation reveals one or two or three consciousnesses in it, and only after that can there be a conclusion about its unity or division.

I prefer those intelligent acts that the author borrows from the normal life of people when they have their intelligence and their speech intact, and when they can themselves assure us that they do not have any awareness of these acts. The most interesting are those habitual acts that Despine describes in a very curious manner. He insists on the unconscious character of habit: it is not intelligence that captures a piece of music and executes it consciously; the artist must have the piece "in his fingers, in his mouth." "When I am searching for a motif that I cannot recall," says one of them, "I let my fingers roam over the keyboard and they find it at once. They have a better memory than I." Further, if the artist thinks consciously about what he is doing, it will not happen as easily; "mistakes are made more often by the mind than by the automaton." This same unconsciousness, so striking in habitual acts, is present in all the actions we perform. We are not conscious of the delicate work that the muscles have to do when we lift an arm or open the mouth: "the self commands the movement, but it is a power that is independent and entirely organic that coordinates the muscular action needed for the execution." Finally, purely organic acts, such as those of digestion, respiration, etc., constantly manifest the most marvelous intelligence which the self not only does not know about, but is not even always able to understand. These are some examples of those very numerous actions that happen within us, without us, which are performed without the participation of the self and consequently without any consciousness, and which ought to be connected to the purely organic functioning of the ganglia and the brain. Acts carried out by cataleptics and somnambulists are nothing so marvelous. They speak or make coordinated movements which very much resemble those that we make when distracted or by habit, *without realizing it.* These acts should therefore have the same nature, and since the former are unconscious, so should be the latter.

I will not dwell on the description of these unconscious actions drawn from normal life. The author describes them in detail with a truly psychological talent, all the more curious since he denies them any psychological character.

But allow me to voice some reservations about the interpretation of these phenomena. We admit that the actions performed in catalepsy (because this would be very inaccurate for actions performed in somnambulism) very much resemble, if not organic phenomena, at least habitual acts. Should one then without hesitation admit the absolute unconsciousness of habit? The pianist mentioned by Despine can play his piece by heart without *giving attention* to the movement of the fingers, but he can also, and very easily, give attention to each of these movements in a way that involves a distinct consciousness.[23] Other actions, on the contrary, remain conscious even when habit makes it possible to do them more rapidly and easily. "Thus the phenomena of memory, the awakening of ideas under the influence of association, are incontestably the results of habit. They are nevertheless accomplished with consciousness."[24] For us what is lacking from our having a perfect understanding of habitual phenomena is attention, much more than consciousness, and, when we are unaware of them, or when we believe we are totally unaware of them, nothing proves that they do not have a consciousness that belongs to them. The smallest effort of attention will make manifest *for us* a consciousness of habitual acts that we have not created and that exists already beforehand. But, someone will say, there are acts of the body that are completely unconscious for us, such as acts of organic life. Agreed, although in reality the cataleptic act of communion hardly resembles the beat of the heart or digestion. It is necessary now to prove that these acts, unconscious *to us*, are unconscious *in themselves.* "The excitation of the soft palate by alimentary bolus, or by a foreign body," says Richet,[25] "produces either swallowing or nausea. It seems that there is a kind of vague discernment of the nature of the irritation. This is a rudimentary psychological characteristic, a kind of discernment of the ganglia." So it is with all the reflexes which everywhere show a kind of sensibility and discernment, although we are not conscious of it. A great number of physiologists have recognized this role of an elementary consciousness. Buffon attributed some species of material sensations to the coordinated organic molecules of the animal body that are alien to thought and the self. Bonnet attributes the faculty of sensation to all the parts of the body and even to plants. Pflüger, Auerbach, Lewes, and many others attribute sensibility and some kind of intelligence to all the nerve centers. There is no reason to discuss all these perhaps adventurous theories, and we will not stay with them very long. But mentioning them is enough to make comprehensible the notion that a habitual or even organic action is not necessarily unconscious just because the self is not aware of it. Also, likening cataleptic acts to similar phenomena, when that is justified, does not in any way prove that they are unconscious.

In reality, we only directly know our one consciousness, that is, our own, at the moment we are aware of it. Every other consciousness is known only by way of an inference or a supposition. No one can ever mathematically demonstrate that the person who speaks to me is not a mechanical puppet with language abilities, and the Cartesians use rigorous reasoning when they say of an injured dog: "He yelps, but he does not feel anything." In this matter of the consciousness of another person, as in many others, we have to accept likelihoods and probabilities. Now, we ordinarily presume we are dealing with consciousness from two indications: speech and intelligently coordinated actions. The first indication, speech, is considered the most decisive, and this is reasonable. But it is actually only a more complex and more perfect instance of the second, an ensemble of movements that are more complicated and more intelligently coordinated than others. And if the first indication leads us to presume consciousness, the second leads us to the same presumption, perhaps with a little less probability. Cataleptics do not speak, it is true (and we must later return to this important fact), but they act intelligently. If I put a weight of two kilos on the extended arm of a cataleptic, the muscles of the arm and of the whole body tighten in such a way that the arm can support the weight without bending. If I make her hands form a peak, the collection of movements coordinate themselves as if I had put them in a position of prayer. There is adaptation, unity of movement; in a word, what one ordinarily sees as a sign of intelligence.

But, one might say, coordination, intelligence, and even sensitiveness to feeling can exist without consciousness. "Many very complicated, *intelligent* actions, attaining a goal that is perfectly defined and *varied according to circumstances*, actions exactly like those commanded by the self … can be automatic"[26] (here meaning unconscious). "Man," says Maudsley, in the same sense "will not be a worse intellectual machine without consciousness than with it."[27] In a word, consciousness is only an accessory, an epiphenomenon, the absence of which does not unsettle anything. Some have, I do not know why, attributed this theory to Ribot, who, however, has opposed it with excellent arguments.[28] I will not attempt to discuss it because, I have to admit, I do not understand it very well. It does not seem to me to be intelligible, either from the point of view of psychology or that of physiology. What does one mean when one speaks of "the reasoning of the ganglia and the intelligence of the brain"?[29] Nothing other than that there is a consciousness other than our own in the ganglia or in the brain, because reasoning without consciousness makes absolutely no sense. On the other hand, if one agrees that consciousness results from a combination of physiological conditions bringing about a certain action, one cannot agree that on another occasion exactly the same combination bringing about the same action would happen without consciousness. Then the same conditions would at one time be causes of consciousness and at another time not. On the contrary, the reality of consciousness seems to us very important in the range of organic phenomena. Its presence or its absence, as we see more and more, considerably modifies things. When we know that a complicated phenomenon, such as movements of anger or gestures of prayer, can exist in us only with a combination of emotions and conscious ideas, we do not have the right to suppose that the same gestures exactly reproduce themselves during catalepsy without being directed and unified by some kind of consciousness. Also, let us suppose – and this is now legitimate at least as a hypothesis – that cataleptic phenomena are psychological phenomena whose nature we have yet to determine. What is now only a hypothesis will, we believe, be verified by other phenomena of the same kind.

1.3 Psychological interpretations: catalepsy compared to somnambulism

Actions carried out during catalepsy are under the domination of psychological phenomena. This is a proposition that seems simple, but is susceptible to very different interpretations. This is because psychological phenomena are extremely varied in nature and it makes a difference whether we explain the facts that we have described by one interpretation or another.

I will not give a facile interpretation, following the timeworn mode. This type of explanation consists of linking all the facts that we do not understand to a framework that is based on a voluntary and perfectly conscious simulation. It is completely false to believe that a psychological or even imaginary illness would always be a simulated illness, and that on the other hand catalepsy consists of all the abnormal phenomena which cannot be easily simulated in this way. But, without linking catalepsy to a complete intelligence which plans its deceptions, one can explain it through a half-intelligence that includes the thoughts of the operator and takes its actions into account, without having the ability to oppose them. In a word, one can liken catalepsy to somnambulism and explain all its actions by suggestion. "To make a limb cataleptic, one must open the subject's eyes, not submit her to a bright light or a loud noise, as is done at the Salpêtrière. It is enough to raise the limb and leave it in the air for a while, in order to make certain that it is not going to lower. The person remains in *suggestive catalepsy*: the hypnotized person, whose will or power to resist is weak, passively maintains the posture imposed."[30] All of this is perfectly correct, and, in somnambulism and the waking state, we study what Bernheim calls suggestive catalepsy and its varieties. But here it is a matter of a collection of phenomena brought into being through different procedures, or rather by the illness itself, and which, since they are psychological, present different characteristics. Catalepsy and somnambulism are only different degrees of each other. This is incontestable, and we see intermediate states between them. But a difference of degree does not mean there is no difference, especially when it comes to mental phenomena. Therefore we will try to make clear the precise point at which the consciousness of cataleptics ends.

(1) *The immobility and inertia of the subject* are very much greater in this state than in any other. A normal person or a somnambulist (particularly when the eyes are open) moves much more spontaneously. This spontaneity is evident in the execution of actions, even actions that are commanded or suggested. Not only can there be resistance – often very strong resistance – but also independence, which never exists to any degree during catalepsy,[31] and also there is variety or alterations in the execution of the same actions. A somnambulist does not always execute the same action in the same way. Sometimes she acts quickly, sometimes slowly, sometimes with good humour, sometimes under protest, sometimes in one way, sometimes in another. This is nothing like the regularity of cataleptics, where there are no changes in their characteristics, no external qualities that distinguish or modify them. Their gestures, their steps are always mathematically the same. Léonie will always make the same number of steps forward and to the right to take communion, and she will run into a wall without moving forward rather than turning to the left. A somnambulist, who is always capable of adjusting her actions to circumstances, therefore demonstrates a different kind of intelligence.

(2) *The preceding difference is, without doubt, only a difference in degree,* although it is very easy to recognize. But it should be noted that the difference in degree of intelligence implies the presence or absence of an important characteristic. One of the most important, albeit negative, signs of catalepsy is this: *the subject does not know how to speak*. It is not a matter of the kind of articulated speech present in the repetition of sounds that occurs in echolalia, rather it is a matter of language as a sign of thought. The cataleptic does not respond to questions, either by speech or some sign. In certain profound states of sleep, Rose's mouth is more or less paralyzed, but she responds to me with a hand signal which signifies "yes," or another which signifies "no." When she has a moment of catalepsy during a hysterical crisis or during somnambulism, she does not respond to me with any signal, although she is not at all paralyzed and she is able to speak in echo or reproduce gestures. I will take the example of two women, Rose and Marie, in a state in which they are externally identical – rigid, eyes closed, immobile – but one of them, Rose, is undergoing a cataleptic attack (there are catalepsies where

the eyes are closed), and the other, Marie, is in a simple state of somnambulism. I approach each successively and, in a loud voice and the same tone, pronounce the same phrase: "Did you sleep well last night?" Rose, without stirring, repeats in the same tone: "Did you sleep well last night?" Marie turns quickly, smiles, and says: "Not too badly, thank you, but I had a bad dream." Am I mistaken to conclude that these two women, perhaps identical in appearance, are not in exactly the same psychological state?[32]

If the cataleptic does not respond to speech, it is because she does not understand it. One can easily verify this by trying to give orders to these subjects by speaking. If one shouts out, "Raise your arm," Léonie does not move and seems not to hear. Rose repeats over and over "Raise your arm," but neither of them actually raises their arm. It is true that I here find myself in disagreement with Paul Richer. This author, although he has remarked that certain cataleptics do not obey oral suggestion,[33] nevertheless writes: "While B is in a cataleptic state, you could attract her attention and, pointing to the ground, say to her that she is in a garden filled with flowers. Immediately the cataleptic state ceases, she makes a gesture of surprise, her face becomes animated: "How beautiful they are," she says, and, bending down, she gathers some flowers and makes a bouquet of them, attaches one to her bodice, etc."[34] For me, a subject who acts in this fashion is no longer in a cataleptic state. One might say that this is merely a matter of words and names. Without doubt, the different states of human intelligence form a series so continuous that it is impossible to precisely distinguish between them, and a subject like this will find herself in intermediate states that one might indifferently label with one name or another. But if one is going to call a cataleptic a subject who understands verbal suggestions and speaks, then there is no difference between catalepsy and somnambulism. In effect, all the other symptoms either are found in all hypnotic states or, as when paralysis is produced by rubbing the tendons,[35] are not general enough, since I cannot establish them in regard to every subject. Furthermore, it is not important to give the state that I have described the name of first somnambulism or of a state of complete suggestibility. The only important thing is to understand the psychological alterations of the subjects in this state, because we only have psychological differences to distinguish all the states. Indeed, consciousness, which exists here as everywhere, since, as I believe, it only disappears with life, is in this state more rudimentary than in any other. This consciousness is capable of sensation, but not of ideas; capable of hearing, but not of understanding. It would be a mistake to conclude that one can speak off the cuff in the presence of cataleptics without any implications for future experiences. They can retain the words, even without understanding them, and if, as we will point out later, this memory is awakened in a later, more intelligent state, it will then be understood and have its suggestive power. But the only certain thing is that the words are not understood now and that it is not an intelligent obedience that manifests in catalepsy.

From this it follows that the subject, while appearing extremely inert and docile, is, in reality, not very manageable and obeys much more her own inspirations than those of the operator. If I show Léonie playing out the scene of communion that I have described, it might seem that she is being obedient to a command that I have given her. In reality I have neither commanded nor foreseen what she was going to do, and the first time it happened I was very surprised. I now know, through experience, that by putting the subject's hands in a certain position and leaving them there for some minutes, I will induce the communion scene. But even now I do not direct the scene. If I should want to change the least thing, to have the subject move to the left, for example, or have her kiss the crucifix before communion, I would not be able to do it. If I speak to the subject, I am not understood, and if I touch her body, I simply halt the scene. I am therefore a simple spectator, rather than an actor. It is from her own self that the subject derives her actions and movements, and although she acts in a manner so predetermined that I can foresee them in an instant down to the smallest movements, she acts spontaneously. It is, therefore, at this moment more than ever, that the automatism of the subject is revealed, and that is why I have begun our study with a description of a state which, although conscious, does not demonstrate normal consciousness or normal intelligence.

Before examining the nature of this rudimentary consciousness, it is necessary to take up a possible objection. Today, when it is the fashion to explain everything as suggestion or simulation, one might say that all the psychological characteristics of catalepsy have been taught to the subject who has been trained in this way. It would be dangerous to push this reasoning to the extreme so that it would quickly become a kind of "lazy argument." Yet it is right to take it into account, because undoubtedly very often in the milieu where these subjects are numerous and imitate each other, certain states that are real for one subject can be artificial for another. But in the present case our subjects do not know one another, and one should not suppose that the operators are so naive as to have suggested, without realizing it, all the positive and negative characteristics of catalepsy. Furthermore, an artificial state is always recognized by some sign, as the following observation may demonstrate. One day I did some experiments with Lucie with a stranger present. This circumstance displeased me very much because it is necessary to keep with one only indispensable persons who are habituated to the attitude one needs to maintain during an experience of this kind. This stranger continually asked me bothersome questions and, as was my wont, I did not want to answer in the presence of my subject. However, an unfortunate word escaped me: "What is catalepsy?" was asked. "It is a state in which the subject remains immobile and leaves her limbs in the position in which they are placed." Hardly had I said this when I greatly regretted my words: "From now on," I thought, "people would be justified in saying that she produces suggestive catalepsy," and I wanted to immediately test the effects of my imprudence. "Listen," I said, "When I clap my hands you will fall into a state of catalepsy." I clapped my hands and behold! – there was Lucie remaining completely immobile with eyes wide open. I lifted her arms and they stayed in the air; I bent her body and it remained bent. Was she cataleptic? It was easy for me to verify that no other sign of catalepsy – neither the expression of the face, the imitation, the *echolalia* – could be confirmed, and above all the subject could understand very well the words I used to terminate the situation, saying to her: "It is over. You are no longer in catalepsy." Indeed, if one tried to stop a true attack of catalepsy, such as Lucie herself had had (although rarely), by simply saying to the subject that it is over, one would see what a difference there is between this state of suggestive docility, formed by a brief somnambulistic sleep, and a true cataleptic onset, during which thought is brought back into a totally rudimentary state, and which is one of the forms of a major attack of hystero-epilepsy.

I therefore cannot believe that the state which is being described is completely artificial. Because it is recognized as a conscious state, it is not necessary to conclude that it is some kind of psychological state. There are differences and very important varieties indeed when it comes to conscious phenomena.

1.4 A rudimentary form of consciousness: sensation and isolated images

Certain philosophers – Cartesians, for example – think of consciousness as invariable, immutable, without nuance and degree. For Descartes, thought exists complete with doubt, reflection, reasoning, and language, or else it does not exist at all and is replaced by mechanism pure and simple, by extension and movement. Leibniz, on the contrary, in his profound philosophy, to which, it seems to us, all the physical and psychological sciences of today can trace their origin, had a totally different conception of consciousness. He posited an infinite number of degrees, and certain of its forms seemed to him to be inferior to normal thought, stating "that human minds are like little gods compared to them."[36] It is the latter theory that we must now bring to mind, in its principle propositions, in order to understand the possibility of inferior and rudimentary consciousnesses. Let us take human consciousness in its ordinary and complete form and successively take away all the perfections that it has acquired but are not essential to it. We all know that it is necessary to separate scientific intelligence – a faculty which exists in us all to a greater or lesser degree and which explains and understands things – from everyday consciousness. This intelligence, properly speaking, involves a coming together (*comprehendere*) of a great number of facts of consciousness into syntheses or general ideas. It does so by discovering connections between particular facts which, remaining the same among different terms, give a unity to things that have a very distinct appearance. Here we obviously have the highest expression that human thought attains. But it should be pointed out that it is not always attained. Perhaps human thought attains it only rarely and less often than we are disposed to believe. As a matter of fact, when we examine the actions of others, we are too ready to ascribe to them ideas and lines of thought that we ourselves have in interpreting their conduct. Very often we believe that an individual has acted with intent, that he has calculated the consequences of his actions, that he has made a systematic whole of his ideas, bound together by well-understood connections, whereas in reality this individual has allowed his thoughts to be evoked mechanically, one giving rise to another, without recognizing any systematic connection among them. We should not confuse law, or the interpretation of facts of consciousness which our intelligence discovers, or believes it discovers, with consciousness itself. If the phenomena of consciousness presented by someone *appear to us* to be connected among themselves by ties of likeness, difference, or finality, that does not necessarily mean that in the mind of this person there is consciousness of the likeness, difference, or finality.[37] The English philosophers seem to fall into this error when they say that all consciousness is perception of a difference. This is also an exaggeration of a kind that I sometimes criticize in the very interesting works of Paulhan, who seems to attribute to elementary consciousness the ideas of finality, of which he sees himself as the interpreter.[38] Consciousness can exist without any judgment, that is, without intelligence. Man can feel and not understand his own sensations. To give an example relating to our subject, if we witness the complicated actions that Léonie performs when I join her hands, we think – *we* think – that she is taking communion and we join together all the actions in the systematic idea that we call "communion"; but it is not hereby shown that *she* has the idea of communion and that she joins together these actions in this general idea. It is indeed more likely that she has images that evoke one another, and nothing more. If later she regains the memory of these sensations – which is possible, as we have said – she can examine them, connect them, and understand them. "Well," she said one day under such circumstances, "I am holding my hands thus, I rise, then I kneel … but that means I am praying! … what a fool I am." She is *now surprised* at the actions which did not astonish her at the time, because she was conscious of them without understanding them.

I would place the phenomenon known as *perception* below intelligent judgment. If we open our eyes and know that we have in front of us a tree of such a colour, such a form, at such a distance – this is, as has often been demonstrated, a complex psychological phenomenon. The actual sensations, already very numerous, have to be combined with a great number of interpretative images which make it possible to appreciate the exteriority, the form, the dimension, the place of the object. These interpretive images which here accompany the principal sensation are accessories. They can be modified, as we see in errors of sense. They can even disappear, while the sensation persists. Animals which have their brains removed seem to provide an example of this. They would appear to hear and see, but they are not able to interpret their sensations, that is, to be able of themselves to add the notions of distance, of fear, of desire, etc.[39] The element of consciousness which subsists when one removes the accessory facts therefore seems to be the sensation or image.

It nevertheless seems to us that to understand the facts that we have presented, and especially those that we will study later on, it is necessary to go further in this analysis of the elements of consciousness. Ordinarily sensation is defined as "the simple phenomenon that occurs within my *self* when *I* see, hear, etc." Perhaps this definition cannot be replaced by a better one, because one cannot define the things that explain them and how our interpretations enter into the mix. But it is evident that it contains an extra term: the word *self* [moi], the word *I* [je]. "It is certain," said Reid,[40] "that nobody in the universe can conceive or believe that odour exists in itself, without a mind or some subject which has the faculty to sense." Garnier stated,[41] "Can some knowledge occur in the soul without the soul being aware of it?" If one takes a metaphysical point of view, as these authors do, if one seeks the origin, the cause of sensation, perhaps one might think as they do, that there is no sensation without a soul to produce it and know it. But if one takes an exclusively psychological point of view, if one considers the *self*, not as a being and a cause, but as a certain idea that for the most part accompanies psychological phenomena, one will be forced to think that there are sensations without the self, that there can be phenomena of vision even though no one says: "I see." The idea of the self is, as a matter of fact, a very complex psychological phenomenon which includes memories of past actions, the notion of our situation, of our abilities, of our body, even of our name, which, connecting all these scattered ideas, plays a large role in the knowledge of the personality. If one considers a simple sensation, it contains nothing of all this, and it alone is not enough to form such a complex idea. No doubt ordinarily most of our sensations awaken these memories by association or simply the word *I* [je], which is their substitute, but it is not necessary to attribute to an isolated sensation what is the result of a complex combination. Stuart Mill[42] said: "Seeing that the only fact that makes it necessary to believe in a self ... is memory ..., I do not see any reason to think that knowledge of the self precedes memory. I do not see any reason to believe, with Hamilton and Mansel, that the self would be an original presentation of consciousness, that the simple impression experienced by our senses implies or brings with it a consciousness of oneself, any more than of a not-oneself."

A great number of philosophers, belonging to all the schools, have expressed this truth very well, this independence of sensation from every idea of personality: Cudworth; Bonnet; Buffon, when, without explanation, he attributes feeling without thought to animals[43]; Flourens, when he gives to animals an intelligence that does not know itself. Gerdy, distinguishing sensation and consciousness of sensation,[44] had admitted that one can sense without having consciousness of being a person who senses. Among the moderns, Lewes[45] and Herzen admit that we sense without saying it, without knowing "that it is we who sense, nor what we sense."[46] Spitta characterizes profound sleep by the absence of consciousness of the self, with persistence of consciousness itself. Radestock makes the same distinction between consciousness of the self and simple consciousness.[47] Dumont, especially in his scientific theory of sensibility, has attempted to distinguish this universal consciousness, which pertains even to "an atom of sensation" from intelligent knowledge of the self and of the person.[48] It would be very interesting to analyze these recent studies.[49] But it is more profitable to return to a French philosopher, more remote in time, who made this distinction the basis of his philosophy and who truly seemed to foresee the experiences we are reporting today. Maine de Biran distinguished three degrees in the development of intelligence, calling them animal life, human life, and the life of the mind. We will not concern ourselves here with the third, the life of the mind. But we must point out the characteristic that distinguishes animal life from human life. "The vital functions," he says, "result in internal effects called animal sensation, general modes of pleasure or pain which constitute the existence of the animal, such that, existing and having these feelings in its own right, it has no need to know that it exists or to perceive that it feels, that is, to have consciousness, *the idea of sensation,* or to be a person, a self, constituted as one, simple, identical, remaining the same when sensation passes and varies."[50] Elsewhere he says, "Between complete consciousness and the mechanism of Descartes there is a place for beings who have sensation without consciousness, without a self, capable of perception."[51] He proposes a special name as a fitting title for these phenomena, and since we ourselves propose to use the name and meaning given by Main de Biran, it is fitting to cite in its entirety this very interesting passage.[52] "*Affection* is what remains of a complete sensation when one separates from it the personal individuality or the self and with it every form of space and time, if I may borrow an expression from the Kantians, every feeling of external or internal causality, or, in the language of Locke, when the idea of sensation is reduced to the simple sensation without any idea of kind, or, finally, from the point of view of Condillac, when the statue becomes sensation without yet being anything more ... This simple affective state is not a pure hypothesis; it is a positive mode and complete in its own genre, which originally formed in its origin our whole existence and which constituted it from a multitude of living beings from the *state that we come close to every time our intellectual thought grows weak and degrades*, every time we doze off, *every time our will is not in play*, every time the self is so absorbed in sensible impressions that the psychological person no longer exists." We should not be too surprised if these passages from Maine de Biran apply exactly to the cataleptic state. This philosopher did not scorn observing somnambulists and he spoke of them again and again. He deserves, more than is generally believed, to be considered a precursor of scientific and experimental psychology.

But before applying Maine de Biran's ideas, we must borrow from him responses to the most serious objection that this conception of the *affective state* can raise. He himself tells us about discussions he had with Ampère, Cuvier, and Royer-Collard, and the pains that he took to make himself understood. "For them a sensation is nothing if it is not joined to the consciousness of the being who experiences it. This discussion showed me how far I still was from having my point of view clearly understood. The theory of Leibniz, who so well described the state in which the simply living monad is reduced to lowly perceptions, from where it is lifted to clear perceptions and to consciousness, will serve as an introduction to the exposition of my doctrine, which I find difficult to make understood."[53] However, he attempted to respond elsewhere: "How does one conceive of a sensation that one does not feel? It is especially here that I observed the defectiveness of language with its natural and necessary forms which, being so imprinted with the self and the human person, cannot be applied to where the self is not. What is a sensation that one does not feel? I, in my turn, asked to what does this "one" refer? Persons feel. They know their sensations because they are identical, permanent persons who distinguish themselves from their sensations … An animal does not feel, does not know its sensation, because it is not a person constituted to know or perceive its individual existence from the inside. It feels without knowing itself to feel, as it lives without knowing itself to live."[54] In a word, we cannot understand a sensation without a self, because the idea of the self is the condition of the knowledge and because we necessarily transfer to consciousness the conditions needed for knowledge every time we attempt to study it, that is, to know it.

The preceding conclusions about the existence of an elementary form of consciousness, drawn from philosophical reasoning, are confirmed by a study of the facts. The most curious, and most decisive, are those facts observed after fainting, and it is very fitting to recall them here, because, as we see all the time, something analogous occurs during nervous crises and during hypnotic sleep. "During syncope," says an author who has been able to study this phenomenon in himself,[55] "there is psychological nothingness, absolute, the total absence of consciousness; then one begins to have a feeling that is vague, boundless, infinite, a feeling of existence in general without any delimitation by one's own individuality, without the least trace of any kind of distinction between the me and the non-me. One is then an organic part of nature having consciousness of the fact of one's existence, but not having any consciousness of one's organic unity. One has, in two words, an impersonal consciousness." "One has 'stupid' sensations, if I might put it thus, that is to say, sensations which – rightly, because they remain isolated – cannot be known, but only felt."[56] Without doubt, the normal state does not present us with such clear examples, but we can nevertheless recognize that the idea of the self is not always equally joined to all sensations that we experience. On the contrary, most so little evoke the idea of the self that we do not hesitate to attribute them to the exterior; instead of saying that it is we who experience the sensation of the colour green, we say that it is the tree which possesses it. Often we do not separate things as much and, in the face of a spectacle that excites us, we only have the sensations of the spectacle in our consciousness without reflecting on ourselves, without distinguishing between what is interior and what exterior. It is true that in ordinary life we can pull ourselves together, come out of these *absorbing* sensations and recognize that it is *we* who have had them. But we can conceive that there are certain beings, inferior animals, for example, who can never disengage their personality from these elementary sensations, and, on the other hand, that certain other more complex beings would be momentarily reduced to a purely *affective* life, without knowledge and without reflection.

1.5 The nature of consciousness during catalepsy

It is precisely a purely affective consciousness of this kind, reduced to sensations and images without any of those connections or ideas of relation which constitute personality and judgments, that we believe it is legitimate to suppose occurs during catalepsy and analogous states. Neither the obliteration of consciousness and mere mechanicalness, nor knowledge capable of understanding and obeying seems to us to be what is involved here. Rather we are dealing with a particular form of consciousness intermediary between these two extremes.

Herzen describes for us the particular state of thought that he observed in himself, with consciousness in a nascent state, so to speak, which manifests when the mind wakes up after a full faint. If we have emphasized these very curious observations, it is because *the cataleptic state* seems to us to present notable analogies with *this nascent state of thought* after syncope. Many authors, such as Pitres and Binet and Féré,[57] have already noted examples of swooning during hypnotic sleep, but they consider them rare and accidental. I, on the contrary, believe them to be both important and frequent, although they might ordinarily be so rapid that the observer barely notices them. With many of the subjects I have studied, the cataleptic state was preceded by another state very much like syncope. Note how things occur at the beginning of Rose's hypnotic sleep, and even in the midst of a somnambulistic seance.

Suddenly she ceases to respond and speak and remains completely immobile, with eyes closed. If one lifts her arms, they heavily fall back down. If one addresses her or shakes her, she does not stir. This is not the state described by Charcot as lethargy, because pressure on tendons, muscles, or nerves does not produce contraction. This is, one might say, a hysterical sleep blended with hypnotic sleep. Without doubt, this exact state is found in the crisis of hysteria, and it has, as we have noted, the same consequences. But what matters is that it is a real state, and, furthermore, that there is not one thing in hypnotic sleep that does not have its analogy in the crisis of hysteria. In this kind of hypnotic syncope, organic functions ordinarily take place in a regular fashion, although sometimes, if the state is prolonged, there may be difficulties in breathing. But psychological functions seem to be totally suppressed, or at least I have not been able to find the least sign of their existence, so I have no grounds for supposing consciousness to be present. This state continues for a longer or shorter period; sometimes it lasts for a quarter of an hour or more; sometimes it is so rapid that one must know the subject well to recognize that it is present. But at the end of some period of time a change occurs in the subject, although no external alteration may be visible. For if I raise an arm or a leg and let it fall as I did before, it remains immobile in the position I put it and continues the movement I have communicated to it. However, if I speak, the subject does not produce any further reaction. Let us take a look at some occurrences. If I now speak and say loudly: "Lift your arm," her mouth opens and repeats what I have said as an echo, "Lift your arm." Sometimes after this period of *echolalia*, the subject no longer repeats the command, but executes it and actually lifts the arm. In another moment the subject may respond to me with increasing liveliness and a consciousness which seems more or less complete. Thus, the subject has passed, in this period of time, from a state in which consciousness was absent to another state where consciousness is sufficiently developed for her to speak intelligently. Is it not natural to suppose that the subject has passed through different degrees of increasing consciousness and that as the state of catalepsy and then echolalia are found, the closer one gets to hypnotic syncope; is it not legitimate to conclude that these states correspond to the most elementary forms of thought, to the nascent state of impersonal consciousness? Almost all subjects, when susceptible to profound somnambulism (a veritable second existence) exhibit, just at the moment in which they fall asleep, a period of transition well known to the old magnetizers, during which they are without response. We know about the fainting which separates the two existences of Felida X,[58] what Azam called a "little death." We find the same phenomena with instructive variations with other subjects. One day I found Lucie ill, half mad, in the state of aura that comes before the grand hystero-epileptic crisis. I wanted her to avoid going into the grand crisis, which would always last many hours, by putting her to sleep immediately, but I had scarcely touched her when she suddenly fell into a very complete state of hypnotic syncope or hysterical sleep (the name is hardly important). She remained in that state for ten minutes, without anything being able to produce the slightest reaction. Then I noticed a curious change that began to take shape: each time I touched her limbs, I provoked a small movement. I ascertained that each muscle, when pressed even lightly, immediately contracted, in isolation from the others, and then quickly relaxed. It was possible to study in her the isolated actions of all the muscles of the body. This was similar to the state of lethargy described by Charcot, with this difference: the muscular contraction did not persist under the form of contracture. Some moments later, the contraction systematically extended to all the muscles of the arm at once, and the limbs now maintained the positions I gave them. I open the subject's eyes and they remain open. I stand before her and she stands to imitate my movements. A few seconds later, she begins to speak and enters into a state of ordinary somnambulism. We note here that, in addition to the preceding facts, a state analogous to classical lethargy is interposed between the syncope and the first catalepsy. This disposes me to believe that this lethargy, although a real state, is not well named: it is not a state analogous to death, a "death trance," and it is probably not an absence of all consciousness. Furthermore, natural lethargy indeed sometimes presents general contractions, but ordinarily it does not involve this neuromuscular hyper-excitability.[59] Hypnotic lethargy seems to me to be rather a degree of elementary consciousness, a muscular sensation so rudimentary that it remains totally isolated and cannot spread itself enough to cause a movement of a whole arm.[60] A third example will be even clearer. A peculiar characteristic of Léonie is that every change of state, of whatever kind, is always signaled by an abrupt sigh, a kind of small respiratory convulsion. With her the state of syncope is very rare, completely accidental, and it always frightens me, because it is always accompanied by respiratory troubles and choking. When it ceases spontaneously or when one brings it to an end by putting a hand on the forehead of the subject, it always stops with an abrupt sigh, after which the subject is in a well-known state, which is, in fact, classical hypnotic lethargy with all its characteristics.[61] But we can see in this lethargy, more clearly than in that of Lucie, the first return of consciousness. When a contraction is produced by striking the tendons or muscles, it is not necessary, as I have already remarked, to strike the muscles that are precisely antagonistic in order to release it. It is enough to strike the muscles at random for other muscular sensations to replace the first. In fact, to release the contraction of a bent arm it is enough for me to lightly touch the fingertips. Does there seem to be a consciousness capable of sensing the extension of the arm, as there is in catalepsy one which senses the position of the limbs? Lethargy ends with an abrupt sigh and the subject has again made progress. The limbs do not contract when touched; they more easily assume the changes one might give them; they maintain, with astonishing precision, the position in which they are placed. But movements given to them are no longer carried through; the arm remains immobile in the last position given. In the past I have thought it useful to give this state, which participates in both lethargy and catalepsy, a specific name. But this naming offers no particular advantage; one can establish as many stages as one wants in this gradual awakening of consciousness. With Léonie these grades, marked by sighs, are fairly clear, but with Rose, the change occurs in a continuous fashion, and when they take place slowly one can observe a considerable number of states between the syncope and the complete somnambulism. The only thing that does not hold true is that the catalepsy does not present itself under a unique form, with open eyes and with the aptitude to present all the phenomena that I have described. With Léonie there are three degrees of catalepsy with eyes closed: first the limbs remain mobile, without continuing communicated movement; next, the limbs are capable of continuing the movement given to it and the face takes on an expression that is in harmony with these movements; finally, the sense of touch seems to return and an object put in the hands provokes certain habitual movements. After the last stage, the eyes open on their own and there are four types of catalepsy with the eyes open. I am not going to make a point of these differences of state which are, I repeat, insignificant or at least very peculiar to the subject. First the sense of sight returns, and the subject is susceptible to carrying out imitations; next comes the sense of hearing, in an *echolalia* which is never as perfect as that of Rose; then there is a beginning of intelligence, or speech, and the possibility of evoking hallucinations; then incoherent words, a kind of delirium, and finally intelligent speech in a state of complete somnambulism. When one reaches the latter stage, the characteristics of catalepsy, imitation, and harmony of expression with movement disappear. This example, therefore, like the preceding ones, proves that the cataleptic states correspond to a very rudimentary thought, to sensations totally isolated and incapable of reacting to each other.

1.6 The nature of consciousness during states analogous to catalepsy

Up to now, we have been studying phenomena that have been artificially obtained, or rather arise from a context of more or less artificial states. It is interesting to examine, from the same point of view, naturally produced phenomena. But we should remember that all these facts have their analogies in a somewhat maladaptive natural state, that is to say, in the crises of hysteria.

Rose's grand nervous crisis presents a development completely identical to that of her somnambulism. After an initial uneasy feeling that lasts for a period of time, she suddenly falls into a faint. The muscles are limp, the face pale, and consciousness does not show itself in gesture or movement. Very often this initial syncope, which lasts a long time with her, leads to profound and dangerous respiratory difficulties. At one moment her breathing is rapid and gasping, at another moment it stops entirely for a minute, her lips turn blue and a little froth appears. But soon the movements start. At first they are small tremors in every muscle, with no coherent movement; then there are movements of the limbs, but completely uncoordinated. I will pass quickly over the details of the convulsions, which have been too well described by the experts to allow myself to dwell on them here. I will only point out the characteristics that, in my opinion, clarify my theme. It seems to me that the movements, at first totally isolated and incoherent, become more and more general and systematized. For example, at the beginning, the muscles of the arm contract randomly, one working against the other, which produces simply a trembling of the arm and various flexions of the fingers. Then the muscles work together enough that the two arms make large movements and bring about a pounding of the fist on a specific place on the chest. Now, I know that she has in that area, under the left breast, a continual ache produced, I believe by a permanent and painful contracture of the intercostal muscles. I believe, therefore, that the movement of the hands is now coordinated by this painful sensation. But, little by little, after this period of convulsions and contractions, and overlapping with it, because there is no sudden transition, all the other movements begin. She sits down on her bed (she does not rise because both legs are in a state of contraction during this crisis), she bows, waves a greeting with her hands and smiles for attention. She has been a singer in a performance café and she probably imagines herself to be on the stage, because she sings some very funny songs for us. Or else she seems to be hearing her companions, because she puts her hand to her mouth as if to ask for silence, and appears from time to time to hear with delight that they are applauding the singer. In her grand crisis, Lucie presents the same kind of phase even more regularly. After the convulsions at the beginning, which last for some time, the poor woman remains in an attitude of terror, with eyes wide open and fixed on the curtains in her room. For nearly an hour, she does not change her position and simply makes movements of desperate defense, or impelled by some inexpressible crisis.

With both of these women, this period is followed by another in which intelligence seems augmented. They no longer obey a fixed idea but begin to chatter about ordinary matters. Lucie has the singular habit of going down to the kitchen and making herself an improvised dinner, which she consumes with a hearty appetite, whereas she refuses to eat when she is awake. This last period of crisis, called hysterical delirium, corresponds exactly, as we have seen, to somnambulism, and for that reason does not interest us here. But in the intermediate period, the period of what is called "passionate attitudes" is also produced between the state of syncope, in which consciousness seems to be absent, and another state, in which consciousness is nearly complete. It seems to be produced by a consciousness that is still rudimentary and corresponds to the state of catalepsy. Furthermore, the symptoms are the same: immobility or indefinite continuation of the same movement, harmonious expressions of the whole body, absence of speech as a means of expression, and repetition of the same phrase.

Finally – and this seems to me to be decisive – there is effortless movement from one state to another. While Lucie is in an artificial state of catalepsy, I place her hands in a posture of terror; she immediately fixes her gaze on the curtains and, if I do not quickly intervene, the rest of the natural crisis will develop itself for many hours. On the other hand, if I come upon Rose or Lucie in the midst of their natural passionate attitudes, all I have to do is make some magnetic passes over their arms to put them into a state of so-called artificial catalepsy; for now I can lift their limbs and they stay in the new position I have given them. With Lucie the transformation is complete and she immediately forgets her terrors and, little by little, enters into a state of artificial somnambulism. With Rose, it is only partial, because there is always a part of her personality that continues in the crisis, while the other part obeys me. We will return later to these complications.[62] Observations of others confirm my own. The crisis of natural catalepsy of Dr. Saint-Bourdin is very often transformed into a veritable somnambulism as a crisis of hysteria.[63] Paul Richer describes the crises of a hysteric whose limbs could be displaced during "passionate poses" which then maintained the position given them.[64] These observations are sufficient to show the analogy that exists between these diverse states.

The great difference that seem to exist between the states we are comparing is that during artificial catalepsy, the origin of the movements and attitudes of the subject is always exterior, in the modifications that are communicated to her. During the hysterical crisis, on the other hand, the origin of the "passionate poses" seem to be internal, in the memories of the ill person. There is no need to exaggerate this difference. To begin with, the internal memories of the subject play a large role in the catalepsy. If I join Léonie's hands together, I get her to take Holy Communion, but it is because of her personal memories which are connected with the sensation of joined hands. Lucie, who is no less religious, when someone joins her hands together, does not take Holy Communion and does not kneel. On the other hand, I am not certain that exterior objects play no role in the poses of the hysterical crisis. Somewhere, and unfortunately I cannot remember in what work, there is a description of a hysteric who, in her crisis, took up the poses of the tableaus that were in her room. This would not surprise me. Lucie always turns her eyes to her curtains, and I have often asked if she had some crisis in a room without curtains. Marie dreams of fire during her crisis, if it occurs at night, but not if it occurs in the daytime. This is very probably because at night she sees a lighted lamp that is close to her bed. But, one might observe, it is very difficult to alter the poses of a hysteric; she does not seem to sense or see you. We have noted that there are exceptions and that we can change the poses of some hysterics while in crisis, but this resistance can very well be explained in terms of the fact that consciousness is so reduced, so small, that she is concentrated on a single sensation and incapable of experiencing others. That is why it would be easier to put oneself in rapport with the hysteric in the last stage of her crisis[65] rather than during the first period.

Besides, the same phenomenon presents itself in artificial catalepsy. Anyone can cause changes in Léonie when she is in somnambulism, but only I can alter her cataleptic poses. When I touch her arms, they are very light, but for another person they are stiff and contracted. We cannot fully explain here this phenomenon of electiveness, which is rare during catalepsy. We will return to it when discussing systematized sensibilities.[66] But it is necessary to point it out now, because it shows that a subject who is in a state of artificial catalepsy for her magnetizer, is, for a stranger, like a hysteric in crisis. It is probably for the same reason that natural cataleptics sometimes exhibit such stiffness in their limbs when a stranger tries to move them. Thus, the differences that we have demonstrated are only differences of degree and leave in place the comparisons we have made.

Note, however, that I have barely touched on the connections catalepsy has with other states. First there is the delirium that is sometimes produced following an epileptic crisis.[67] "We know," says Luys,[68] "that there are some epileptics who, in each period of absence, repeat the same acts and utter the same cries or the same words." An epileptic at the hospital of Havre had an unusual habit of this kind. He would get next to a pillar and make the movements of one ringing bells at full peal. No one could get him to interrupt this action, which would continue earnestly and in silence, for nearly a half-hour, until he was fully awake. This idea of ringing the bells probably entered his mind when he lived in the countryside, and, in the cataleptic state in which he found himself when awakening from an epileptic coma, was reawakened and completely took over. Indeed, some of the states called ecstasy are of the same kind. It is enough to see Léonie immobile, with hands joined and eyes raised to heaven, to understand what the middle ages called an ecstatic. Saints Teresa, Hildegard, Marie Chantal, Catherine Emmerich and many others were simply subject to attacks of catalepsy, during which dominant religious ideas or ideas sometimes communicated at the very moment of the attack, gave the whole body a harmonious and expressive attitude.[69] One person might take the pose of the Immaculate Conception,[70] another successively express all the attitudes of the stations of the cross. A most curious case from this point of view is that of Louise Lateau, described by Dr. Lefevre and summarized in Despine's book.[71] She would suddenly cease speaking; her eyes would become fixed and immobile and she would remain unmoving for many hours in the attitude of most profound contemplation. "After about two hours, the ecstatic would slightly bend forward, rise slowly, and, with a kind of projecting movement, fall down with her face to the earth. In this position she would be stretched out on the ground, lying on her chest with her head resting on her left arm. The eyes would then be closed, the mouth half-open, her lower limbs extended in a straight line. At about three hours she would make a sudden movement, extending her upper limbs transversely in the form of a cross, with her feet crossed with the right foot resting on the sole of the left foot. She remains in this position until about the seven hour mark. The ecstasy is terminated with a frightening scene: her arms fall to the side of the body, her head inclines onto her chest, her eyes are closed. Her face takes on the pallor of death, she is covered with cold perspiration; her hands are frigid, her pulse imperceptible; there is a rattle in her throat. This state lasts for ten to fifteen minutes; then her life reawakens, warmth returns, the pulse starts up again, and the cheeks regain their colour. But for some minutes still, there is the indefinable expression of ecstasy." Is this not a very exact description of a cataleptic acting out the scene of the death of Christ, instead of simply portraying, as Léonie does, the scene of Holy Communion? In this way, in natural ecstasies, in crises of hysteria, as in artificial catalepsy, we find the same initial phenomenon: a sudden and complete stopping of consciousness which lasts for an indeterminate period of time, and which can, "like a dizziness, have only an imperceptible duration,"[72] but which always occurs. At the moment of the return of consciousness, when the reawakening is not too rapid, the ecstasies, the "passionate poses," and the catalepsy take place. It is this nascent consciousness, "these witless sensations" of which Herzen speaks, that produce the phenomena that we are studying.

1.7 Interpretation of the special phenomena of catalepsy

Guided by the preceding research on the general nature of consciousness during cataleptic states, let us recall the various phenomena which we have described, that is to say, the continuation of an attitude or a movement, the repetition of movements that have been seen or sounds that have been heard, the harmonious expressions of the whole body and the movements associated with them. Let us attempt, through some hypothesis, to interpret each of these phenomena.

(1) *Continuation of an attitude or a movement.* Here we actually see the superiority of real experience, no matter how imperfect, over purely theoretical speculations. Indeed, some philosophers, particularly Condillac, asked themselves what happens when one introduces an isolated sensation into a statue devoid of thought. They thought up a multitude of things that were more or less true; they said that this sensation would produce attention, memory, pleasure, pain, etc., but they

did not define the principal phenomenon that this sensation would produce. They did not tell us that with each new sensation the statue would bestir itself. Even our simplest experiments immediately reveal this important phenomenon. Given a lack of consciousness, as soon as a sensation is introduced, of whatever kind, produced in whatever way, there will be movement. Such, we believe, is the law manifested by the simplest phenomena of catalepsy.

How does one explain the fact that the arm of a cataleptic which I lift or move maintains its position or its movement? The physical forces of gravity tend to make it fall. To sustain the situation, there must be a delicately coordinated contraction of all the muscles. What gives the muscles their unity, their persistence? I do not see any other possible response than this: a persistent sensation. When I raise the arm I provoke a certain conscious muscular sensation, one that is entirely determined, that is, corresponding precisely to a particular position of the arm, the wrist, the fingers, etc. This sensation, being entirely in the mind, does not encounter any antagonistic or weakening phenomenon; it does not disappear with the removal of the excitation; it subsists and endures. But at the same time as it endures, by its persistence it retains the position of the arm to which it is tied, or rather, from which it is inseparable.

Let us look separately at the various issues raised in this explanation. That the position in which I place the arm can produce in the subject's mind a muscular sensation that is determined and different for each posture – this is a proposition that is almost indisputable. *Kinesthetic* sensations, as Bastian says,[73] are perhaps provoked by the displacement of muscles, the rubbing together of the surfaces of the joints, the crinkling of the skin, or a thousand other modifications of the limb. Thus, their origins are still obscure, but their existence and preciseness are indisputable. In the present instance, it is necessary for the subject to have sensed the position of her arm in order to maintain that position or reproduce it later on, as we have seen often occurs. Now, if precautions are taken so that the subject cannot see the displacement of the arm, then it is by means of the kinesthetic sense that she experiences this sensation.

Can this kinetic sensation reproduce or, in the present case, maintain the posture? This is what is most debated. Ordinarily, one draws a great distinction between sensation and motor phenomena. The important discovery of the difference between sensation and motor nerves has led to the less certain (if I may venture to have an opinion on this matter) distinction between sensation centers and motor centers, and this has given impetus to the desire to find an analogous separation between the phenomena of sensibility and the functions or the phenomena of movement in psychological phenomena. In certain cases – very rare, it is true – we observe the two distinct phenomena in consciousness: I see an object approaching my eye and I sense the movement of my eyelid, which closes. But in most other cases we note only one or the other of the two phenomena, the consciousness of the sensation without the consciousness of the movement, or the feeling of movement without the notion of the preceding sensation.[74] Then one can make various suppositions. Some, such as Wundt and Charcot, are struck by the fact that there is always a sensation of movement coincident with the emission of nerve force and preceding all movement. Others, such as Bastian, considering kinesthetic sensations to be completely centripetal, coming exclusively from the exterior, are struck by "the completely unconscious nature of all centrifugal currents"[75] or in general of all motor actions. Without prejudging all the difficulties that underlie this question, which we will perhaps encounter later, I believe that the cataleptic phenomenon of the conservation of posture offers us a simple "privileged" case in which the question of the connections between sensibility and movement can be more easily studied than in any other.

Indeed, we have acknowledged a phenomenon of sensation following the displacement of the arm. Is there now some reason to suppose there is another psychological phenomenon that produces the necessary movement to maintain the posture? I for my part have not seen any, and furthermore, this supposed psychological phenomenon would be a determined motor image, exactly corresponding to the position of the arm which it must maintain. This would be exactly the same thing as the preceding image already produced by the kinesthetic sensation. Why posit two phenomena which are indistinguishable? We would like to illustrate these things here in a simple form:

The excitation E' produces the kinesthetic sensation KS, which suffices to produce, in its turn, the movement M. There is no reason to posit any other intermediaries. In this simple case there is no room for the underlying difficulties that Bastian speaks about: we do not have to try to see if the motor phenomenon has or does not have a consciousness distinct from that of the sense phenomenon, since the two phenomena form one and the same thing.

With respect to the third point, the persistence of the muscular sensation, it follows naturally from our preceding remarks. If the supposition of a conscious image has been judged to be necessary to explain the coordination of the movements and muscular contractions, insofar as this coordination persists, we are forced to posit the existence of a psychological phenomenon that accounts for it.

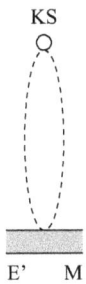

Figure 1.1 Movement *M* produced by the excitation *E* via the kinesthetic sensation *KS*.

Now, we know that the cataleptic posture can persist for a very long time. It is therefore likely, as we would say, that the kinesthetic image, not encountering any obstacle in the completely blank mind, continues, in that we have not replaced it with any other displacement of the arm.

In regard to these muscular sensations, it may rightly be said – perhaps more than for any other phenomenon of the mind – that sensation and movement are one and the same thing, presenting under two very different aspects, because they are known in two very different ways.[76] Although, in our confused and complex mind, this law may often be modified, it can be said that regularly, and in a simple being, there is no movement without a sensation of movement and no sensation or even an image of movement without a movement.

(2) *Imitation and Repetition.* Actions produced by imitation and by repetition help us advance a bit more in our study of the same problem. Instead of lifting the arm of the subject, I show her my raised arm and she puts her own in an identical position. Here the sense phenomena (to see a movement) and the motor phenomena (to raise the arm) are not mixed together as before, and it seems natural to separate them. Indeed, one can explain things in this way:

The visual excitation E' produced by my movement brought about the visual sensation VS; this, by association, awakened the kinesthetic sensation KS, which was just now directly awakened, and this image, according to the preceding law, led to the movement M, to which it corresponds. This explanation would be very simple and likely. It explains why, in certain cases, movement by imitation takes a long time to produce. It does not raise any difficulties in respect to consciousness of motor phenomena, for it only introduced two phenomena of sensation, of which one is simply of its nature inseparably tied, as we have shown, to a real movement. If we were to study only cataleptics, we would not have any reason to reject this hypothesis. But, anticipating difficulties that the study of the anesthesias and paralyses will later present, we should remark that the phenomena can also, for the most part, be explained in another way.

Can the visual sensation VS directly produce the movement M without the intervention of any muscular image?

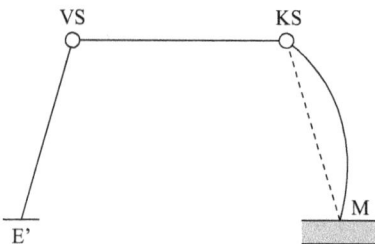

Figure 1.2 Alternative schema on the production of the movement M.

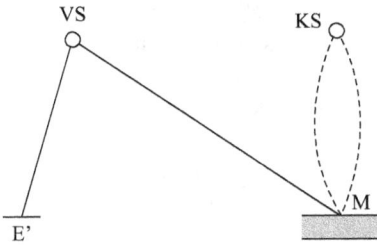

Figure 1.3 Movement *M* directly produced by the visual sensation *VS*.

The muscular sensations *KS* can be awakened secondarily from elsewhere following a movement brought about (or not). Once awakened they can contribute (or not) to its perfection and precision. This hypothesis is supported first of all by certain well known experiences.[77] We know that every excitation of the senses, of whatever kind, produces an increase of general force and a disposition to movement which sometimes finds expression in an elective movement. This movement is completely natural. It is the external manifestation of the visual and acoustic sensation, just as the contraction of the muscles would be, so to speak, the reverse of the muscular contraction. But if this movement remains general when the sensation itself is vague (such as the simple colour red or some kind of noise), should it not become precise when the sensation is itself more precise? Féré has shown that the sight of a moving object, of a disk in rotation, produces a different motor reaction following the sensation of the rotation.[78] Why would the image of a specific movement in some cases not of itself produce another precise movement? This hypothesis is confirmed by research on hysterical anesthesias, of which we will speak later. In my opinion, it is impossible to explain how these individuals can often maintain their movements despite the complete absence of sensation and even of kinesthetic images if one does not admit that the movement can be produced directly by visual or auditive images. Finally, since the fine work done by Charcot, this hypothesis is universally accepted when it is a matter of the movements of language. There are, from the point of view of language, visual, auditive, or motor individuals who, in order to represent words to themselves, employ visual, auditive, or motor graphic images. These representations play a large role in speech itself, and there are individuals who speak with an auditive sense, that is, for whom the auditive image of a word suffices to bring about the pronunciation. We can extend this celebrated theory to all movements and say that certain movements of the arm or leg can immediately accompany the visual image of the movement without an intermediary kinesthetic image.

However, this supposition encounters a grave difficulty, one which Paulhan very much insisted upon.[79] The sight of a rising arm does not resemble the real movement that must be made to really lift the arm, any more than the sound of a word resembles the movement of the mouth that must be made to pronounce it. How can one thing bring on the other and be mistaken for it? We first of all point out that one finds a similar difference between the muscular sensation of a movement and the movement itself. It is the general difference which exists between the physical and the mental, and which stops us from ever finding an analogy between a physical phenomenon and a psychological one, even when they are intimately united. Next, we do not experiment with individuals who come to us from birth and who, in their mind and body, do not have an already existing association. It is probable that in infancy we all begin as "movement types", acting and thinking by means of images of the muscular sense. Only much later would visual and auditive for the first time associated with motor images, become dominant and by themselves capable of producing movement. This would be an application of "this coordination, this psychic synthesis" which Paulhan has shown to be necessary; this would be "a pre-established systematization"[80] of psychic phenomena and organic phenomena which would make it possible for any image to play the role of a motor image.

A similar remark allows us to resolve another difficulty. One might note that in the preceding explanation we did not take into account phenomena of pleasure and pain that certain psychologists give such a large role in the formation of movements. For Bain in particular, "at the beginning of every voluntary natural impetus there is some kind of pleasure and pain, whatever form they may take."[81] For him, "some kind of pleasure or pain is needed to produce the motor impulse,"[82] and sensations only play an accessory role in directing the movement, making it precise, and adapting it to circumstances. We, on the contrary, have not at all spoken about the phenomena of pleasure or pain and, in fact, have found nothing that implies such phenomena in our subjects when cataleptic. This contradiction can be easily resolved if one considers that we are not studying the same problem as Bain. Indeed, this author is studying the origin and first manifestations of activity in a being from birth. We also study elementary activity, but of a kind that exists in a mind already formed. It may be that, at the beginning of life, movements would be uniquely determined by pleasure and pain, because then there are no psychological phenomena except those general and vague sensations that are manifested by movements equally vague and indeterminate. But, little by little, the sensations and their movements are refined. The child has learned to feel a movement by learning to do it, and the inverse is true. The union that once existed between a vague pleasure and a vague movement exists today between a determined sensation and a determined movement. It suffices that the sensation itself be experienced even without pleasure or pain for the movement to take place.

It is therefore necessary to generalize our previous law and say about every sensation and every image what we have said about the kinesthetic sense. An image of movement in consciousness always manifests on the outside, for an exterior observer, in the form of a real movement, and on the other hand this image tends to endure, to persevere, and consequently to bring about the continuation of the movement, as long as it is not replaced by a new image.

(3) and (4): *Expressions of the physiognomy and associated acts*. These phenomena seem more complicated than the preceding ones, and it appears that one single

persisting image can no longer suffice to explain them. It is necessary that in connection with the first sensation, that of the closed fist, the hands held in prayer,
etc., a great number of other images emerge simultaneously and successively,
each of which leads to the next, one a gesture, another a facial expression, here
the action of standing up, there the act of greeting. How is this possible?

We see here in its simplest form the phenomenon of the association of ideas,
which is one of the most important manifestations of psychological automatism.
Without any doubt, the images which were once produced at the same time as,
or following, the provoked sensation now reappear in the same fashion and in
the same order. It is this automatic succession of images which brings about the
regular succession of gestures and movements.

But how is one to understand this law of association? May one not, in some
sense, link it to the preceding law of the persistence of a psychological state?
We think that we can. Hamilton already understood the association of ideas in
an interesting manner when he said: "Thoughts which previously belonged to
the same unity, to the same act of knowledge, are suggested one by the other."[83]
Taine likewise considers associations as the partial rebirth of totalities which have
a tendency to re-form completely.[84] Paulhan, in the articles which we have already
cited, also tries to link association with the act of synthesis considered as a general
function of the mind. These theories seem to us, at least in part, very accurate and
they can be applied easily to the facts which we are studying. The sensation of
the closed fist or of joined hands, at the same time that they form a unity in themselves, a complete sensation, have been united previously with a great number of
other sensations, simultaneous or successive, and have been part of a synthesis,
of an ensemble which was the state of anger or the act of communion. One may
suppose with some justification that the ensemble of very different sensations
experienced by the mind during the act of communion has formed a common
sentiment, a particular coenesthesia, which is not the same as that experienced in
a state of anger or of gaiety. In now evoking the sensation of joined hands, I also
evoke, or rather I begin to evoke, the general sentiment that exists during the act
of communion. This sentiment thus becomes a sensation like the others which
tends to manifest itself and to perdure. But in order for the sentiment to persist, it
is not sufficient that the sensation of joined hands alone remains in the mind; this
would only be the beginning of the sentiment. In order for it to persist, it is necessary that it complete itself and that the other constitutive sensations reappear, one
after the other, in the form of images and bring with them the expressions and
movements corresponding to them.

In order to better understand this general explanation of associated acts and
to make use of it later, it is necessary to add some further remarks. One is too
disposed (and this is a slight mistake on the part of Hamilton and, I believe, of
Paulhan himself) to consider this general sentiment, this coenesthesia, as an idea,
a veritable knowing, to liken it to a judgement or to an abstract idea of finality.
Genuine knowledge, judgement, or general ideas ought not to be confused with
these automatic phenomena of rudimentary thought; the former imply means of

emancipation and a relative liberty of which we see no sign in the latter. This coenesthesia seems to me to resemble much more an image which is sensible and conscious, but which is not understood, more like a vague religious emotion than an idea of prayer or communion. The emotions are precisely this ensemble of diverse sensations coming from all the parts of the body: "the special activity of muscles is not simply a sign of passion, it is truly an essential part of it; if, at the moment when the features express a passion, we attempt to create another type of passion, we shall not succeed."[85] The emotions designated by language under the name of fear, anger, love, etc., are not numerous and are not precise. But their varieties must be, in reality, innumerable and correspond in each individual to a determined ensemble of images and movements. It is one of these very precise emotions which we attempt to bring to life in cataleptics and which brings with it its expressions and its associated actions.

Another important remark is that in catalepsy we are only able to provoke old feelings already experienced by subjects, and that we cannot teach them to experience new ones. A subject who is not religious and who has not previously formed the synthesis of movements which constitutes the emotion of prayer will not enact the prayer scene during catalepsy. The hands will remain one against the other, but the other acts will not follow. Automatism does not create new syntheses. It will only manifest syntheses which were organised already at a time when the mind was stronger. We have remarked previously that simple cataleptic acts do not provide us with an explanation of the true origin of the activity, but show us only the manifestation of a sensation formed already, just as more complex cataleptic actions show us only the manifestation of an emotion already organised.

Finally, let us make one last remark which we shall have occasion to recall later: these emotions, these associations of ideas can exist, like the sensations themselves, in a rudimentary consciousness such as the one which we have described. Now, we have said that the character of this consciousness will be impersonal and not awaken the idea of the self or personality. The association of ideas is thus not necessarily linked with the formation of the personality, and the one can develop without the other. So far, we have only looked at the simplest form of automatic association, which suffices to explain all the phenomena presented by the subjects in the states which we have just described.

1.8 Conclusion

To sum up, in our normal thinking, phenomena are always very numerous and very complex. They collide with each other and modify one another, and also one cannot easily ascertain their true nature and the laws that regulate them. We have studied a state of illness where the phenomena of thought present themselves, quite to the contrary, as almost isolated. One of the best expressions for characterizing this state has been proposed by Ochorowicz.[86] Catalepsy is, he said, a state of *monoideism*. "Certain subjects, capable of presenting the two opposing phases of "*a-ideism*" (hypnotic loss of consciousness) and "*poly-ideism*" (somnambulism), do not pass or cannot pass directly from one to the other. They remain for some length of time in the *mono-ideic* phase. It is a brain which concentrates all its action on one single idea, which is unique and dominant and not counterbalanced by any other." A well-known comparison can help us understand these phenomena: "The brain may be compared to a room furnished with an immense number of gas lamps, but lit only by a relatively few and relatively constant number of lighted lamps which are not always the same (ones), but which, on the contrary, change at every instant. In the measure that some lamps are extinguished, others are relit. They are never all lit, and from time to time they are all extinguished."[87] In addition, we would add that there are times when only one is lit. No doubt one must not exaggerate the importance of this expression of monoideism; to begin with, it is a question more of sensations than of ideas properly speaking. Besides, these sensations, except in cases which start with the simplest experience, are not reduced to a unity. But what is true is that the initial sensation which evokes the other images is unique, and then that each image remains isolated, without uniting with the others and without reacting upon them. Each image or each emotion develops in isolation, in accordance with its laws.

Here are the three principal laws to which these isolated phenomena always seem to submit: (1) a great number of sensations and images (the preceding studies do not permit us yet to say all) are accompanied by a bodily movement and cannot exist without producing this movement; (2) every sensation or image evoked in consciousness perdures and persists so long as it is not effaced by another phenomenon; (3) every sensation or emotion tends to develop in order to complete itself by manifesting the movements and actions from which it is inseparable. In this way, one of the most fecund ideas of our philosophers is verified by experiment: "Every idea is an image, an interior representation of an action. Now, the representation of an action, that is to say of an ensemble of movements, is the first movement of that act, the beginning, and is thus the action in its commencement, the movement being at one the same time begun and suppressed. The idea of a possible action is therefore a real tendency, that is to say, a power already acting and not a purely abstract possibility."[88]

Notes

1 Saint-Bourdin, *Traité de la Catalepsie*, 1841, 7.
2 Ballet, *Langage Intérieur et les Diverses Forms de l'Aphasie*, 1888, préface, xv.
3 Descriptions of catalepsy are found in a large number of works. I quote here only the ones I know and consult: Saint-Bourdin, *Traité de la Catalepsie*, 1841. P. Baragnon, *Etude du Magnétisme Animal Sous le Point de Vue d'une Exact Pratique*, 1853, 226. Delasiauve., *Traité de l'Épilepsie*, 1854, 263. Despine, *Étude Scientifique sur le Somnambulisme*, 1880, 194. Axenfeld, *Traité des Névroses*, 2nd edit., 1883, 908. Bottey, *Magnétisme Animal*, 1884, 29. Paul Richer, *Hystéro-épilepsie*, 1885, 610, 668, 775. Culler, *Magnétisme et Hypnotisme*, 1886, 124. Binet and Féré, *Magnétisme Animal*, 1887, 114.

4 Richer, *Op. cit.*, 292.
5 *Ibid.*, 614.
6 Saint-Bourdin, *Op. cit.*, 46.
7 *Ibid.*, 64.
8 Saint-Bourdin, *Op. cit.*, 53.
9 Observation of Tissot, reported by Saint-Bourdin, *Op. cit.*, 9.
10 Richer, *Op. cit.*, 669.
11 Saint-Bourdin, *Op. cit.*, 30.
12 Charcot, *Maladies du Système Nerveux*, 1887, 111, 337.
13 Despine, *Psychologie Naturelle*, 1868, I, 490 and sq. *Étude Scientifique sur le Somnambulism*, 1880.
14 Despine, *Somnambulisme*, 80.
15 *Ibid.*, 17.
16 *Ibid.*, 98.
17 *Ibid.*, 102.
18 Gurney, *The Problems of Hypnotism, Proceedings of the Society for Psychical Research*, 1884, II, 282.
19 Cf. Chapter 2, Section 2.3.
20 Despine, *Somnambulisme*, 99.
21 *Ibid.*, 49.
22 *Ibid.*, 31.
23 On the subject of the unconsciousness of habit, see the study of L. Dumont, *Revue Philosophique*, 1876, I, 326.
24 *Ibid.*, 328.
25 Richet, *Essai de Psychologie Général*, 1885, 69.
26 Despine, *Psychologie*, I, 491.
27 Herzen, *Le Cerveau et l'Activité Cérébrale*, 1887, 212.
28 Ribot, *Maladies de la Personnalité*, 1885 16.
29 Despine, *Somnambulisme*, 85.
30 Bernheim, *De la Suggestion*, 1886, 94. – Cf. Liébeault, *Du Sommeil*, 1866, 412.
31 Cf. Richer, *Op. cit.*, 689.
32 Cf. Binet and Féré, *Op. cit.*, 210, and Cullerre, *Op. cit.*, 162.
33 Richer, *Op. cit.*, 781.
34 *Ibid.*, 697
35 *Ibid.*, 612.
36 Leibniz, *Erdm.*, 125, a.
37 On this subject, see Rabier, *Cours de Philosophie*, 1884, I, 74 and I, 254.
38 Paulhan, *L'Associationnisme et la Synthèse Psychique, Revue Philosophique*, 1888, I, 32, and *Finalité comme Propriété des Éléments Psychiques*, id., 1888, II, 105.
39 Soury, *Les Fonctions du Cerveau*, 1886, 46 et sq. – Mosso, *La Peur*, 1886, 38. – Sergi, *Psychologie Physiologique*, 1888, 114.
40 Reid, *Œuvres*, Trans. Jouffroy, 1829, II, 53.
41 Garnier, *Traité des Facultés de l'Âme*, 1872, I, 380.
42 Mill, *La Philosophie de Hamilton*, Trans., 1869, 249.
43 Buffon, *Discours sur la Nature des Animaux, Œuvres*, 1839, III, 1.
44 Gerdy, *Physiologie Philosophique des Sensations*, 1846.
45 Lewes, *Physiology of Common Life*, W. Blackwood and Sons, Edimburgh-London, 1859, II.
46 Herzen, *Op. cit.*, 255 ff.
47 Cf. Delboeuf, *Le Sommeil et les Rêves, Revue Philosophique*, 1879, II, 335–339.
48 Dumont, *Théorie Scientifique de la Sensibilité*, 1877, 103.
49 Cf. Fouillée, *L'Homme Automate, Revue des Deux Mondes*, August 1st, 1886, 552, and elsewhere: "We respond," he says, "that to feel does not at all imply that I feel myself,

that the immediate consciousness of pain does not imply reflexive consciousness, that these feelings can be stirred in a distressing way without the individual, as an individual, feeling it." *La Conscience: Revue des Deux Mondes*, October 15th, 1883, 902.

50 de Biran, *Anthropologie*, in the *Œuvres Inédites*, 1859, III, 362.
51 *Ibid.*, III, 405.
52 de Biran, *Essai sur les Fondements de la Psychologie, Œuvres Inédites* II, 11 et 19.
53 de Biran, *Journal intime*, 1877, 139.
54 de Biran, *Anthropologie, Œuvres Inédites*, III, 397.
55 Herzen, *Op. cit.*, 236.
56 *Ibid.*, 245.
57 Binet and Féré, *Op. cit.*, 118.
58 Azam, *Hypnotisme, Double Conscience...*, 1887, 66.
59 de la Tourette, *L'Hypnotisme et les États Analogues*, 1887, 223.
60 Without intending, in this purely psychological work, to discuss the very controversial question of the three stages of hypnotism, the importance of which is moreover sometimes exaggerated, I would like to make some remarks concerning the preceding observations. Catalepsy and the same state improperly called lethargy with neuromuscular hyper-excitability seem to me perfectly real states which follow naturally in the course of a grand crisis of hystero-epilepsy or even during the state of somnambulism brought about in some subjects who have already had crises of this kind. But it must be added that these states, especially the latter, are very rare, since they are indeed psychological rather than physical modifications and that consciousness remains, although very altered and even reduced, in lethargy, so that a great many subjects reproduce these states through simple automatism when they are heard to speak or when they can see. Cf. Chapter 3 in this volume.
61 I have already described this state of Léonie and its accompanying features in my article on *Les Phases Intermédiaires de l'Hypnotisme, Revue Scientifique*, 1886, I, 577.
62 Cf. Chapter 1 of the second volume.
63 Saint-Bourdin, *Op. cit.*, 96.
64 Paul Richer, *Op. cit.*, 279.
65 Cf. de la Tourette, *Op. cit.*, 242.
66 Chapter 2 of the second volume.
67 Despine (*Somnambulisme*, 294) makes a very strong comparison between epileptic vertigo and somnambulism. To clarify, it would be necessary to cite almost all his remarks. My only reservations are about his interpretation of the phenomena already cited in section 1.2 of the present chapter.
68 Luys, *Maladies Mentales*, 1881, 146.
69 For a description of a great many ecstatic attacks, see Gauthier, *Histoire du Somnambulisme chez tous les Peuples*, 1842, II. –Desages, *De l'Extase*, 1866.
70 Richer, *Op. cit.*, 217, 220.
71 Despine, *Somnambulism*, 376.
72 Azam, *Op. cit.*, 88.
73 Bastian, *Le Cerveau Organe de la Pensée*, II, 165.
74 See Richet, *Les Réflexes Psychiques, Revue Philosophique*, 1888, I, 228.
75 Bastian, *Op. cit.*, II, 129.
76 On this subject, see the theories of Lewes in the *Psych. angl.* of Ribot, 401, and the works of Dumont.
77 Féré, *Sensation et Mouvement*, 1887.
78 *Ibid.*, 83.
79 Paulhan, *Revue Philosophique*, 1888, I, 45 and 59.
80 *Ibid.*, 45.
81 A. Bain, *Émotions et Volonté*. Trans., 1885, 345.
82 *Ibid.*, 342.

83 Cf. Ferri, *La Psychologie de l'Association*, 1883, 231.
84 Taine, *Intelligence*, 1870, 1, 144.
85 Maudsley, Cf. Bain, *Esprit et Corps*, 7.
86 Ochorowicz, *La Suggestion Mentale*, 1887, 112.
87 Herzen, *Op. cit.*, 216.
88 Fouillée, *Liberté et Déterminisme*, 1884, 3.

Chapter 2

Forgetting and various successive psychological existences

It is only in very rare and extraordinary circumstances that human actions are isolated and impersonal in this way. Ordinarily they seem to be the manifestation of a character and depend on a personality. In order to pursue the study of automatic actions in the more complex conditions that approximate the normal state, we must find psychological states which are susceptible to experimentation, but in which, nevertheless, character and personality are beginning to develop. It is the state known as *somnambulism* that best fulfils these conditions.

Indeed, in somnambulists we see the automatic life of the mind grow and extend to form a special memory and give birth to a character and a new personality. To discover the nature and main characteristics of this new form of psychological life is to see the activity of the elements of our thought under another face.

2.1 The different characteristics that have been proposed for recognizing somnambulism

This state is well known on the surface. Sometimes, as we know, it occurs spontaneously in connection with sleep; at others, it forms an important part of a nervous crisis; at still others, it is artificially induced by procedures that have been too often described for me to say more. Nevertheless, it is very hard to find a distinctive property which characterizes it in a general way, and most of the characteristics that have been assigned to it seem to us to be inadequate. In reviewing them, we will see certain subordinate properties of this state, but it will remain for us to search out its distinguishing mark.

Some of these characteristics have been called physical, not because they are true, visible modifications, but because we ascertain them through various experiments made on the body of the subject.

Most of the old magnetizers considered the absolute insensitivity of the skin to be the invariable rule and infallible sign of somnambulism: "To have somnambulism," said Lausanne,[1] "it is necessary that the exterior senses do not produce any distraction and experience nothing." "There is no magnetic sleep," wrote Baragnon,[2] "without complete insensibility of the body and the senses, so that convincing ourselves of insensibility is our best guide for deciding whether sleep

DOI: 10.4324/9780429287671-2

has been established." Also, magnetizers went ahead and tested their subject with burns and pin pricks once the sleep had begun.[3] In the celebrated report presented to the Academy of Medicine in 1837, Dubois (d'Amiens) complained that to verify somnambulism he had only been allowed "a simple tattooing of a pin on the face and hands." He would have liked to do more. Indeed, the procedure of Dubois would not have produced much of a result if applied to the somnambulists that I have studied. Most of them – nearly all, in fact – were already anesthetic on quite a large part of their bodies in their more normal state, before any hypnotic sleep. Moreover, it was by no means usual for them to be anesthetic while in somnambulism. On the contrary, for some of them and in some instances, I have come to consider the return of sensibility a proof of the most profound somnambulism.

The same authors draw attention to another curious characteristic, although not as frequently: the complete absence of swallowing during certain somnambulistic states.[4] This feature strikes me because with one individual, Léonie, it is always present. She never swallows during somnambulism and I have never been able to get her to drink a drop of water. In a recent article, Dufay draws attention to the same fact in his somnambulists.[5] But this phenomenon, far from being characteristic, is very rare. Most somnambulists eat and drink without any discomfort in their sleep state. In natural somnambulism, Lucy will come down to cook a cutlet and eat it very well. Rose is never so happy as when she has lunch during somnambulism. There are even hysterics who are dysphagic in the waking state but eat very easily when asleep, and this is a fact that is useful to keep in mind. My brother succeeded in feeding a hysterical woman of this kind who, because of uncontrollable vomiting, was in danger of dying of starvation.

Despine, a modern author who has a good understanding of somnambulists, believes that he sees a clearly distinctive quality in their exterior attitude. Popular belief is that in general somnambulists are people who speak with their eyes closed. This belief probably results from the idea –- in reality very false – that somnambulism is a sleep. We say to somnambulists that they are asleep, from which they conclude that they should have their eyes closed. But if you allow somnambulists to act in their own way, very many, such as Lucie, nearly always have their eyes open. But then, Despine claims that their gaze always has a singular and distinctive character: "The eyes, he says, are wide open …; the pupils are largely dilated and do not change with the introduction of light; the conjunctive is without feeling and does not have the need to be lubricated by tears; also, the blinking of the eyelids is suppressed, or very rare."[6] The author is so convinced of the importance of this characteristic that he claims "to be able, through an inspection of the eyes, to discover attempted fraud by a false somnambulist." I must confess that I have had neither such audacity, nor such a conviction.

No doubt, sometimes it happens that way, and Despine indicates very well in what particular circumstance: "when the retina is paralyzed"; when, indeed, "this unseeing gaze is like enough to that of an individual who is sufficiently myopic to be unable to distinguish objects in the environment." Thus, during catalepsy, when one does not excite visual sensation, the eye takes on this characteristic. If one forces the eyes of a hysteric open at the start of somnambulism, at the moment when, ordinarily (because there can be exceptions) she does not see clearly, her eyes have an unseeing gaze. But does that mean that a somnambulist always has a paralyzed retina and is always blind? According to a very old opinion, one held by Maine de Biran himself, she behaves in a fashion that accords with her dreams, with the hallucinations that represent objects to her, such that she knows them and not her true visual sensations. This opinion seems to me to be completely incorrect. If one allows the somnambulist to develop sufficiently, there are subjects who open their eyes on their own, or indeed one can have them open their eyes to verify the moment when they see clearly. Obviously one recognizes that a somnambulist then finds her way guided by her view of real objects, seeing that one could easily verify that by leading her down a passage she does not know. Then the eyes do not have this bizarre look; they are entirely normal and, even during catalepsy, if one would fix them on an object, through acts of imitation, for example, one would see them move and take on a normal appearance. In regard to this attitude of somnambulists, I have many times conducted an experiment that I consider decisive. I have often sent Lucie, in full somnambulism, to speak to persons unknown to her, who were not forewarned about her, and she was always taken as a normal person. Marie could be left in a somnambulistic state in a hospital room without other patients suspecting her state. No doubt there are for me, who knows her well, some characteristic traits, and I have never had to inquire about their sensibility or memory in order to know what state they were in: Maria is paler in somnambulism than in her waking state; Lucie, who often has facial tics when she is awake, has calm and regular features in her second state. But these are individual traits of minimal importance, and they do not provide the basis for a scientific distinction.

Finally, to bring to an end this enumeration of physical traits that have been proposed, Charcot, along with Paul Richer, Binet, Féré, etc., have seen in hysterics, placed in somnambulism, a particular contracture which is produced in the muscles following a superficial rubbing, or even a simple blowing on the skin. Seeing that in this work I especially want to give an account of what I observed, I should say that I have looked for this characteristic in a dozen hysterics placed in a somnambulistic state, and I have only found it in two subjects. On the other hand, one hysteric – Rose – who never exhibits this characteristic in somnambulism, sometimes exhibits it in the waking state. This is enough for me to say that I do not see this feature as characteristic.

In reality, I am now convinced that there is no physical sign which allows one to recognize if a woman is in a state of somnambulism or not, and it goes too far to claim that one can recognize this state at a glance. Despine held that psychology should not deal with somnambulism[7] and that physiology alone can explain it. Well, physiology, far from being able to explain it, does not even recognize it. Certain authors, such as Bertrand and Braid, and more recently Gurney and Bernheim, to their great credit have recognized that somnambulism is a psychological phenomenon and that its presence can only be established from features that are uniquely psychic. However, not all the mental phenomena that have been attributed to it are of equal importance.

Dr. Carpenter talks about the state of distraction of the hypnotized subject. He compares this state to the reverie of a poet contemplating a beautiful passage or the distraction of a scholar absorbed in researching a problem.[8] This is vague and inexact. There are somnambulists who are hardly distracted at all and who study a problem with great attention. Moreover, Stanley-Hall has said, to the contrary, that hypnosis is a fixing of attention on an object. Gurney, who cites this author, justly remarks that a hypnotized person can have a series of fixations of attention on different objects without awakening in passing from one to another. I would add that somnambulists are not always attentive, any more than they are always distracted. Léonie, when one needs her attention for subtle experiments, from time to time asks for a little recreation to rest and amuse herself.

Bertrand, Braid, and especially Bernheim, have sought the characteristic feature of somnambulism in the state of activity or of willing, and have noted that the somnambulist has no personal will or active spontaneity, and obeys all orders. Without at this moment investigating the matter of suggestion, which is indeed one of the most important phenomena involved in this state, I would only like to remark that nothing is more variable than the state of will in somnambulism, as well as in the waking state. One of the more curious studies I have done – and one to which I will later return – is that of a young girl, sixteen years old, with significant cognitive impairment and probably epileptic. During her waking state, she was most normal and, throughout her whole life, more suggestible and more subject to hallucinations than the most docile somnambulist. Furthermore, Bernheim has clearly recorded suggestions in the waking state and has admitted that this phenomenon is merely more accentuated in somnambulism. So, how then to explain that subjects such as Rose, Lucie, and many others become more and more independent as somnambulism deepens, and come to a state in which their will is perfectly normal and more spontaneous and independent than in the waking state?[9] In fact it seems to me that the will is a secondary phenomenon, depending on many other things, and it is among the most elementary facts that we must seek the distinctive signs of somnambulism – that is, in the state of memory and sensation.

2.2 Essential characteristics of somnambulism: forgetting upon waking and alternating memory

The phenomena of memory are perhaps the most important in our psychological make-up, and their slightest modifications have great repercussions on our lives. Now, in all mental pathology there is no modification of memory more complex and yet more consistent than in the memory of the somnambulist. We note regularly in the thought of individuals who, for one reason or another, have periods of somnambulism, three characteristics or three laws of memory which are peculiar to them: (1) complete forgetfulness in the waking state of all that has occurred during somnambulism; (2) full memory during a new somnambulism of what has occurred in previous somnambulisms; (3) full memory during somnambulism of what occurs while awake. There are perhaps more exceptions and irregularities in regard to the third law than the other two; so in this study, whose main purpose is to present a general idea of somnambulism, we will lay less stress on it. But the first two – despite the diversity inevitable in phenomena that are so complex – are so general and so important that they might be considered the characteristic sign of somnambulism.

The phenomenon of forgetting upon waking what has occurred during som- nambulism is so curious and striking that it has been noted from the earliest stud- ies of this kind. "When returning to the natural state," says Deleuze,[10] "he loses the memory of all sensations and ideas that he has had while in the state of som- nambulism. So that these two states seem to be so alien to each other that the somnambulist and the waking man are two different beings. This single charac- teristic is constant and essentially distinguishes somnambulism." "Forgetting all that has occurred during magnetic sleep," also writes Baragnon,[11] "is an invariable effect, without which there is no sleep." Braid also characterizes somnambulism by forgetfulness on waking and calls it a doubling of consciousness. There is no use multiplying these citations which one can glean from all the writers – old and recent. It is simply a matter of giving a few examples to convey the importance of the phenomenon. One day, about two hours after noon, I came to put Léonie in a state of sleep, and I had already had her in somnambulism for some time when I received a letter from Dr. Gibert, who, not being able to join me, asked me to bring Léonie there. Instead of waking the somnambulist, I showed her the letter and proposed that she come with me as she was. "I would very much like to," she responded, "but I must dress; you would not want me to come like this." She went upstairs and dressed. Then I took her with me in a carriage, which put her in a state of great joy, like a child. She remained in somnambulism the whole evening and was very lively and happy. She participated in certain experiments we wanted to make, and during the breaks she talked about a great many things. It was nearly midnight when I brought her back home, and there, in the same place where I had put her to sleep two hours earlier, I brought her back to full wakefulness. Note that after this stirring session, she awoke calm, tranquil, convinced that she had not stirred all day and that she had only just been put to sleep. But she was astounded to see that she was dressed differently, and I was obliged to put her back to sleep and make suggestions to prevent her from becoming preoccupied with this anom- aly. Here is another example. During a somnambulism, Lucie got it into her mind to be angry with me, I do not recall why. Believing that she was in one of the hallways that she frequented, we did not keep watch well enough and she took advantage of that to make her escape into the street in full somnambulism. It was necessary to find her and make her return – something that was not easy to do. As the situation went on, I found it very easy to awaken her. Immediately, as if by magic, she was rendered pleasant and amiable, with no sign of her bad humor and no thought of reproaching anyone. Back home, the lack of memory was so complete that she, like Léonie, did not remember having been asleep for some time. If she is put to sleep in the middle of an action or a conversation, she nearly always continues with her action or speech on waking as if nothing unusual had occurred. The somnambulism, no matter its length, seems not to have happened and the two moments of waking life seem to join together. Rose has remained four and a half days in a somnambulism (we were trying in this way to heal a paralysis of the legs which had resisted all other treatment and we were, as it turns out, completely successful); but during these four days she spoke to many people and even received visitors. On waking, she forgot all, was mistaken about the day of the week and believed it was four days earlier. Thus it is for all somnambulists whom I have seen: that whether their abnormal state is short or long, whether the events are insignificant or important, their forgetting is always complete and absolute. It is a page completely erased from their lives.

The second phenomenon, the return of memory in a new somnambulism, is very easy to establish. When Léonie was again put asleep on the day after the one I have just narrated, she suddenly re-experienced the excitation she had had when awake. "You did not want to allow me to return on foot," she told me afterwards, "You saw that I walked easily and was not fatigued." In the case of Lucie, when, on the following day, I again put her to sleep, she immediately recommenced the experience that waking had interrupted. This time I succeeded in calming her and, happily, obtained a reconciliation. Another somnambulist, N, whom I put to sleep two times a year apart, in the second somnambulism regained a detailed memory of all she had done in the first and recalled to me details that I myself had completely forgotten. Everyone who has frequently put people to sleep has noted this common but singular phenomenon.

Ordinarily the second state also possesses the full memory of actions and ideas of normal waking. During somnambulism, the subject can recall what he has done or felt during the day and is still acquainted with the same people. One time only I assisted at a somnambulism of Rose which was accidentally different from the others, during which she no longer recognized me and appeared to have forgotten most of the events that had occurred since her stay at the hospital. But this kind of case is very rare and I have not seen it repeated. Nevertheless, it is necessary to take it into account if one is trying to explain the modifications of memory.

To consider the state of memory as the essential characteristic of somnambulism is not to put forward a sign that is easy to simulate and difficult to establish. We respond that up to now we do not have anything better. Also this criterion is more certain than one might think. Contrary to general opinion, I consider psychological phenomena to be much more difficult to simulate than physical ones, and I believe it would be much easier even to feign an attack of epilepsy than to pretend madness for many days in the presence of an alienist. In the case of the former, all that would be needed would be a few pieces of information and a bit of practice to simulate a contracture. On the other hand it would require a great deal of knowledge, attention and memory to not mix up memories acquired during somnambulism with memories acquired during the waking state and never be caught in a mistake. One could conduct a very thorough examination with questions that would verify the state of memory. It is true that it is sometimes dangerous to interrogate the subject directly. The question, acting as a kind of suggestion, might awaken a memory without her realizing it. I do not believe that in general the danger of this is very great, because suggestion in regard to memory is not that easy, and one does not awaken memories in a subject by asking about what she has said or done when she was asleep. Nevertheless, the danger exists and Gurney,[12] who has often pointed this out, also mentions quite a good way to avoid this: by verifying the memories through conversation, without giving the impression of direct interrogation. "Give them a seemingly neutral question, to which they respond in one way if they have certain memories and another if they do not know what it is about." This is an excellent approach and easier in practice than it may seem. But, as I have already said, to do this it is necessary to know the character of the subject and all about their life, and be prepared to spend a great deal of time with them. Psychological experiments require specific precautions and cannot be done quickly. It is through this procedure that, at least whenever there could be doubts, we have carefully verified the state of memory of the persons of whom we speak. But we do not attempt to show here, for each person, the experiences and conversations which we have used to make these verifications – that would uselessly lengthen this presentation.

These disappearances and recoverings of memory occur in other states besides artificial somnambulism. We also find them very distinctly in natural somnambulism. A young man, cited by Georget,[13] passed suddenly, after an initial cry, into a new state in which he, while maintaining his faculties, had a different character than in his normal state. "He returned to himself, if one surprised him by squeezing him around the waist, and then he forgot everything. He remembered everything in the following episode and nonetheless thought himself to be in his habitual state, so that it was as if there were two different existences." "I treated a very spiritual young woman," recalls Erasmus Darwin,[14] "who was subject to a state of reverie which came back day after day and which lasted nearly the whole day. Since, during her crisis, she retained ideas of the same kind that she had had on the previous day, and which she no longer remembered the moment the crisis was over, her parents imagined that she had two souls." I have cited these two comments because they are less known, but it would be easy to gather together many others. We know about the patient of Dr. Mesnet who, one night, tranquilly put some pennies to soak in a glass of water and wrote that she wanted to die. She put her concoction in an armoire, hid the key, and awoke. The following night the attack recurred and she found the key and rushed to the armoire to get her glass.[15] We also know about the dreamer of Despine who would steal gold pieces from himself and always go to hide them in the same place.[16] In regard to the study of Dr. Azam[17] on Félida and on Albert X., and as to the description of the somnambulist de Dufay[18] – today they are classics.

The same kinds of things are easily shown to occur during the delirium that follows an epileptic attack[19] and especially during an attack of hysteria. Rose had the bad habit of regularly calling a servant of the hospital names at the end of her attack. She would not remember this upon waking, and she could not believe it when she was told about it. Even so, in the following attack, she would continue her insults at the same point, shouting: "I have good reason for saying this or that; it is entirely true," and she would repeat the details of the preceding delirium.

Certain authors have shown that memory has an analogous quality during ordinary dreams, which justifies Dupotet[20] saying: "There is no sleep without somnambulism." In Myers,[21] we find good examples, too lengthy to report here, in which a dream is clearly the memory of another dream that has been forgotten when awake. It seems to me most interesting to remember, as well as most useful for clarifying the issues around memory, that similar facts have been established during the intoxication of opium,[22]as well as the intoxication of alcohol. The facts are particularly clear in the case of alcohol. Everybody knows that an inebriated person forgets on waking what they have done during his intoxication. Occasionally, I have had the opportunity to carry out a very simple experiment: One proposes to persons … who are overly merry … a good way to prove that they are still in their normal state. One shows them a number and asks them to remember it so as to be able to repeat it the next day. In general, if the intoxication was complete enough, they will, despite their effort, be unable the next day to recall the number which had been mentioned to them. However, I have not verified the return of memory in the next intoxication. Here is a very clear illustration of this matter. A black man, completely drunk, stole some surgical instruments from a Dr. Keulemans.[23] The next day, he insisted that he had not touched them and looked for them in vain; he was unable to find them. Two days later he was again made drunk and was asked again about the loss of the instruments. This time he thought about the matter, immediately went out and, despite the darkness, went right to them, finding them in a box where he had hidden them during his first intoxication. These facts relating to drunkenness, as interesting as they might be, do not reduce the value of the feature we have chosen to characterize somnambulism. They simply show that certain troubles of the mind ought to be compared to it, and we do not hesitate to note that there are in fact still other features which connect intoxication and somnambulism.

We encounter a most serious difficulty in the often noted fact that some somnambulists, after their sleep, retain a certain amount of memory. The fact is incontestable. It is a matter of seeing in what circumstances this happens and how one can interpret it. Let us begin by putting aside all the data of memory which are related to suggestion. It is very clear that if I order a somnambulist to carry out some action on waking, she can only execute the order if she in some way retains the memory. The memory needed to carry out the suggestion presents itself in a variety of forms: it might be completely conscious; it might be unknown to the subject; it might subtly evade the mind as a compulsion whose origin is unknown, or it might slowly take its shape. Later on we will discuss the various ways suggestions can be executed. For now it is enough to say that there is a memory involved, however superficial and passing. First of all, this memory contains only the order that needs to be carried out at the moment. If we direct our attention to the case of G, in which this memory is very clear, note that we gave her two orders during her sleep: (1) to walk around her room when she awoke; (2) to come the next day at 4:00 to a particular room. In addition to that, we made her do various other things. On waking she did not remember anything of the conversation she had had with us, and she no longer remembered the second command which was to be executed the next day. But she did recall that I had said to her to walk around her room, which she now did. The memory of the second command reappeared the next day at 4:00, and as to the memory of the conversation, it only reappeared in the next somnambulism. In the second place, this memory is temporary. Beaunis[24] has fully demonstrated this fact, which I have often observed. If a subject executes a suggestion with consciousness and memory at the moment of execution, a few moments later they rapidly and completely loses not only the memory of the suggestion, but also of its execution. N, whom I ordered to pick some flowers on awakening, carried out my command. I came up to her and asked her what she was doing, and she told me she was picking flowers and that there was nothing wrong with that, etc. A moment later, she maintained that she had not risen from her chair and did not know where the flowers had come from. We find the same things if, instead of suggesting an act, we suggest a memory of certain words spoken during somnambulism.[25] Léonie, when asleep, wanted to retain the memory of some pieces of information I gave her in answer to her questions. I ordered that she remember them with ease. When she awoke it was easy to show that she remembered what I said very well. But the next day, when awake, she again asked me about this information: the memory had therefore not stayed with her. Perhaps it is possible in this kind of situation to make more durable suggestions, but then one changes the natural phenomenon and creates something totally artificial.

Nevertheless, a certain degree of memory does naturally remain after a very light hypnotic sleep, which then comes very close to the waking state. "A subject hypnotized for the first time," wrote Gurney,[26] "remembered everything – not only the actions he had performed, but even the feelings of surprise he experienced in doing them. It seemed that he had two selves, one observing the involuntary actions of the other, without thinking that it was useful to stop them." Charles Richet[27] similarly refers to an individual who not only remembered his suggested actions during somnambulism, but still imagined that he always performed them freely. I have myself noted this persistence of memory in a young man whom I have hypnotized many times, but very lightly. His eyelids remained closed despite himself, and, despite his efforts, he could not alter the position in which I had placed his arms. On waking, he could easily remember everything. It is right to remark that in this case the sole criterion for the somnambulistic state had been the phenomenon of suggestion. Now, we know that this phenomenon occurs perfectly well in the waking state. So why would we not say that with these individuals it is a matter of suggestive phenomena in the waking state, that they do not change their state to experience paralysis of their arms or eyelids, and that they have simply demonstrated certain unconscious phenomena, the memory of which is naturally retained?

Delboeuf has made a most interesting remark about the memory of somnambu-lists. Having noted that in certain circumstances the memory of dreams suggested during somnambulism persists after waking, he had been led to conclude that "the hypnotic dream has the same nature as the ordinary dream and is subject to the same laws, and that hypnotic dreams lend themselves to recall under the same conditions as ordinary dreams."[28] It is without doubt true that, in many cases, especially with somnambulism that is not very deep, it works well to deal with hypnotic sleep and normal sleep from the same point of view, but the facts do not allow us to say that they are completely identical and that in the case of hypnotic sleep there are not great modifications of memory.[29] Here it is that we find the dif-ferent degrees so important in psychology. When one suddenly awakens a subject in the midst of carrying out a suggested act, she remembers it as a dream. During somnambulism, I got Lucie to believe that her dress was on fire and she squeezed the material to put out the flames. Awakened suddenly at that moment, she mur-mured: "Well, I was quite a fool to think that my dress was burning." Memory persists in the same way, as I have elsewhere remarked,[30] when it is not a matter of actions or movements, but of a simple hallucination. I told Lucie that there was a green Bengal light in the room and she looked at it admiringly. Then, choosing a moment when she was wrapped in its contemplation, I suddenly awoke her. I simply clapped my hands, our predetermined signal, and, upon awakening, she looked around, very surprised: "Why did you put out the Bengal light ... Oh, it was a dream!" The same experience occurred, around the same time and in the same way, with Marie, who, when she was suddenly awakened, retained not only the memory, but even a faint and persistent hallucination of the somnambulistic dream: "Well," she said, "so you have lit a Bengal light ... but it is damaged; it is going out little by little." It seems, therefore, that in this experience, waking up did not destroy the memory of the somnambulism and that there had been no splitting of her psychological life.

We note that this experiment can only be replicated with subjects who can experience a sudden and rapid awakening. It makes sense to say that these sub-jects are those who are less asleep and whose somnambulism is less profound. Two things prove this: (1) When a subject is put to sleep for the first time, the sleep is normally light and she can be awakened abruptly. When she has been often put to sleep, she experiences a profound sleep, from which she can no longer easily be aroused. At the very beginning of my study of Lucie, I could easily replicate the experiment just described. After a period of time, I could not make it happen. Because she needed at least a minute to awaken, the somnambulistic act was completely interrupted and no memory could persist. (2) I have been led, wrongly or rightly (the evidence will be seen later), to believe that somnambulism is profound when the psychological state of the subject, the various feelings, the character, the intelligence, all become very different from what they are in the waking state. Indeed, subjects who experience this kind of change cannot be eas-ily awakened. Difficulty awakening always accompanies deep somnambulism.

Rose and Léonie, who display all the phenomena of catalepsy, all the changes in sensation, etc., need many minutes to wake up completely, and never recover even the smallest memory on awakening. Therefore, the persistence of memory is found only with light somnambulisms.

Even for these it is necessary to make an important remark: memory retained with rapid awakening does not last long. It exists at the very moment of awakening and one can get a hold of it if one questions the subject at that moment. But it disappears little by little and before long there is no trace of it left in consciousness. Marie, who, on awakening, complimented me on the Bengal light that I had lit, first stated with regret that the light was fading; then she only had the memory of it and said: "The Bengal light was very nice, just now, but it has too quickly gone." Finally, five minute later, she affirmed that she had seen nothing and only knew what I had said when I spoke of the Bengal light. It is true that if I had put her back to sleep, the memory would have completely returned, but if I were to simply leave her in the waking state, the forgetting would be permanent. To explain this I can only make the supposition that she was first of all badly awakened, and then she was awakened gradually. Furthermore, for the experience to turn out well, it is necessary that the act begun during somnambulism continue a little after the moment of awakening, and for it to continue in that way, it is essential that the somnambulism does not disappear quickly. In reality, psychological states are continuous and the subject does not jump from one to the other. There is a post-hypnotic period that can sometimes stretch out for a long time after waking, and it is entirely natural that the memory of the somnambulism would exist for some time during this period.[31]

If my explanation does not apply to every case, it is because psychological phenomena are extremely complex and it is always necessary to take into account abnormal circumstances that modify the general law. It seems that in the Middle Ages forgetting after somnambulism was seen as a sign of sorcery. The unfortunate somnambulists, for fear of being burned at the stake, says Bertrand, would suggest to themselves that they would retain the memory, and sometimes they were successful. Today, we make our experiments before a public meeting convened specially to find out about memory on waking, we allow the subjects to see each other during the somnambulism, we prepare them to think of it as entertaining when they keep their memory and boring when the contrary happens, and finally, we sometimes revive memories in having them often retell their dreams and we create an artificial memory. It is not surprising that we thus so often encounter this post-hypnotic memory. If we were to correct the faulty conditions, this phenomenon of memory on awakening would be completely absent, we believe, after deep somnambulisms, rare and of short duration after others. Also, we maintain that the feature of forgetfulness on waking is the most important sign of the state of somnambulism, and persist in our belief that if it is completely lacking, we are dealing with suggestibility in the waking state and not somnambulism.

2.3 Varieties and complications of alternating memory

These forgetfulnesses and returns of memory that are so striking in somnambulism sometimes present themselves with a degree of complication that is greater
than is very useful to know. No subject always enters into the same state of somnambulism. She enters into a variety of states that indeed are all analogous to
hypnotic sleep, but are not identical with each other. It happens, then, that after
being in an induced state, she presents a different memory: she remembers or does
not remember from such and such another state in which she had previously been
placed. In other words, the perturbations of memory that ordinary somnambulism
produces in the memory of the subject when she is brought back to her waking
state can be equally well produced when the subject re-enters the first state.

Here is a very interesting observation that was first published in the *Bibliotheque
du magnétisme*, and then represented in Bertrand's *Traité du somnambulisme*.[32]
A young girl, thirteen or fourteen years of age, would fall into various nervous
states distinct from waking, and into nervous crises, natural somnambulism, and
artificial or magnetic somnambulism. "Although the patient had the free exercise of her intelligence in all the different states, in her ordinary state she did not
remember anything she had done or said in each of the others. But what seemed
astonishing was that in magnetic somnambulism, which dominated, so to speak,
all the other kinds of lives that came into play for her, she remembered all that
happened, whether in somnambulism or in her nervous crises or in her waking
state. In sleep-walking she lost her recall of magnetic sleep and her memory only
extended to the two lower states. In her nervous crises, she had less memory than
in sleep-walking. Finally, in her waking state, as the lowest state, she lost the
memory of all that happened for her in all the higher states." Dr. Herbert Mayo
cites a case of quintuple memory where the normal state of the subject was interrupted by four kinds of morbid states, for which she had no memory on awakening, each of these states presenting a kind of memory proper to it.[33] In May 1887,[34]
I myself reported a phenomenon of this kind that I observed for the first time in
Lucie. After ordinary somnambulism, she had a second somnambulism in which
she presented a complete memory for all psychological states, even the crises of
hysteria. On waking from this new state, she re-entered the first somnambulism
and did not retain there anything of what had happened. On the contrary, she discovered the memory of this second somnambulism when I returned her to it. In
the same year, de Rochas[35] remarked on the same finding with his subject Benoist:
"If one continues this application with Benoist" (the application of a magnet to
a subject who has already gone through somnambulism and is in a state of lethargy), "one comes across a fifth state, like the somnambulistic state, in which the
subject retains possession of his intellectual faculties. His memory and most of
his senses are hypersensitive, except for vision. On waking the memory of what
has occurred in this state is lost, but is recovered when the subject one returns
there." Finally, Gurney,[36] in a very interesting study, shows that certain subjects

have "distinct stages of memory that they go through in their hypnotic sleep." These states of memory are somewhat different from those I have just described. Each state of consciousness, as a matter of fact, preserves only the memory of itself. Here is how the author expresses these difficult phenomena: "After having induced a particular state of sleep that we call state A, we converse about one specific thing with the subject. He is then put into a deeper state, state B, and if one wants to continue the preceding conversation with him, he finds himself quite incapable of remembering it – even of remembering that anything at all had been said to him. One then begins a new subject with him and asks him to remember it, after which one returns to state A. He cannot recall what was said to him in state B, but continues the discussion started in the prior state A, in which he now finds himself. Put anew into state B, he similarly remembers what had been said to him in that state, but has forgotten what had been communicated to him in state A. Awake, he remembers nothing of what has been said to him."[37] Thus the author establishes three states of memory[38] during hypnotic sleep, which, for this subject, taking into account his memory during the waking state, adds up to four forms of distinct memory.

We now return to the very interesting study of these variations of memory in our subject. Since these phenomena are extremely complex and very difficult to describe clearly, we ask permission to use a conventional notion. In the past we have designated the subject in each of these states by various first names and have said: "state of Léonie," "state of Léontine," etc., for the successive states of the same person. Some have pointed out to us, with reason, the confusions that result from this way of doing things. So following the example of Azam, we now say "state 1," "state 2," "state 3," of the same subject to refer to the phases through which she passes, and to designate the subject in these states, we say, as Jules Janet has fittingly proposed, the first name of the subject with the number corresponding to the state in which she finds herself. Thus, "Lucie 1" is the subject Lucie in the waking state; "Lucie 2" is the same subject in the second state, which here is ordinary somnambulism. What follows in this work will increasingly clarify how justified we are in employing these notations.

I began by simply putting Lucie to sleep in the ordinary way, and I have noted, in regard to this second state, the phenomena of memory that occur for all somnambulists. One day, in relation to a suggestion that I wanted to give her and which was not successful, I tried to get her to sleep even deeper, hoping to thus increase the degree of suggestibility of the subject. So I recommended making magnetic "passes" on Lucie 2, as if she were not already in somnambulism. Her eyes, which were open, closed, she slumped down and she seemed to sleep deeper and deeper. There was first a general contracture, which quickly dissipated, and the muscles remained flaccid, as in lethargy, but without the disposition toward induced contractures. No sign, no word could bring about the least movement. This is the state of hypnotic syncope that I have already pointed out. Since then, I have often seen it again, and in certain subjects it seems to me to form an unavoidable transition between various psychological states. After a half hour of this sleep, the subject arose on her own, and, with eyes at first closed and then open, at my question, began to speak spontaneously. The person who spoke with me then, Lucie 3 according to our convention, presented a host of very interesting phenomena.[39] For the moment I can only point out one of them – her state of memory. Lucie 3 remembered her normal life very well. She also remembered the preceding induced somnambulisms and everything Lucie 2 had said. Further, she could recount for me in detail her crises of hysteria, her terror in the face of the men that she saw hidden in the curtain, her natural somnambulisms during which she would prepare a meal or do housework, her nightmares, etc. – all things that neither Lucie 1 nor Lucie 2 had ever had shown the least memory for. It was a long and difficult task to then awaken this subject. After passing for some minutes through the syncope just described, she found herself in ordinary somnambulism, but Lucie 2 could not tell me anything of what had occurred with Lucie 3. She claimed to have slept and had nothing to say. When, much later and with much greater ease, I re-induced the same state, Lucie 3 immediately recovered the memories that had appeared to be lost.

This observation – so peculiar that I believed it then to be more unknown than it really is – inspired me with the desire to repeat the experiment on another equally interesting subject – Léonie. This person had a first somnambulism, the state of Léonie 2, that was very easy to produce. To begin with, we expected that this state would be very complete and very developed, since it took two or three hours to form. Then we attempted to put Léonie 2 to sleep, as if she were a normal person, using the same technique that she was accustomed to – touching with the thumb, magnetic passes, etc. … Léonie 2 gradually ceased to speak, went profoundly asleep, and ended by falling into a state of lethargy. We continued the passes, despite the lethargy. The subject heaved a sigh and seemed to awaken. But this peculiar awakening was very slow. The senses seem to revive, one after the other: first the muscular sense, because the subject now kept her limbs in whatever position they were placed; then the sense of touch, when an object placed in her hand caused a movement; finally vision, when the subject saw and imitated movements made in her presence. These cataleptic phases, already described in the preceding chapter, were, as we have seen, forms of consciousness of a nascent state. Indeed, if we continued passes, especially on the head, during the same somnambulism, the state of the subject was transformed and the catalepsy developed into a new somnambulism. The subject, who was sitting up during the catalepsy, gradually reclined, sweetly closed her eyes and seemed to sleep deeply.

Neither pressing her tendons, as in lethargy, nor rubbing her skin, as in somnambulism, produced contractures, and her arms still remained in the position in which they were placed, if I insisted a bit. Her face was pale, her eyes sunken, her lips pursed with an expression of sternness and sadness, which was not usual for her. This state seemed to approximate, and develop from, the catalepsy. But there was an important difference: the subject could now understand and respond to speech. It is true that she spoke in an unusual manner. She began by repeating my questions as in cataleptic echolalia, but she then responded. "Listen to me," I say. "Lis-ten-to-me." "Yes, Monsieur," she responded after a moment of silence. This speaking did not always happen, because in the second somnambulism, as in the first, there was an alternation of waking and sleeping, and they could only be distinguished from one another by the presence or absence of speech. If one succeeded in preserving this state for some period of time, an hour for example, which was difficult, her intelligence seemed to increase, and the subject, whom we can now call Léonie 3, repeated the questions less and responded more. As with Lucie 3, we were able to establish some interesting psychological facts, to which we shall return, but now we are going to examine the state of memory only. (1) The subject in this state remembers all that she has done or heard in somnambulisms of the same kind; (2) the subject easily remembers what has been done during the waking state of Léonie 1; (3) finally, the subject in this state remembers the ordinary somnambulism and the actions of Léonie 2. I thought that I was the first to have induced this state of Léonie 3, but she told me that she had frequently found herself in the same state when she had been put to sleep by Dr. Alfred Perrier, who came across her, as I did, when trying to deepen the sleep of Léonie 2. This resurrection of a somnambulistic personage that had disappeared for five years was very peculiar and when I spoke to her I naturally retained the use of the name of Léonore, which her first master had given her. Here we call her Léonie 3 in order to avoid confusion.

The most important characteristic of this new somnambulism only revealed itself when the state was terminated. As a matter of fact, this state is brought to an end in a variety of ways. The subject returns to a state of lethargy and then awakens in ordinary somnambulism, the state of Léonie 2. As such she resumes the conversation at the point at which it had been interrupted when she was in the same state, and she never has any memory of what occurs in the state of Léonie 3. This loss of memory is not caused by the intervening lethargy, since Léonie 2 remembers all of her life, even though she has undergone numerous lethargies. In a word, Léonie 2, who no more remembers Léonie 3 than Léonie 1, when awake, remembers the somnambulism. Therefore, this state of Léonie 3 is indeed a new somnambulism, by virtue of its connection to the state of Léonie 2, just as the latter is a somnambulism by virtue of a similar connection to the waking state.

Our description of these two subjects would be sufficient for understanding this phenomenon of memory, and we would not discuss our examination of a third subject, Rose, had she not presented the same phenomena with a far greater degree of complication and given us the opportunity to make an important point: the analogy between some of the natural phenomena of hysteria and certain diverse somnambulistic states. When hypnotized, this woman can present four forms of somnambulism, each distinct from the other. Her memory in these different states depends on very complex conditions and varies from one state to the other. The first two states are ignorant of each other, although they both remember the waking state. The third and fourth are superimposed on each other, as are the successive somnambulisms of Lucie and Léonie, the latter state having the memory of all the others and of the whole of the subject's life. But outside the somnambulistic state, the life of this person exhibits a great many extremely varied hysterical symptoms – convulsive crises; hysterical deliriums that last sometimes for days on end, and of which she retains no memory; also amnesias, unique losses of memory which have already been often described. Without our knowing why, she comes to completely forget important parts of her life which seem normal. For example, one day, after a crisis, she lost the memory of the three preceding weeks. Indeed, the memory of one or other of these forgotten states is easily brought back when she returns to certain specific cycles of her artificial somnambulism. Thus, the memory of hysterical delirium is complete during the second somnambulism, but the memory of periods of her life overcome by amnesia is not yet brought back. It is only completely recovered in the fourth period, during which the memory of the subject no longer displays any particular lacuna. I believe that this return of memories allows us to compare the states that are in this way connected by memory: the second somnambulism of Rose would be a psychological state analogous to her delirious state, and her fourth somnambulism would be a state analogous to those periods of her life which were suddenly forgotten. This is a hypothesis which, up to now, has only been supported by one feature – memory – and which our studies justify more and more.

The description of these alternating memories, even though made in a superficial manner and without entering into detail, can seem complicated and obscure. Nevertheless, we are convinced that psychology should to a degree leave aside abstract generalities and take on these details if it is one day to be a useful and practical science. It is through a knowledge of these diverse psychological states of hysterics that we can heal their paralyses and contractures, and we ought to enter into these studies even deeper if we seek one day to have a genuine mental treatment for insanity, which is very much more complicated than hysteria. However, in this essay, it has been enough for us to show that forgetting on awakening and alternating memory does not only apply to ordinary somnambulism, but are found with many variations in many states, and allow us indeed to establish varieties of somnambulism.

2.4 Study of a particular condition of memory and the forgetting of images

It is not enough to establish the existence of a phenomenon; it is also necessary to try to explain it. Where do these changes in psychological state come from? Why do these forgettings and returns of memory occur? All possible hypotheses have been proposed and to review them all would be to review the whole history of animal magnetism. Since most of these theories have already been summarized in the works of Maury, Despine, and Ribot, it will be enough for us to cite the best known among them and to show how little they take into account the actual components of the problem. Some contend that during somnambulism attention is too weak and the psychological phenomena too slight.[40] Others say that, on the contrary, the concentration has been so strong and the phenomena so fierce that the mind has become exhausted and can no longer reproduce what has happened on awakening.[41] These two hypotheses refute each other and do not take into account the variety of somnambulistic phenomena, which are sometimes very strong and sometimes very slight, so that it is very difficult for them to explain the return of memory, which is so perfect, in a new somnambulism. As we have already seen, Despine explains this forgetting as the total disappearance of the self and of consciousness during the abnormal state: "We can only explain it by the non-participation of the self and personal consciousness in this act, which is due to unconscious (that is to say, automatic psychic activity of the brain during a momentary suspension of the conscious activity of this organ."[42] There is, perhaps, some truth in this theory of the disappearance of the self; but to conclude that all consciousness is suppressed during somnambulism seems to us truly paradoxical and inadmissible. There is more that is useful, I believe, in the theories of Maury[43] concerning the role of the association of ideas in memory. But, as he himself remarked, the forgetting of somnambulists cannot be entirely explained as a rupture in the chain of associations. If, immediately on awakening, they always have before them an object or movement associated with the preceding acts and which recall those acts for them, it nevertheless seems likely that, in the course of the day, it would happen that they would see objects or perform acts identical to those which had been done in somnambulism. Why would not the power of association be brought into play at that moment to reawaken the memories? Léonie in a somnambulistic state had picked a bouquet of flowers; when she was awakened, I gave her this bouquet to take with her. Why did she not realize where they had come from? Why, by association, had she not remembered having picked them?

Some of the old magnetizers expressed a very valid idea, one that we can profit from, when they spoke of changes of sensibility which are produced during somnambulism. Bertrand says,[44] "In every sleep there is a lack, more or less complete, of sensibility and motility in the external organs. Sensibility flows back to the interior and the somnambulist experiences new perceptions provided by the internal organs; their succession constitutes a new life, different from that which we usually enjoy." Nearly the same kind of idea is expressed by Ribot when he admits of variations of coenesthesia or general sensibility during somnambulism, variations which may become the center of new associations and a new memory. These ideas seem to us to be generally true, but we have to confess that they remain very vague and difficult to apply to particular cases. That is why we have tried, in our turn, to sketch an explanation of the bizarre phenomena of forgetting and of memory. Our hypothesis will not be more definitive than the preceding ones and it lays no claim to being very general. It is simply meant to explain the facts that I have observed, and it has the decided advantage over the others of being supported by some observations and specific experiences that have occurred under good conditions. To explain the facts presented by other somnambulists, it would probably be necessary to enlarge and transform our hypothesis, but its general direction would in all likelihood remain the same.

Every hypothesis, say the logicians, has three parts: a chance observation, a set of ideas and arguments meant to explain it, and experiences set up to verify the consequences of the supposition. We have followed this order in the exposition of our inquiries.

One of the women whom I have observed for a long time, Rose, before entering the hospital had presented nearly all the symptoms of severe hysteria. Among other things, she had had unusual losses of memory which occurred suddenly following a crisis or a kind of lethargy, and which included one or several of the weeks which preceded the symptom. Very recently she had a symptom of this kind and, following a cataleptic or lethargic sleep that had been badly resolved, she totally forgot the preceding three months. The lethargic attack had occurred quite unexpectedly towards the end of September, after an interval in which she seemed to be fine, and she awoke without any memory of the months of July, August, and September. Understandably, I was very interested in this natural amnesia and, through several attempts using somnambulism or suggestion, I tried to revive these memories, but I have to say that I had no success. Much later, the habit of being put to sleep and the curious influence of magnetic passes brought about in this woman a great many diverse somnambulistic states, which were, as I have said, separated from each other by periods of syncope and catalepsy. In one of these new periods which came into being, she spontaneously said to me one day: "You have often asked me what took place during the months from August to September. Why could I not respond? It is so simple. I now know it very well …, I did this and that …, etc." The memory of the three forgotten months had totally returned, as far as I could see. But as soon as this somnambulism changed and the subject entered the state of waking or into another somnambulism, these memories once again completely disappeared. Was there something special in this state of somnambulism, which had occurred by chance, so that the memories would occur at this moment and not another? My attention went to one particular phenomenon, which may or may not have been important, but which for me constituted the only visible difference between this state and the others. In the waking state and in all the other states, as I have known for a long time, Rose was totally anesthetic and not conscious of any tactile or muscular sensation. In the particular somnambulism that led to the return of the memories, Rose unexpectedly recovered tactile and muscular sensibility on the right side and became hemi-anesthetic. On the other hand, when I sought information about the state of the subject during the three months for which her memory had been lost, I discovered that she was in quite good health and at that time had tactile sensibility at least on the right side. Indeed, at that time she had received a slight injury caused by a knife cut on her right arm and had suffered from it a great deal. Now, at this time, when she is awake, she is so lacking in sensation that she does not suffer from any injury, even when, in her crises, she inflicts real wounds on her limbs. Therefore, during those three months she was not anesthetic, as she is today. She had sensation, at least on the right side. If we compare the state in which the memories had been acquired and the state, which is now a particular somnambulism, in which these memories are restored, we see that these two states have something proper to them which they hold in common: the existence of tactile and muscular sensibility on the right side.

This chance observation very naturally led me to suppose that there should be a relationship between the state of sensibility and the state of memory. Memories acquired by a certain sensibility seemed to be recallable or reproducible only if this sensibility continued to exist in the same state. To discuss the value of this hypothesis and apply it to new cases, it seemed to me that it was necessary to distinguish the two cases and study two kinds of memory separately. First there is elementary or sensible memory, which simply consists in the memory of such or such a particular sensation considered in an isolated way, and then there is a complex or intellectual memory, which gives us the recall of complicated ideas and which can only exist in human beings because of language. To begin with, we will concentrate only on the first memory and find out under what conditions it is possible.

Memory contains very important elements, but ones that are in fact subordinate: recognition and localization. These distinctions are, as Ribot[45] says, the contribution of intelligence in memory, nothing more; they do not constitute memory. The essential element of memory here is, as we know, the reproduction, in the form of an image, of the previously experienced sensation. Now, today, since the studies of Galton, it is admitted that the image is, with a complexity that is ordinarily less, identical to sensation. For the image to be produced, and, consequently, for the memory to occur, it is absolutely necessary that the capacity to experience this sensation still exists, at least in part. An individual who has completely lost one of his senses and who can no longer in any way experience the sensations that belong to that sense has at the same time lost all images and, consequently, all memories relative to these sensations. But, one might say, a man who suddenly becomes blind through an accident still preserves, despite the fact that he can see nothing, the memory of visual sensations. This is because the individual has lost only the eye, the external organ of vision, and not the psycho-physiological faculty of seeing. If he had lost the nervous centers of vision, the faculty needed to experience visual sensations, he would no longer have the memory of having seen, and, as one blind from birth, he would no longer know what it is to see. There are individuals who fall into this category, and one can show that this kind of thing happens in hysterical anesthesias.

In this illness the external organ is not touched – it is perfectly intact. It is the centers themselves which no longer function, or at least function in an abnormal manner, as we shall see later.[46] Also, opposite to the man-made blind through an accident who still has dreams and hallucinations of seeing after the loss of the sight, hysterics who experience a complete and profound anesthesia do not in any way preserve hallucinations of the sense which they have lost. Let us examine this fact and then show the consequences for the exercise of elementary memory.

At one point, Rose was totally anesthetic and at the same time dyschromatopsic in both eyes; that is, she could not feel any contact on any part of her body and she could distinguish colour with neither her left eye nor her right – she saw all objects as gray and white. At that time I could not get her to experience any coloured visual hallucination, nor any tactile hallucination. If I suggested that she see flowers, costumes, etc., she saw them as gray and white. If I suggested a soreness, a pain, an abnormal temperature, she felt absolutely nothing. At the same time, I could awaken auditive hallucinations with a simple word, proving that she was very suggestible. When I asked her about her dreams, she assured me that in her dreams she saw objects in the same way as in waking – in gray and white – and never experienced sensation on contact. In this subject, images have disappeared at the same time as sensation.[47]

Inversely, when, as is sometimes possible, one goes to induce a hallucination despite the anesthesia of the subject, one thereby causes a return to normal sensibility. It must also be said that among certain subjects in which anesthesia is not very profound and of recent origin, suggestions can awaken sense images, particularly by means of other images which have been preserved.[48] For example, for some days, Marie had been totally anesthetic. When I suggested to her that there was a short caterpillar on her hand, she declared that she felt nothing. I told her to look and see the caterpillar; she saw it and at the same time felt it – the visual image had awakened the tactile image. But what is interesting to note is that at the same moment her whole arm became sensitive in reality, and Marie now sensed all pricks and all contacts. The sensible image could not be induced without bringing with its real sensation. This demonstration shows, in an inverse manner, the dependence that exists between the image and the sensation.

Now let us look at the consequences such a phenomenon might have on the state of memory and note that it is easy to understand, and verify by experiment, that this loss of images leads to the loss of all memories connected to them. One of the main symptoms which, I believe, demonstrates for us this loss of memories is the well-known indifference of hysterics in regard to everything connected to their anesthesias.[49] It seems to me that if I awoke one morning with neither tactile nor muscular sensation, and I, like Rose, suddenly lost the sensation of colour and could only perceive the universe in black and white, it seems to me that I would be terrified and would immediately ask for help. These women, on the contrary, find their states so natural that they never complain about them. It is I who, because of such experiences, have pointed out to Rose that she could not distinguish colours; she did not realize that fact. When I have pointed out to Lucie that she does not feel any pain or sense contact, she responds to me: "So much the better." When I help her to realize that she never knows the position of her arms without looking at them, and that she loses touch with her legs in her bed, she answers me: "But that is entirely natural, because then I cannot see them. That happens to everybody." In other words, they are not able to make a comparison between a former sensation, the memory of which is entirely lost, and their present state, and they no more suffer from their present insensibility than we suffer from not hearing "the harmony of the celestial spheres." If a hysteric like Marie complains of not having sensation, it is when she is not totally so; when her insensibility is complete, the absence of memories is also complete.

It is very easy now to verify this point by some precise experiments. One can cause certain persons to have a particular sensation when they have full sensation, wait for the course of the illness to render them anesthetic and see if they then still have the memory of the preceding sensation. But this experiment would be a very long one and difficult to oversee. It would be better, I believe, to make use of artificial changes in sensibility brought about by means of esthesiogenic agents. After some attempts, I found out that one can produce sensation in part of Rose's body by three procedures: either by the prolonged application of a strong magnet, by the application of plates of tin or lead, or finally – and most easily – through the application of an electric current of medium intensity (20 or 30 elements Trouvé).

We have here, if I may discuss this question, an interesting study of the effects of these procedures. It seems to me that in the present case it is very difficult to explain their influence in terms of "expectant attention," or by the phenomenon of suggestion, since we are here dealing precisely with a subject with whom the suggestion of tactile hallucination did not work and who no longer possessed tactile images. Suggestion makes use of a psychological state; it does not create it. Here, under the influence of one of these three agents, tactile sensibility reappears in the right arm and then one can suggest tactile hallucinations for this limb, although previously this would have been impossible.

So, when Rose was in the waking state, I induced tactile sensibility in her right arm by an electric current and assured myself that she could clearly feel pricks and touches. Then in her right hand I placed a small object that I asked her to identify by touch, without looking: "This is a small pencil," she said to me. Then I stopped the electric current and for some minutes spoke of something else. After some time I asked her, "What do you have in your right hand right now?" "A small pencil," she responded. I examined her right hand and found that it was still sensitive – it was an examination that could be done quickly and without warning. Coming back nearly an hour later, I repeated the same question, and she then answered, "You did not put anything into my hand; I do not remember anything." I then quickly examined her right hand and established that she was again completely anesthetic. But, someone might say, in an hour she could forget something as unimportant as contact with a small object. All right, but let us pursue this experience. The next day I returned to see her and noted that naturally she had neither sensibility in her right hand nor memory of the pencil. Then I applied the same electric current to her hand; after two or three minutes, the arm was again sensitive and she spontaneously said, "Ah, it was a small pencil that you put in my hand yesterday."

In this experiment, which is interesting and which I have often repeated, we see that the two moments, when the memory has been acquired and when it is reproduced, are both moments of waking when the right hand has been made sensible by an electric current. What would happen if these moments belonged to two different states, one to the waking state and the other to somnambulism? We have seen that Rose presents various somnambulisms, at least four characterized by distinct memories. In two of these states, the third and fourth, she is naturally sensible on the right side, that is to say, under the influence of passes or a prolonged sleep, and there comes a moment when Rose clearly senses everything on the right side, and if one awakens her in this state to put her, for example, into her second state, she no longer feels and she forgets what happened during the third somnambulism. Indeed, during this particular state, in which she is sensible, I put an object in her right hand: "It is a coin," she said without looking. I had her close her eyes and I myself moved her right hand: "You are having me make the sign of the cross," she said. This done, I awakened her; she passed through the lower somnambulisms, arrived at waking and, as always, was completely anesthetic. Without asking directly, I established, through conversation, that she had no memory of the somnambulism, nor of the object that she had held in her hand for a very long time. Moreover, I could even ask her directly and beset her with questions, nearly suggesting the response, and still she remembered nothing. Then I applied the electric current to her right hand, which once more became sensible, and Rose spontaneously said to me, "It was a coin that you put in my hand ..., you had me make the sign of the cross while I slept – what a funny idea!" There is no use going on any further about this person; the phenomenon is constant with her: use a procedure such as electricity, metallic plates, somnambulism, etc., to bring forth a particular sensibility, and you bring at the same time all the elementary memories which have been acquired by this same sensibility at any other moment.

It is more interesting to recapture the same experience with another subject, and I have tried to reproduce it with Marie. From the beginning of my pursuit, I ran up against a difficulty, and the results of the experience seemed to me to contradict the previous ones. Indeed, Marie's memory persists longer than the sensibility. Does this mean that the experiments with Rose were false? No. We too often forget that a fact cannot be false, but it can depend on complex circumstances, and if one cannot verify it, it is because, without realizing it, one has taken up one's position in different conditions. With a little thought, this is what I believe can be said. Marie is not anesthetic in the same way that Rose is. While Rose has completely lost the images of tactile sensation and no suggestion or word can revive them, Marie, on the contrary, can experience tactile hallucinations induced by speech. If I strongly insist that a caterpillar is crawling on her neck, though she is insensible, she feels the caterpillar, and this tactile sense image – and this is as bizarre as anything we have seen – even revives for a moment real tactile sensation. So it is the word that comes in here to introduce an element of confusion in the experience. It is necessary to avoid speaking, because the memory of the word stands in the place of the memory of tactile sensation and can even bring about its rebirth.

One can proceed in this way. Out of thick cardboard I cut ten shapes measuring approximately two centimeters at the most[50] and having forms sufficiently irregular that they would be difficult to name with words. If one were to name them, one would have to say: a scalene triangle, a trapezium, etc. – something this good woman from the countryside would be entirely incapable of doing. I wanted her to touch one of these figures without asking its name, since, to verify the memory, I wanted her to use touch to recognize, among the ten shapes, the one she had already touched.

During a profound somnambulism, Marie also became sensible – this time in her whole body. I would have her touch a figure and then awaken her. At that moment she would still have some of the sensibility of the somnambulism, especially if she had been awakened abruptly. If I put the shapes in her hand, she would feel them and hold out to me the one she had already touched, saying: "I have just been holding this one." Here we see that the memory persists after a quick awakening, but that is because the somnambulistic sensitivity persists.[51] We repeat the experiment, this time leaving a larger interval after awakening so that all sensibility can be obliterated. When I let her look at or touch the shapes, she does not recognize them and says she does not know what they are. Now let us try to make her sensible without putting her back to sleep. Marie does not become sensible through an electric current – I do not know why. So we use Burcq's plates and, after several tries, end up using the iron plates, which act very strongly. Application of an iron plate makes her hand tremble and causes painful tingling, and then, when the shaking and tingling have completely disappeared, renders her arm completely sensible. Then she touches the shapes with her hand and immediately holds out to me the correct shape, which she now recognizes. Again here disappearance of the sensibility means disappearance of memory, and persistence or return of sensibility means persistence or return of memory. One might say with Bastian, "Sensory activity forms the basis of thought; when it is extinguished, thought disappears or is put to sleep."[52]

2.5 A condition of memory and forgetting for complex phenomena

After this all too rapid study of the conditions of recall for elementary memory, let us move on to complex or intellectual memory, complete memory of ideas and actions. Here our task is made much easier by the excellent psychological work of Charcot on language and its different sensorial types. Indeed, we know that complex actions and ideas can hardly be comprehended and retained in memory except through language. To seek out the conditions of complex memory of ideas or actions is to seek out the conditions of the memory of language.

Language is formed by a large number of images that are associated with our ideas and our movements, and these images, as the medical men have been telling the psychologists,[53] are not the same for all individuals. Some, perhaps the greatest number, think by means of motor or kinesthetic images, of which we have already spoken, and which have a tendency, when isolated, to find expression on the outside through actual movement or actual speech. This kind of person thinks, while speaking very loudly or in a whisper, but always with images of the movements of speech. The others think through auditive or visual images, and their thought is formed by a series of images of words that are heard and not pronounced, or by a series of images of writing, or of gestures seen and not heard. How do these people speak and act? Do their visual or auditive images first evoke somewhat feeble motor images which are expressed in movement? We have already discussed this question and concluded that perhaps it was so at the beginning of life, but that now things happen more simply. The sound of a word should find expression in movements that express this word exactly as the motor image itself. The habit of speaking or even acting by means of auditive or visual images ought to be added to the habit of thinking by means of these images and contribute to further separation of these different types from each other. All thoughts and all actions thus depend on only one type of image, so that all memories end up depending on the persistence of these same images.

In the work of Ballet, we see very well how one and the same lesion produces very different effects on intelligence and memory, depending on the category of images habitually used by the individual. With an individual for whom all memories crystallize around motor images, the loss of visual images is of no great importance. For another subject, one who makes use of visual images, it suppresses all memory and all speech. For the latter, a new education, which may or may not be easy, can now group ideas and actions around a different category of images – that of the muscular sense, for instance, or the auditive sense – and this man, apparently cured, can once more think and act. But he would live entirely from these new memories and never be able to retrieve the old,[54] unless, by some miracle the old visual images would one day be restored to him. This restoration of lost images did not occur with the aphasic patients studied by Charcot, because cerebral disease has completely destroyed them. But is it not possible that in other subjects these images could simply be momentarily suppressed, and so able to be restored in different conditions? The preceding study of elementary memory has shown us that it is precisely this that occurs with hysterics and somnambulists.

Let us revisit this study with a particular example that will serve as an illustration and a proof. Anyone who carefully examines the conduct of Lucie in the waking state will easily recognize that she is very clearly "a visual type." She thinks, speaks, and acts almost totally through the sense of sight. She does not retain the sense of touch anywhere in her body, and she has no muscular sensation. One can move her limbs, even fasten them behind her, and stop her spontaneous movements – all without her being aware of it, provided she does not see what is happening. This very deep anesthesia has removed all memory of tactile sensations, and she insists, as we have just seen, that everyone is like her. In addition to this loss of tactile sensation, Lucie has almost completely lost her sense of hearing. She does not hear someone speaking unless the voice is very loud and quite nearby; she does not hear the tick tock of my watch, even if I put it against her ear. Her sight, although very diminished (visual acuity one-third; restriction of visual field 20%), is still her best sense. Also, she uses it continually. She neither moves nor walks without constantly looking at her arms, her legs, the ground, etc. Also, it is in this same way that a great number of hysterics are able to maintain the ability to sew, knit, and write without any muscular sensation. One is often deceived in this matter, and this is why many authors assert that muscular anesthesia is rare in hysteria, whereas it is really very frequent. In some cases, visual images can even make up for the missing sensations and allow them to make movements with eyes closed. It is that way with Lucie. One can put a screen in front of her eyes – something that makes her furious – and she cannot do anything. She cannot walk, she cannot move her arms, she cannot even move her hand, and she is unsteady and cannot stop herself from falling. If, then, one has her completely close her eyes, she can no longer even speak, and ... she goes to sleep. We already have examples of the kind of subject[55] who will fall asleep when one suppresses the one sense that remains to them. That is why one should never touch the eyes of a hysteric when studying them in their waking state. I have observed four subjects of this kind who live only by their visual sense and who sleep from the moment one closes their eyes. If one avoids this sleep and if one interrogates Lucie when awake, one discovers that when she thinks about people, she always represents them to herself in terms of their visage and their dress. To sum up, in the waking state all of her memories, whatever their origin, are remembered under the form of visual images.

Now let us place her in a profound sleep and, in order to have clear distinctions, let us pass by her intermediate states and put her into her deepest somnambulism, the state of Lucie 3, which can be attained only after a half hour of passes. Note who comes forward and opens her eyes, as I have said: what kind of person do we have in front of us? The senses that she has in the waking state are not lost, but, on the contrary, are augmented. But what is most striking is that she has recovered completely, and in a refined form, all tactile and muscular sensation. She knows perfectly well where her limbs are situated. She distinguishes the smallest objects by touch. She recognizes my hand by simple contact. She walks and even writes without looking at her feet or hand. These new sensations are in no way suppressed, and she finds them very natural. But we see that she is no longer so attached to the visual sense and that she does not complain, nor does she seem in any way to be changed, if we close her eyes. Is it not natural to suppose that she does not now produce movements, and especially speech, by virtue of the same images as before, but that she now makes use of those coming from the muscular and tactile senses? In a word, she is no longer a woman of the visual type, but a woman of the motor type.

This affirmation raises some difficulties. How, one might ask, did she change her sensory type so easily, and become capable so quickly of speaking by means of one category of images when she had just been speaking by means of another? Charcot's patients had needed a lengthy reeducation to effect such a change. I answer: her education as a motor type had already long been in process, because she is hysterical, that is, she exemplifies a kind of psychological instability. She has been ill for fifteen years. She has spent a lot of time changing her sensibility and practicing speaking and acting now with one, now another. In his classification of types of language, Charcot has spoken of an indifferent type who, at the same moment, uses one image or another. I request a small place for an alternative type, one which successively uses now one sense, now another.

What proof do we have that Lucie has before been a motor type, as she appears now to be in this artificial state? We find a very good one in the state of her memories. Let us now interrogate her in the state of Lucie 3. She tells us about her childhood up to age nine, which Lucie 1 has entirely forgotten. She speaks to us about the great fear she had one day when some men were hidden behind some curtains and suddenly jumped out at her, the emotion that constituted the principle framework of all her hysterical crises. She recounts to us these crises themselves and the movements she made and her wanderings in the house at night in a state of natural somnambulism. She especially tells us about the year which had been so painful for her, when she had been kept in a dark room because she had some eye problem and could not see clearly, and because the physician, believing he had found some small lesion, kept her in darkness. Now, just before this, Lucie had been totally ignorant of all these stories and could not tell us any of them. Could we not legitimately suppose that, in these circumstances unknown to Lucie 1 but known to Lucie 3, for various reasons her memories were not associated with visual images? At one time, in her childhood, she was in good health and thought, as perhaps all children do, by means of muscular images; at another time, the muscular sense operated only during her crises; at another time, her visual sense was suppressed, as in her attack of ocular anesthesia, and it was necessary to think in other ways, and her memories were then centered on other images. These images did not reappear in the waking state, by virtue of the law referred to in the preceding paragraph, and neither did the memories. The passes – I do not know why – acted the same as the metallic plates (for her, gold plates), or as the application of a static electricity machine, and restored her lost senses. As we have shown, the images all returned and, with them, all the memories. But the conversation we had with Lucie 3 was in turn associated with this particular memory and increased the amount of muscular memories, but not that of visual memories. Also, when we awoke her, that is, simply took away from her the sensations that had been added by a certain excitation, Lucie was the same as at the beginning; she looked around in every direction and began to once more think in terms of visual images. She now had neither muscular nor tactile sensation, and therefore she had no images from these senses and absolutely no memory of anything that was connected with them.

This demonstration would be endless if it were necessary to reproduce it with all subjects. We believe that it would be easy to show that Léonie is visual in the waking state, auditive in ordinary somnambulism, where she exhibits supersensitive hearing, and motor oriented or tactile in state 3. But the study of Rose was especially interesting. In the waking state she exhibited the following characteristics: she totally lost the sense of touch in her whole body and she totally lost the muscular or kinesthetic sense in her two legs and her left arm, but preserved it in her right arm; her vision was very weak and, because she had been overtaken by a complete dyschromatopsy, she could only distinguish black and white. On the other hand, she had hearing that was almost normal; she loved music and had been a singer in a concert cafe and became irritated when she heard bad singing. This analysis of sensibility shows us that it is the auditive sense that is very rare among hysterics in the waking state, because they are almost always visual. But note what effects this repair of her senses had on her movements. A person can speak well with the auditive sense, but not walk well, because the movement of the limbs does not easily mesh with images of hearing. Also, this unhappy soul became paraplegic when she lost muscular sensibility in her lower limbs. It is not good for a hysteric to be a musician. She had learned, for good or ill, to move her left arm by visual images and could only use it when she saw it; her only free movements were those of the right arm through the muscular sense that she retained and those of language through the auditive sense.

When I began to put her to sleep, I encountered a singular difficulty – one that rarely happens: I was unable to get her to speak in somnambulism. Nevertheless, she understood me; she made the movements I ordered and seemed to experience hallucinations, but she did not succeed in speaking. It was as if she were affected by hysterical mutism. After many sessions of this kind, I was giving up trying to get her to speak, when I was struck by something new: visual hallucinations brought about speech. I ordered her to see roses. She seemed to experience the hallucination. She became agitated, opened her eyes, seemed to breathe in the scent and murmured: "Roses." In that way, I was able, in some sessions, to develop language in her, but always by means of visual images.

Moreover, it was easy to verify that she was no longer dyschromatopsic and had a visual sense that was nearly normal. Although I cannot say for sure, it seems that with the recovery of her visual sense she entered into a state to which she was not accustomed and in which she did not know how to use language. Since, unlike Lucie, she did not know how to move her legs by means of visual images, I could not remove her paraplegia in this state. In another somnambulistic state, which I could only induce much later after many difficulties, she recovered her tactile and muscular sense, first on the right side and then on the left, and then all that was required was a small effect to release the contracture of her legs and get her to move them at a simple command from me. She became mobile – something that she probably was for a great part of her life – seeing that now she spoke very easily, recovered all the memories that seemed to be lost in the waking state, and had absolutely no paralysis. When Rose rewoke, she once more lost all of these sensibilities, forgot everything, and, unfortunately, did not know how to walk.[56] All of the phenomena, whether of movement or memory, clearly seem to depend on modifications in the state of sensibility.

In other words, all complex psychological phenomena, ideas, voluntary movements, and language, are constituted, for each individual and at each moment of life, by sensible images of a determined nature, and the memory of complex phenomena depend on the reproduction of these elementary images. If these images can no longer be reproduced, all memories that are tied to them disappear, and even though the person can still think and speak with new images, she will no longer be able to remember former thoughts and words. If the reproduction of the first images again becomes possible, all the memories will once more be present. Now, as we will see, this reproduction can only take place if the state of the sensibility itself is also restored. Therefore, memory and forgetting of complex phenomena are attached to the same reality – the persistence or variation in the state of sensibility.

2.6 The interpretation of forgetting on awakening after somnambulism

After all that has been said, the application of the above remarks to somnambulism seems so natural that it will suffice to emphasize a few details.

To understand the alternating memory of somnambulists we have been led to suppose that it is due to a *periodic modification (whether spontaneous or induced) in the state of sensibility,* and consequently, in the nature of the images which go into forming complex psychological phenomena – particularly language. This modification is produced particularly in subjects who are more or less anesthetic in their normal state, and it therefore consists in *the temporary restoration of certain categories of images* that the subjects ordinarily no longer possess. These modifications can be more or less complete and, in certain subjects who are *distracted* rather than truly anesthetic, simply consist of the *temporary predominance of certain images* that are ordinarily neglected. Let us now examine each of these points in order.

(1) We have already had occasion to show *these periodic variations in sensibility and images* in most of our subjects. We have seen that one individual will be a visual type in the normal state, and then, temporarily, a motor type during somnambulism, while another is an auditive type when awake, then a visual type when in a certain kind of abnormal state – there is no need to go all through this again. We would simply like to remark that in all those cases where, for one reason or another, analogous modifications of sensibility are produced, one can find phenomena of memory analogous to those of somnambulism.

Who has not been struck by the fact that a hysteric who is anesthetic in the waking state is no longer anesthetic in catalepsy? If you close the left fist of Léonie or Lucie during waking, they are not aware of that fact. Meanwhile, if I close their fist during catalepsy, even without them being able to see what I am doing, it will suggest to them a feeling of anger. If one puts a key in the left hand of Léonie in the waking state, she does not know what it is. If we put the same object in her left hand during catalepsy, she will make the movements of opening a door. Therefore, there is a tactile sensibility during catalepsy that is not there in the waking state. So we should not be surprised if these women do not recall their catalepsy when they are awake, but do recall it in the second somnambulism, when they have recovered their tactile sensation.

A hysteric, such as Lucie or Léonie, remembers night dreams upon wakening when they were *visual*, but has no memory of them when they were *motor*, and when she rises from her bed, this is something she cannot do in darkness without the help of her motor sense.[57] The crises are, as Moreau (de Tours) tells us, muscular deliriums. There is nothing surprising in the fact that memory reappears in somnambulism only where the muscular sense is complete. Finally, we understand how, during the normal waking state, there occur peculiar losses of memory through sudden changes in the dominant sensibility that constitutes the sensorial type. "A woman who was anesthetic could only remember a small part of her life … In somnambulism, she had no anesthesia and remembered her entire life."[58]

These changes in sensibility, brought about by hypnotic sleep, or by passes, can be produced through other means of whatever kind, if they temporarily restore to a subject the sensibilities which she has lost. Charpignon[59] says, "There are somnambulists whom one can put to sleep by means of an electric machine." Here is a great truth; we have seen the partial effects of a small electric current. We know about the excellent effects that electric baths have on hysterics. The celebrated Louis V "regained all his sensibilities from the electric bath …,[60] and when his mind was opened in that way, he remembered his whole life."[61] I am convinced that electrical apparatuses will soon become a genuine scientific instrument for producing at will and with regularity all the variations of somnambulism. But in fact other procedures attain the same result: the magnet, the metallic plates of Burq, etc. Jules Janet has demonstrated that, in the excitation phase of chloroform, an anesthetic hysteric will recover her sensibility and enter into a genuine somnambulism. We can find the same observation in Despine. In a work of Dr. Ball, I read a very striking observation in this regard: "Among the most paradoxical consequences of the hypodermic use of morphine, we must cite the re-establishment of cutaneous sensibility in subjects who had lost it … An anesthetic hysteric who was daily given an eight centigram dose of morphine saw her pains disappear and her normal sensibility return … When the medication was not given, the hysterical symptoms returned."[62] It is unfortunate that the author did not give us more psychological information and did not tell us about the state of memory. It is very likely that morphine here produced a state analogous to somnambulism, because every modification of sensibility leads to a modification of memory, and that is precisely what somnambulism is.

(2) This modification nearly always consists in a *restoration of a sensibility and a group of images* that are ordinarily lost to the subject. This explains the third characteristic of the memory of somnambulists, which we have not particularly emphasized: according to the previous explanation, in the abnormal state, memory of all that takes place during the waking state, obviously ought to return. Somnambulism has always added new sensibilities and new images to the mind of our subjects, and never subtracted them. For a subject asleep to lose the memory of the waking state, it would have to be that in somnambulism she no longer possessed images around which her waking memories were grouped; for example, that she was visual when waking and no longer visual in somnambulism and had neither the sensation nor the images of vision. Now, we know that this does not

occur, at least in the studies we have made. On the contrary, images increase without diminishing. In my day to day notes on Léonie, I find a striking observation that I made some time ago without understanding it. She claims that in her waking state, when she thinks of me, she *sees* me, even to the point of sometimes having visual hallucinations. In her first somnambulism, when she thinks of me, *she sees me and hears me speak to her*. In her second somnambulism, *she sees me, hears me, and touches me*. I remember that I explained this in terms of her habits: she barely spoke to me in the waking state, she was very talkative in her first somnambulism, and she would always hold my hand in her second somnambulism. But it is more than that. It must be noted that first of all she displayed only visual images and the memories attached to them, then she displayed auditive images, without losing the visual, and finally she possessed tactile images without forgetting the former kinds. In hysterics, somnambulism is an increase in the mind through some kind of excitation, not a diminution.[63]

Perhaps there are different kinds of somnambulism. Hypnotization of healthy subjects who possess all their senses and all their images, can somewhat, if possible, diminish them and suppress their diverse sensations. For example, sensible subjects can become anesthetic. It would be interesting to discover whether, in subjects of this kind, the suppression would not sometimes pertain to images that they use more habitually in the waking state, and whether in this case somnambulism would produce a forgetting of the phenomena of the waking state. The well-known patient of Macnish may be a somnambulist of this kind. I have seen nothing that would verify this supposition. It is true that I have almost exclusively hypnotized the ill. I cannot, therefore, speak about an observation I have never made. Henceforth, in psychology, as in the other sciences, one can only speak about what one has seen.

It seems to me that this hypothesis explains multiple somnambulisms and different varieties of alternating memory. As we have seen, there is not just one kind of somnambulism, but many, each characterized by a particular memory. Somnambulism does not depend on a single, unvarying mental modification. It varies according to all the possible modifications that can be brought to the state of sensibility. We believe that, with a subject who is strongly anesthetic in her normal state, one can produce not just one, but many more or less complete restorations of sensibility, which lead to many alternating memories and many somnambulisms.

If one only considers one single subject, such as Lucie, one can come to believe that the division of somnambulism into two parts has some importance, and that there are thus always three memories. This would be an error analogous to the one that caused me at one time to give specific names to all the degrees of catalepsy of Léonie. In reality, there were neither two, nor three necessary memories. There could be any indeterminate number of memories. Rose had at least four or five different somnambulisms, each having a specific memory. There were subjects, such as N, who were so unstable that they could not return to the same somnambulism when being put to sleep by the same person in the same manner. Or else they entered into a different sensitive-sensorial state and could not recover the memories of the first somnambulism. Later, this important fact explained for us certain difficulties in regard to suggestion. Now it is enough for us to know that the somnambulistic state is not one, but that, depending on the modifications of sensibility, it can manifest, for one single person, in a great variety of forms and lead to a most peculiar variety of memories.

Nonetheless, in this series of states of sensibility and memory that can be produced according to one single law, one can, as mathematicians do with their series, distinguish points of interest. Thus, one can determine the normal state of a subject in which she naturally finds herself at the moment when she is being studied, and which has a sensibility and memory which are natural for her. One can take note of the first somnambulistic state, occurring when one modifies the subject through some procedure, that is, the first very important modification in sensitivity that produces a loss of memory when the subject returns to the waking state. But one should especially take note of the final somnambulism, what I call the state in which the subject has recovered the full integrity of all sensibilities that are natural to healthy people, and consequently, the absolute integrity of memory – in a word, the state in which the subject has no anesthesia or amnesia. This is the most important state of all states, especially from a therapeutic point of view, which we will not take up at the moment.[64] But it is sometimes very difficult to obtain, and subjects attain it at different speeds, sometimes after a single intermediary somnambulism, as with Lucie or Wittm. (in the study of Jules Janet), or after many intermediary somnambulisms, as with Rose, or even never completely, as with Léonie, who, in the last somnambulism that I was able to obtain with her, still had anesthesias. In this chapter, dedicated to the study of somnambulism in general, we are not going to spend more time on this particular state. It is enough to show how it is connected with the others and is only a point of greater interest in what is actually a continuous series.

(3) *This modification can be more or less complete, and visible.* Indeed, in this work we have cited only three or four subjects for whom the characteristic phenomena of somnambulism manifest in a, as it were, gross fashion. We all know, as I was struck from the very beginning by the fact that, Lucie makes use of the sense of sight when she is awake and the sense of touch when she is put to sleep – this is clear. But with other subjects the modifications are very much less visible. In particular (and this is an objection that is often made) one can put to sleep subjects who do not manifest any clearly characteristic anesthesia in the waking state. I respond that I myself have noted cases of this kind – although more rarely than one might suppose – but that in this chapter I have neglected them in order to concentrate first of all on the simpler and more characteristic phenomena. Nevertheless, I believe that in these different, less clear cases, the explanation ought to be the same.

Indeed, the subjects who can be put into somnambulism without manifesting obvious anesthesia in the waking state, present a completely analogous phenomenon that has the same consequences for memory – that is, *distraction*. No doubt, if we turn our attention successively to each of our senses, we realize that we possess them all, or at least *could* possess them all. But in practice we do not use all of our senses and all of the images of our senses. We are not capable of joining together all of our senses and we neglect many of them to deal with our predominant and habitual images. *Somnambulism changes these predominant images* without exactly producing new sensibilities. By altering them, it brings into relief certain specific images and turns them into a new center around which thought orients itself in a different way. When awakened, these subjects regain their habitual thought, and, by distraction, neglect these images and, consequently, the memories associated with them. They can no longer recall them because they are incapable of making the small effort needed to slightly modify the habitual form of their thought.

A specific form of forgetting therefore results from distraction, just as another kind results from anesthesia. But it is obviously much weaker. It does not take much to draw attention to these images – which are more neglected than lost. A young man, H, who had a somnambulism of this kind, had forgotten everything upon awakening, but little by little, during the course of the day, recovered, one after the other, all the memories of the somnambulism. The next day he could recount everything for me. It is subjects of this kind with whom one can evoke memories by having them pay attention and directing their efforts. Just as with certain subjects anesthesia is only a slight distraction that one can modify with a word, for these same subjects forgetting too is only a consequence of distraction and does not have any greater importance. At this point we are not going to spend any more time on this explanation. The connections between anesthesia and distraction will be the subject of a later section of this book.[65] For now it suffices to have shown that, through this way of looking at things, cases that seem to be irregular can be included in the general theory.

Paulhan said, "Every time there is a change in what might be called the general orientation of the mind, it results in a kind of split in memory that is greater the more pronounced the change."[66] "What produces the forgetting of dreams on awakening is that the orientation of the mind is suddenly changed."[67] Another author said, "When the original conditions of memory reappear, memory itself reappears."[68] I have tried to further clarify this general explanation of the phenomena of forgetting and to adapt it more exactly to the facts that I have studied. No doubt the examples I have given are not sufficient to demonstrate that it is always so, and we do not always have means that are precise and sure enough to discern the differences in the images which lead to differences in memories. Furthermore, it may be that, in certain cases and for certain light somnambulisms, the modifications of the mind are less pronounced. It may be that in somnambulism certain subjects do not have sensibilities that are completely new, but only a little different from those they have in the waking state. The separation between the two groups of memories, systematized around sensations while awake and those of somnambulism, still exists, but is not as strong. In other words, we have only explained very clear and relatively simple cases. An explanation of somnambulism will be more complete, but will remain, we believe, of the same kind.

2.7 Various successive psychological existences: spontaneous modifications of the personality

When a certain number of psychological phenomena are brought together, as a rule, a new and very important reality comes into being in the mind: their coming together, when observed and understood, gives birth to a particular *judgment* that is called the idea of the self. We state that it is a judgment, and not an association of ideas. The latter reproduces phenomena, one after the other; it automatically juxtaposes them and gives us the occasion to note their unity and judge their resemblance, but it does not of itself constitute this connection of unity and resemblance. Judgment, on the contrary, synthesizes different facts, ascertains their unity, and, in regard to various psychological phenomena evoked by sensible impressions or by the automatic activity of association, forms a new idea – that of personality. We do not, in this study of the automatic part and not the active part of the mind, need to study this judgment of unity. We are content to show that the psychological phenomena that occupy the mind can, as we have seen, be very different in diverse states. This judgment, this idea of personality ought to undergo similar changes and vary in the same subject according to changes that occur in sensations and memories.

A psychologist has said: "In the course of a long life, a man can be successively many persons, persons so different that, if each of the phases of this life could be incarnated in distinct individuals and if we were to bring those diverse individuals together, they would form a very heterogeneous group: they would oppose one another and despise one another, and would quickly split up, never wanting to see each other again."[69] At some point, reviewing the memories of our past life, we might say with astonishment: "Was it I who trembled before this imaginary danger? Was it I who fell in love with this coquette? Was it I who espoused these beliefs? This cannot be! I do not recognize myself!" Nevertheless, it was real. If we do not recognize ourselves, it is because we have changed. Fortunately, the changes occur gradually, and they really only have to do with complex secondary phenomena of our mind: our beliefs, our ambitions, our desires. If these changes had to do with the basic phenomena of our thought in a way that would modify our memories, the differences would have been very much more pronounced and the continuity of our life would have been broken. We have gone on saying "I" at each moment of our existence, that is, to make a judgment of unity in regard to groups of phenomena actually joined together, but we have ignored or *failed to recognize* the greater part of our life, which has been for us as though it were that of another person.

Let us quickly examine the modifications of personality that occur spontaneously. They are too well known to spend a lot of time on them, but they will prepare us to understand those produced during artificial somnambulism. Individuals who are mentally completely healthy, in their dreams nearly always present the first sign, the first hint of changes that are often of the most serious kind that can be produced in the personality of certain ill persons.

Every night we have a particular kind of mental life that is not at all like that of our conscious life when awake. No doubt, the ideas of the dream seem almost always to borrow from normal life, but they are presented and arranged differently. They are presented in the form of images of a kind we hardly ever use in waking life. If I were to describe them in the language of experiment, they would be of the "motor type." Awake, when I think while speaking aloud or writing, my thought always involves an inhibited gesture. At night, on the other hand, as I have consistently established, I maintain absolute immobility; I am a simple spectator and no longer an agent. Images and sounds form pictures and scenes that pass before me. I see myself acting or hear myself speaking, but rarely, and I always maintain at the same time a vague sense of my immobility and powerlessness. Furthermore, precisely because of this marked difference between my dreams and my waking thoughts, I find it difficult to remember my dreams.

During sleep, a group of isolated psychological phenomena takes shape out of the great mass of ideas that form our life. These phenomena develop to a certain extent, following the law of isolated phenomena. But seeing that they are of sufficient number to create mutual opposition, and that, on the other hand, they hardly contain any visual and acoustic images which we do not hold, for ourselves, to move ourselves, they rarely become movements. Furthermore, they are sufficiently grouped for a very simple personality, for if the isolated phenomena of catalepsy do not present the idea of personality, this is not the case for the complex groupings that exist in dreams. Further, it is certain that in healthy people this tendency to form a memory and a secondary personality in the dream remains rudimentary. Even if certain memories of different dreams become tied in with each other, what remains is only a tumult of fragmentary images which are incapable of unification or systematization. Instead, the dream is like the state of sluggishness that certain elderly people exhibit in which the cerebral substance is softened.[70] Attention is impossible, the will and judgment are almost totally absent. It is more a thought in a state of disaggregation than a personality on the way to being formed.

If we somewhat increase the activity of the dream, and if we also bind together its scattered images, we will already have a psychological state with a life more independent and distinct than the waking life, one comparable to the state of somnambulism.[71] Erasmus Darwin wrote,[72] "One of my friends remarked that his wife, who often spoke a great deal and distinctly in the state of sleep, could never remember the accompanying dreams, but could, on the contrary, recall them well when she had not spoken during sleep." I have observed the same thing with Léonie who, during the waking state, remembered the dreams she had had without speaking and could only recount in somnambulism the dreams she had in which she both moved and spoke. The latter had, therefore, already formed a secondary personality and had an independent life. When ether, chloroform, and alcohol are used for the first time, they do not do more than disaggregate normal thinking and prevent the formation of judgments of unity, while leaving only sparse psychological elements during the delirium. But with the repetition of these poisonings, these thought fragments come together and form a new psychological synthesis, with its own proper memory, similar to a somnambulistic experience.[73]

Illnesses which are called "nervous maladies" and which, if I am not mistaken, also very much deserve to be called "psychological maladies," show us with still more clarity the development of this secondary group of phenomena and the formation of many distinct forms of psychological existence. We do not include those periodic convulsions that return at regular intervals with certain epileptics, and which can rightly be called a "muscular delirium.[74] In post-epileptic or hysterical deliriums there is a true mental life, different from normal life, that often stretches out over many hours and which regularly begins with a memory and a character all its own.[75]

The possessed of Morzine present a good example of this kind of modification of character, which frequently survives under diverse influences during the delirium of the hysterical crisis. During their attacks, they demonstrate a real rage against religion, insulting priests, the Holy Virgin, etc., and all their responses are sprinkled with every profanity they know. After the attack, they awaken in a state in which they are calm, polite, and religious.[76] These ingenious young women spout revolting obscenities. "But," writes a witness, "we then say of them that it is not they who express themselves in this way; it is the devil who possesses them and he speaks in his own name. The young girl Blaud was a passive instrument. She was calmed, as if by enchantment; she knitted beforehand and she knitted afterwards, and she experienced no fatigue, *not remembering anything* and not wanting to believe that she had addressed insults to us."[77] We admit that they have a diabolic character during the crisis, but it is clear that they are not always that way and that they have two forms of existence that are independent of each other. All hysterical deliria show us the same kind of reduction of phenomena. Rose insults people who approach her during her delirium, but is very polite in the waking state. Lucie thinks only of cooking and doing housework during the last two hours of her crisis but is not interested in such things in her normal state.

Crises of this kind are, in general, of a very short duration. The personality is not very complete, since the duration of a psychological state is ordinarily in proportion to the perfection of the being involved. Like the atoms of Epicurus, these isolated psychic elements come together to form a personality, but they cannot be combined into a viable one. Too many elements are missing. In one case the visual sensation is missing, in another the motor sensation of the pharynx. In this person it is the motor sensation of the limbs, in that the sensation of hunger or of thirst is totally absent. Moreover, the grouping is not very coherent. At certain times it disaggregates, and simple convulsions, the elementary form of this new life, recommence.

Also, this unstable compound can actually bring about its own destruction, and then the older, more complete compound, which formed the person's normal life, reappears. But let us suppose that, by a combination of chance happenings, the coming together of intellectual atoms has formed a more complete and stable compound. Here the new psychological life, which has formed little by little and which is abnormal for the subject, resembles a normal personal life. The elements, as numerous or even more numerous than ordinary, are assembled around another center – it is as simple as that. This is "an allotropic crystallization," as Myers well names it,[78] but it can form crystals as durable as the preceding crystallization. Let us say that the subject, who was formerly visually oriented, is now motor oriented. Undoubtedly this will cause difficulties later, because if he reverts to the first state, he will no longer remember the second, but will be like someone who is normally motor and is none the worse for it. This, we believe, is what happened with those people well known in the history of science – Félida X, Louis V, and many others. If we do not summarize their stories here, it is because they have been so thoroughly and deeply studied that it seems to us to be enough simply to recall a memory present in all the memories.[79] I simply want to recall that the second state of Félida develops, after a sleep, a kind of sudden syncope[80] that wipes out the first personality and from which, little by little, the second emerges. It is the same with the young man described by Myers, who, over a period of time manifested similar alternations of personality.[81] Furthermore, this period of transition became more and more brief, as we have seen with artificial somnambulists who have been frequently put to sleep. I would also remark that if, in this second state, Félida has a more complete memory, it is because she also has a more complete sensibility and, in re-entering her first state, she loses both certain memories and certain sensations. Finally, Azam leaves us to understand that, during the second state, she sometimes attains a kind of crisis which clearly seems like the beginning of a third state.[82] The somnambulist of Dufay,[83] when entering a second state, no longer experiences the nearsightedness she has when in the first state. She uses an infantile language and speaks pidgin French: "Moi pas bête maintenant" ["me not dumb now"], she says. This is probably a new language that has formed itself by means of other images. Another remarkable patient has two naturally occurring states: one in which she is mute, but can drink and eat, and another in which she can speak but is unable to drink.[84] Most likely, with this patient speech and swallowing depend on two different kinds of images which do not coexist in the same psychological existence. The famous Louis V presents a most remarkable example of modifications of personality and memory tied to sensory and motor modifications. One cannot modify the latter through some kind of stimulation without changing the former. At one time his states unfold during the development of a great crisis. At another he remains for some time in one of his states, after he has been artificially placed there. "Each page of his life is independent of the others."[85]

All of these people, as we know, change in character and behavior when they change in sensation and speech. Félida, who is sad and contemplates suicide in her primary state, is happy and courageous in her secondary state. She is egotistical and cold in her first state, but has more affection and devotedness in her second. Louis V is now sweet, obedient and timid, now angry, insubordinate and arrogant, now a fearful infant, now a fiery young man. From no point of view does he remain the same.

The transition between natural modifications of the personality and those which occur during artificial somnambulism can be easily made. As a general rule, although we do not always see this, it is possible through hypnotism to lead the subject from one to the other of his various abnormal personalities and produce the character and memories which he possesses in the latter state. This has often been verified in the states of Louis V and in general for all delirious hysterics.

What is curious is the easy passage from natural delirium to artificial somnambulism, a passage which is analogous to the changing of hysterical poses in catalepsy. On one occasion I came across Marie in a great hysterical crisis, having been writhing on a cushion and crying for two hours. I said to her, "My goodness, what are you doing? Could you contain yourself a bit more?" Continuing her convulsions, she squeezed my hand and answered, "Oh! If only you knew the pain I am having in my side." "If you get up and go to lie down in your bed, I can treat you there." She arose, with eyes closed, and went to her bed. I calmed her a bit and she said to me, "It is fortunate that you came along. I was seeing horrible things – blood, fires – and I was in great pain." Here we have a somnambulism which is a slight transformation of her hysterical delirium, seeing that she retained her memory and that, with a word, I could get her to recall what happened. Another hysteric, G (of whom I have not previously spoken because she is too similar to others that I have described), one day experienced something even more unusual. She was having convulsions and being held by two servants when I approached her. Before I could touch her, she said to me: "Well! So there you are," and the convulsions immediately stopped. These kinds of things happen with people who have often been put into the state of artificial somnambulism: in the end this state absorbs all the other abnormal states. But with other subjects, it produces the inverse phenomenon, with the artificial somnambulism degenerating into a hysterical crisis, or simply reproducing the crisis. In this regard, nothing is more decisive than the observation of Grasset, who describes for us artificial sleeps of a patient which were totally identical with her spontaneous crises.[86] At the Pitié hospital, Jules Janet showed me a young woman of the same kind. Jos had spontaneous attacks of sleep during which she remained immobile, with eyes closed, but spoke the whole time. Her dream revolved around two or three ideas (always the same), amusing anecdotes that made people laugh, or wrongs attributed to the doctors and interns, whom she called "butchers, pig's heads, etc." If, in the course of the day, one attempted to hypnotize her using some procedure or another, she would take up exactly the same attitude and continue the same dream about "these villainous doctors who have again brought in a poor woman to cut her up." The old magnetizers were not wrong to say that nervous crises are nothing other than imperfect somnambulism.

2.8 The various successive psychological existences – changes of the personality in artificial somnambulism

We have explained how modifications in memory can easily be explained in terms of modifications in the nature or the quality of images which, at a given moment, are a part of consciousness, and how these modifications of memory produce modifications of personality or of the whole psychological being. It is now possible for us to have a general idea of artificial somnambulism or the state of magnetized individuals, which for a long time have been thought of as supernatural and inexplicable. As we have shown at the beginning of this chapter, the somnambulistic state does not present characteristics that are peculiar to it or in some way specific. If you examine an individual at any particular moment of his life, it is impossible to establish what state he is in.[87] The characteristics of the somnambulistic state are relative and can only be determined in connection with another moment in the life of the subject, the normal or waking state. "When one has occasion to observe (somnambulists)," say the old magnetizers who know about these things, "one is convinced that there are two very distinct lives, or at least two ways of being, in the lives of somnambulists."[88] This is in fact true; somnambulism is a *second* existence whose only characteristic is of being the second.

This is how we can explain the oft-repeated truth that there is no single phenomenon established during somnambulism – anesthesia or sensory excitation, paralysis, contractions, emotion, intellectual weakness, etc.[89] – which cannot be frequently found in other persons in their ordinary life. Only, for the latter, the characteristic is constant and normal during the whole of their lives, whereas for the former it is accidental and only exists during their second life, even though in reality it is the same characteristic. A subject who is foolish, or blind, or intelligent in somnambulism is not different from someone who is foolish, blind, or intelligent in the normal state, but is not so in their whole life. Rose, in one of her profound somnambulisms, was hemianesthetic on her left side. For her, this is actually a completely normal state, because during the seven months in which I have observed her daily, she has always been totally anesthetic. This state does not last, because if I awaken her or even allow her to rest quietly, little by little she loses sensibility on her right side and returns to her normal state, in which she feels nothing. But this state that we qualify as somnambulism in Rose is what is normal for Marie, who for a month has been hemianesthetic on the left side, and the characteristics of this state are exactly the same for her. Furthermore, we have observed that Rose herself has on one occasion spent three months being hemianesthetic on the left side. Therefore, for those three months she was naturally in a state that has now become somnambulism. But if you awaken her, she forgets all. True enough, but we should note that she had also forgotten everything when, after three months of being partially healthy, she was *reawakened* totally anesthetic. It is the change in the sensory state, not the awakening, that produces the forgetting. Also, if I should suddenly find a way to give to my neighbor, who is a painter and visual, my own state of consciousness, which is motor, he would no longer remember his past life, which, nevertheless, would appear to be perfectly normal.

This conception of somnambulism also explains for us the infinite diversity of somnambulists that is as great as that of people around us. They can possess all possible psychological characteristics, provided they are not precisely those of their normal state. There are very intelligent people who, when somnambulistic, are very much like the mentally deficient. R, an epileptic[90] whom I could easily put to sleep, presented an insignificant somnambulistic life. He had little muscular sense, since he would leave his arms in whatever position I placed them. He had little hearing, since he responded with grunts to whatever I would say. Moreover, he did not understand anything and consequently did not obey suggestions. He did not speak, and teaching him was more difficult than the famous Laura Bridgman. It was useless to try. All one could do was to awaken him and return him to his first life, which, although unremarkable, was superior to his second. Lem, when somnambulistic, was subject to a deplorable infirmity. He had no memory and, similar to the somnambulist described by Dr. Philips[91] who would forget one syllable the moment he moved on to the next, he would forget what I said to him as soon as I had said it. He could exactly execute simple commands at the moment they were given to him, but could not execute them later, because he always forgot them. Teaching him was very difficult. N, on the contrary, is endowed with a remarkable memory[92] in her somnambulistic state. As I have said, she can remember the smallest details of her preceding somnambulism, even a year later. All the other somnambulists that I have spoken about have an ordinary or sometimes remarkable intelligence in their second state, with sensations and ideas that no one would expect in their situation.

When subjects in their second state have this kind of sensation, memory, and intelligence, they immediately present a curious but not unexpected phenomenon. During this new state of being, they acquire an education, knowledge, a character such as they have acquired during their first state of being.

One can therefore foresee what will happen when the somnambulisms are repeated and prolonged. To begin with, the secondary personality who is about to be born is subject to the influence of the ideas and practices of her magnetizer like an infant is subject to the influence of its parents. She takes on the habits, manners, and beliefs that have infused into her almost without any conscious intention to do so. It is said: as the magnetizer, so the somnambulist. Show me a somnambulist and I will quickly know who has put her to sleep and the opinions and beliefs, scientific or otherwise, of her first master. Why is Léonie a practicing catholic when awake and a convinced protestant when in a state of somnambulism? It is simply because her first magnetizer was a protestant; there is no further mystery about it. Why do certain somnambulists always carry on with a dramatic attitude? Because they have been exhibited on stage like bizarre animals and they have learned to play a role and do imitations, although they are really in a state of somnambulism.[93] The education of the somnambulist by the one who puts her to sleep is the great danger of these experiences. It shows us that our somnambulists always verify our own ideas.[94] In our introduction we have indicated the particular precautions we have tried to take, but we well understand that only the confirmations of other experimenters can give a general verification to our studies.

The influence of education on a subject brings into play in this new life, as with infants in their normal state of being, certain predispositions and particular abilities. Beaunis tells us that he has never encountered lying on the part of a somnambulist.[95] He has been very fortunate. There are somnambulists who lie, such as Lucie, or who are honesty itself, such as Léonie, just as in ordinary life there are both bad and good.[96] It is important to take into account not only the influence of the magnetizer, but also that of all others who speak with the subject in her new state and contribute to her development. To illustrate this, it is sufficient to describe one of our subjects, Léonie, on whom all these influences have exerted a very curious effect. This woman, whose life is a veritable novel, unbelievable but real, has had attacks of natural somnambulism since age three. From age sixteen she has repeatedly been put to sleep by all sorts of people, and she is now forty-five. While her normal life took shape in a rustic and poor environment, her second life has passed in salons and parlors and has naturally taken an entirely different direction. Today, this poor peasant, in her normal state, is a serious and slightly sad woman, calm and deliberate, very sweet with everyone and extremely timid. On seeing her, one would never suspect the kind personage locked up inside her. Barely having been put to sleep, and having passed through a transition phase, there follows "the awakening to another existence,"[97] and she is entirely transformed. Her countenance is no longer the same, her eyes remain closed, but the acuity of the other senses compensate for the loss of sight. She is merry, rowdy, and restless in a way that is sometimes intolerable. She remains nice, but now has acquired a notable inclination to irony and caustic jokes. Nothing is more curious than to chat with her at the end of a séance, when she had been visited by new people who had desired to see her put to sleep. She gives me a picture of them, mimics their mannerisms, claims to know their little absurdities and petty passions, and weaves a story about each of them.

This new character also has an enormous quantity of new memories that she has no knowledge of in the waking state, since she always experiences a total forgetfulness on awakening. Recently, a doctor of Le Havre, who had frequently seen this woman in her somnambulistic state and who was among her friends (because at the time she had her favourites), recounted seeing her very much awake outside the town. Forgetting in what circumstances he had seen her, he went up to meet her to say hello. The poor woman was stupefied, not recognizing the man who was speaking to her. So it was that there were a host of things that she did not know outside her somnambulistic state. It would be contrary to very laws of elementary psychology that this collection of sensations, memories, habits, and characteristics would form a synthesis and a system identical to that of the normal personality. Thus it is an entirely different person in the waking state: she knows the one, but has no idea of the other.

We know that somnambulists in their secondary existence retain the memory of their primary existence, and that, consequently, they can themselves make a comparison between the two personalities. It is interesting to see what they think of this alteration.

Most often, especially in the first somnambulisms, when the subject has many memories of her first state and not so many of her second, she simply senses being *changed*. Many express this difference by saying that they are asleep,[98] and nothing is more curious than people who, with eyes closed, chatting easily, from time to time say, "It is true that I am sleeping. Yes, I am sleeping very well." I believe that here we have a commonly used phrase that does not make any sense. Somnambulists say that they sleep because it has been said to them that they sleep and that, in popular thinking, "to magnetize" is the equivalent of "to put to sleep." It is a mistake to keep on repeating this to the somnambulist, because she comes to believe that she is obliged to really go to sleep, she takes on a dazed expression which is not necessary. More intelligent persons, such as N, have said to me, "But I do not go to sleep and it is absurd to say so. I am merely changed; I am a bit odd. What would you have me do, anyway?" Now we have suspicions about what has been done to these somnambulists. We realize that someone has used their psychological instability to change the state of their senses by paralyzing or, more often, exciting one or the other of them. This modification of the subject sometimes manifests grossly and in an objective fashion. One subject is deaf in the waking state and now hears.[99] Another feels or sees nothing, and now has exquisite touch and sees even in darkness.[100] All subjects that we have cited have sensorial alterations of this kind, often with corresponding motor alterations. Seeing that they retain the memory of their former state and can compare the two, they naturally find that state "very odd." Sometimes somnambulists stop with that and never modify their expression. The difference between the state of somnambulism and the waking state is not very great, since they are aware of the split in their personality. Lucie, in her first somnambulistic state, even after many séances, always remained the same and would always say, "It is I, Lucie, but you have changed me." Sometimes the alterations could be considerable, but be brought about little by little, by steps so numerous and so subtle, that the subject habituated in this way of changing kept her identity. It was similar with Rose who, in her three or four somnambulistic states, continued to say, when questioned on this matter, "It is indeed always me … but not entirely the same."

However, often things are otherwise and, whether gradually, by the development of the secondary existence, or suddenly, following a very powerful alteration, the subject refuses to recognize herself, mocks herself about her former personality, and claims to be a new person.

This singular habit of somnambulists to double themselves in this way is very common and has been noted from the very first studies of this subject.

"Somnambulists speak of themselves in the third person," said Deleuze,[101] "as if the individual of their waking state and that of their somnambulistic state are two different persons … Miss Adélaïde never brought together the identity of Adélaïde with that of Petite, the name she received and gave herself during her mania (somnambulism), etc." Aubin Gauthier[102] says, "Their minds in the waking state and in somnambulism are two different things." All those who write about animal magnetism have described this fact, which is as frequent as it is curious.

N, when she found herself changed, immediately claimed that she was someone else. "Who are you, anyway?" I would ask her. She would reply, "I do not know … I believe that I am a patient." Not dwelling on this response, which is perhaps not so absurd, I asked her by what name she wished to be addressed, and she indicated the name "Nichette." We should not smile about this name; no detail is insignificant in these delicate matters. In this case it was the name she was called in her infancy, and she reclaimed the name in somnambulism. This is not rare. We have seen a somnambulist of Deleuze who was called "Petite". Dr. Gilbert has told me that a woman of thirty, when put to sleep for the first time, spoke of herself as "Little Lilie." Why this return to infancy? Is it because of the fact that hysterics, who are ordinarily visual in the waking state, regain their muscular sense in deep somnambulistic states, and that this sense is the one that probably dominates in infancy? We must at another time come back to this matter of the return of the somnambulist to the state of infancy, which is one of the major factors in suggestion. Lucie, who by her own account remains the same in her first somnambulism, completely changes her opinion on the matter when placed in her second somnambulism. In all likelihood the alteration is so great, that she no longer recognizes herself. At that point she spontaneously takes on another name, that of Adrienne (Lucie 3), which she chooses in circumstances which we will come back to later on.

Finally, it is possible to conclude that every alteration of state might be sufficiently exaggerated so as to produce the illusion of doubling the personality. Léonie, since the first somnambulism that we described, refused her ordinary name and took that of Léontine, to which her first magnetizers had habituated her. "This good woman is not me," she says, "She is too foolish." She adds, "She is the other, too true, too true." But this is a habit that has been imposed on her. With respect to herself, she believes she is as real as "the other." The new character, Léonie 2, attributes to herself all sensations and all actions – in a word, all psychological phenomena – which have been conscious for her during her somnambulism; these combine to form the history of her life, which is already quite lengthy. On the contrary, she attributes to Léonie 1, that is, the normal waking person, all phenomena that are conscious in the waking state. Now, I have been struck by an important exception to this rule and I have become disposed to think that there is something a bit arbitrary in this distribution of memories. In her normal state, Léonie has a husband and children. Léonie 2, during somnambulism, attributes the husband to the other personality, but the children to herself. This choice might be explainable, but it does not seem usual. I have come to realize that the old magnetizers, every bit as audacious as certain hypnotizers today, induced somnambulism for first childbirth experiences, and that the secondary state was re-experienced spontaneously in latter ones.[103] Léonie 2 was not mistaken to attribute the children to herself, because it was indeed she who had them. So the rule remains intact and the first somnambulism for her did lead to a doubling of existence. But, curiously, it is the same for the second. When, after lethargy and catalepsy, she enters the state I have described by this name, she is not the same. Instead of being a restless child, she is serious and grave; she speaks slowly and moves little. At that point she distinguishes herself from Léonie 1 in the waking states. "She is an honest woman, somewhat simple," she says, "but she is not me." She also distinguishes herself from Léonie 2: "How could you think I am like this madwoman?[104] I am absolutely nothing to her, fortunately." This separation of one being into three successive characters, who are mutually scornful when aware of each other, forms a most striking spectacle and produces a multitude of incidents that I could not relate without indefinitely expanding my book. Léonie went into a sleep state on a train and passed into state 2. After some time, Léonie 2 wanted to get off and go to look for this poor Léonie 1 at the preceding station: "She was left there," she said, "and must be helped." If I show Léonie 2 a portrait of Léonie 1, she cries, "Why does she have my bonnet? This is someone who is dressed like me." When she comes to Le Havre, I have to say "good day" successively to three persons who successively repeat the same emotion in a very amusing manner. There is no use going on with these anecdotes; one can imagine the odd situations that will result from a subdivision of this kind.

But, someone will say, these secondary states are not real existences, because they do not last very long. The subjects always wake up after some hours. No doubt, *some* subjects cannot remain indefinitely in *certain* somnambulistic states. Léonie can eat nothing in the state of Léonie 2, and so cannot remain in that state for more than a day, but that is not because her secondary state cannot last, but because it does not contain certain elements necessary for life. Some authors write that it is dangerous to leave a subject in somnambulism for more than twenty-four hours because they will begin to catch a chill. Certainly, if one leaves a subject incapable of moving or eating, she will catch a chill very quickly. But if, on the contrary, one chooses to bring about a complete somnambulistic state which undoubtedly forms a secondary life, but a secondary regular life, analogous, as we have said, to the normal life of a normal person, there is no reason why a subject cannot remain in that state for a very long time.

Also, putting aside natural secondary existences that can prolong themselves, such as that of Félida, we have often seen artificial somnambulisms that have stretched out for a long time. The celebrated Abbé Faria claimed that some of his subjects remained asleep for years and that, when awakened, forgot all that had occurred during that extended period.[105] The magnetizer Chardel put two women to sleep in the winter and did not awaken them until some months later, in the middle of spring. They were very surprised upon awakening to see leaves and flowers on the trees which, before being put to sleep, they had seen covered with snow.[106] One author recounts: "I would frequently leave my somnambulists asleep the whole day, with eyes open, so I could walk with them to observe them, without arousing public curiosity. In the case of a young woman who was in my service, I succeeded in prolonging the somnambulism for fourteen or fifteen days. In this state, she continued with her work as if she were in her ordinary state.... She found herself awake, in a bewildered state, in the house, unaware of what had been taking place."[107] These accounts should not be considered false, for it is very easy to verify them. I myself kept Rose in somnambulism for four and a half days without any difficulty, because she handled the situation very well during this period, eating and sleeping much better than in her ordinary state. Jules Janet, who has closely studied that interesting period of these somnambulisms during which a hysteric, in contrast to her waking state, recovers all her senses and is like a normal person, has stretched out this state longer still. Can one leave subjects in their secondary state indefinitely? This would be a very good way to easily bring about a complete cure of hysteria. Unfortunately, this seems to me very difficult to do. This state seems, at least for my subjects, to be one of fatigue, and it rapidly exhausts them. Some of them, such as Léonie and Lucie, need to sleep frequently for several minutes to get their rest, and hysterics in general can only maintain this state of sensory integrity through excitations repeated from time to time, such as passes, electric current, etc. Most likely, hysterics gradually regain their deficiencies, their habitual anesthesias, and re-enter their normal state, forgetting what has happened during their more complete existence. However, my observations on this matter are very incomplete and I cannot present any final conclusions.

There is one last question to ask regarding these new forms of psychological existence. Are they inferior or superior to the waking state? Are we dealing with a degeneration or an advance when a subject passes from one state to the other? Many authors hold the latter view. "The latter phenomenon, forgetting upon awakening, leads us to think that the state of magnetic somnambulism is the perfect state."[108] Myers, in his very careful study of automatic writing, asks whether the somnambulistic state instead of being "regressive," is not rather sometimes an "evolutive" state.[109] Here, as with all of these kinds of things, one cannot give a generalized response, due to the many varieties of somnambulism. There is an infinite number of forms of psychological existence, from those that contain only one rudimentary isolated characteristic, without judgment and even without personality, to the thought of the superior monad that Leibniz speaks about and which represents, in short, the whole world. We have seen that hypnosis can put subjects into the primary state that we have called catalepsy. This is proof that it can give them a very inferior form of existence. Can it also bring them closer to a superior form of thought? I believe that this depends on the nature of their thoughts in their normal state. When one considers hysterics for whom thought, sensation and memory are diminished, that is, reduced to below the normal limit, then the least excitation of their nervous system, whether through passes or an electric current, which for them is very powerful, can restore to them faculties that they had lost and give them a superior form of existence. It is evident that Lucie 3, Rose 4, and Léonie 3 are very superior to Lucie 1, Rose 1, and Léonie 1. But here we are dealing with hysterical women, and the superior state of being given them is simply a normal state of being, one that they would have enjoyed continuously had they not been ill. This state is not much better than that of the real life which, for these women, occurs in moments of health that they might experience. Is it possible to go beyond that? Can one surpass the somnambulistic states of these subjects or give to other subjects, who are healthy, and who already possess this kind of existence, another form that is superior? Almost all the old magnetizers thought so when they examined the new sensations and supernatural faculties of their subjects. This is also Myers' thinking when he speaks of new adaptations of our personality in response to new needs. This is a study that we are not able to engage in; it is sufficient that we have shown at what point it touches our subject matter and how it is possible.

2.9 Conclusion

In the previous chapter, while studying isolated psychological phenomena, we saw that the movements of limbs and sensations on one side of the body, the expressions of the face, the series of gestures, and the emotions of the other formed unities and syntheses with coherent and inseparable elements. If one part of a sensation or emotion was given, the rest necessarily came into being and contributed to the formation of the group, which tended to complete itself and subsist. In this chapter we have studied a group that is more complex, but of the same type – one that is formed by sensations and memories, and in this new study we have established a similar law. When a sense, or even a more special sensibility, disappears, the images and, consequently, the memories of the phenomena otherwise provided by the sense also disappear. When a sense remains intact, the images of past sensations, their memories, also persist. "No sensation, no ideas," says Lamettrie in his *Homme-machine*.[110] "The less sensation one has, the less ideas." We say at least, "No sensation, no memories; the less sensation, the less memories." Memories which persist, therefore, are joined together and united around a principal sensation which serves to express and evoke them. And when there are many of them around it, they form a system, all parts of which are held by and belong to a single memory. An individual who is perfectly healthy from a psychological point of view will have but one memory of this kind, and, since all phenomena of thought will be attached to images that are always the same and always present, he will be able to easily and instantly call them forward. But no man is perfect. A thousand circumstances – the state of passion, the state of sleep, intoxication, or illness – diminish or destroy certain images, while reviving others, and change "the whole orientation of thought." In virtue of these laws, secondary groups are formed around certain images that are abnormal for this particular mind. These new images can never reappear, but if they are periodically reproduced or artificially produced, they bring with them all the memories tied to them, and these different memories become alternating memories.

A group of images crystallized in this way can give birth to a particular judgment that acknowledges and establishes its unity, and the alternating memories produce different, successive personalities. Somnambulisms are existences of this kind, having their own peculiar memory and personality. Their essential character is to be an abnormal psychological state which does not constitute the whole life of the individual but alternates with other states and other memories, the memory of which it cannot retain. Often imperfect and rudimentary, somnambulisms can form a new existence that is more complete than the normal existence of the individual. For this, it suffices that circumstances favor the automatic development of elements which enter into the second life and render their grouping more coherent and stable. Thus, these systems of psychological elements seem to have their own life, as does each particular element, and it is this life of a psychological system that constitutes the different personalities and their diverse somnambulisms.

Notes

1 De Lausanne, *Principes et Procédés du Magnétisme Animal*, 1819, II, 54; also in Teste, *Magnétisme Animal Expliqué*, 1845, 285.
2 Baragnon, *Étude Pratique du Magnétisme Animal*, 1853, 33.
3 Lafontaine, *L'Art de Magnétiser*, 1860, 99.
4 Baragnon, *Op. cit.*, 103.
5 *Revue Scientifique*, 1888, II, 241.
6 Despine, *Somnambulisme*, 107.
7 *Ibid.*, 80.
8 See Gurney, S. P. R. *Proceedings*, 1884, II, 266.
9 See Chapter 3.
10 Deleuze, *Histoire Critique du Magnétisme Animal*, 1819, I, 187.
11 Baragnon, *Op. cit.*, 173.
12 Gurney, *The Stages of Hypnotic Memory. Proceedings S. P. R.*, 1887, 517.
13 Georget, *Maladies Mentales…*, 1827, 129.
14 Erasmus Darwin, *Zoonomie, trad.*, 1810, II, 163.
15 Régnard, *Sorcellerie*, etc., 1887, 221; Gilles de la Tourette, *L'Hypnotisme et les États Analogues*, 1887, 236.
16 Despine, *Op. cit.*, 93.
17 Azam, *Hypnotisme, Double Conscience*, 1887, 129.
18 Dufay, *Revue Scientifique*, December 1st, 1885. Gilles de la Tourette, *Op. cit.*, 260.
19 See Myers, *Automatic Writing. Proceedings S. P. R.*, 1887, 230.
20 Dupotet, *Traité du Magnétisme Animal*, 4th edit., 1883, 470.
21 Myers, *Op. cit.*, 226. See also Charma, *Du Sommeil*, 1852, 36 and Maury, *Le Sommeil et les Rêves*, 1861, 94.
22 Myers, *Op. cit.*, 227.
23 *Ibid.*, 228.
24 Beaunis, *Somnambulisme Provoqué*, 1887, 122.

25 The magnetizers cite a number of instances of memory retained on waking when it was ordered by the person who put the subject to sleep. *Journal du Magnétisme*, 1855, 223, and Bertrand, *Traité du Somnambulisme*, 1823, 81.
26 Gurney, S. P. R. *Proceedings*, II, 67.
27 Richet, *L'Homme et l'Intelligence*, 1884, 169.
28 Delboeuf, *La Mémoire chez les Hypnotisés, Revue Philosophique*, 1886, I, 441.
29 Cf. Chapter 3 in this volume, and Volume 2, Chapter 4.
30 *Les Actes Inconscients et le Dédoublement de la Personnalité, Revue Philosophique*, 1886, II, 577.
31 For further details on the post-hypnotic period, see Volume 2, Chapter 2.
32 Bertrand, *Op. cit.*, 318.
33 *Appendix to the Report on Mesmerism*. Proceedings S. P. R. , 1882, 288.
34 *L'Anesthésie Systématisée et la Dissociation des Phénomènes Psychologiques, Revue Philosophique*, 1887, I, 449.
35 De Rochas, *Les Forces non Définies*, 1887, in the Appendix.
36 Gurney, *Stages of Hypnotic Memory*. S. P. R. *Proceedings*, 1887, 515.
37 *Loc. cit.*
38 *Ibid.*, 522.
39 For the alterations in will which occurred, see the next chapter.
40 Dugald Stewart and [AC208] A. Lemoine, *Du Sommeil au Point de Vue Physiologique et Pathologique*.
41 Maury, *Op. cit.*, 188.
42 Despine, *Op. cit.*, 98.
43 Maury, *Op. cit.*, 206.
44 Bertrand, *Op. cit.*, 1843, 467.
45 Ribot, *Maladies de la Mémoire*, 2.
46 Cf. Volume 2, Chapter 2.
47 When experimenting with hemi-anesthetics, this phenomenon does not occur in the same way and there are special difficulties of interpretation. We will speak of this later, in Chapter 3.
48 Cf. Richer, *Hystéro-épilepsy*, 1885, 710.
49 Cf. Pitres, *Des Anesthésies Hystériques*, Bordeaux, 1887, 26.
50 One could perhaps make shapes of this kind with different dimensions and in that way obtain veritable scales of tactile sensibility analogous to the letters of de Wecker used to measure visual acuity.
51 It is often the same with Rose.
52 Bastian, *Le Cerveau et la Pensée*, II, 123.
53 Cf. Ballet, *Langage Intérieur*, 1886.
54 In this regard, see a very complete observation by Charcot that was reported by Ballet, *Ibid.*, 101.
55 Cf. Richer, *Op. cit.*, 259.
56 The famous Estelle of Dr. Despine (d'Aix) developed a somnambulism analogous to that of Rose. During her waking state she was helpless and paralyzed, but during somnambulism she could jump and run. – Cf. Despine, *Op. cit.*, 188, 277 – Gauthier, *Histoire du Somnambulisme*, 1842, II, 373 – Pigeaire, *Electricité Animale*, 1839, 271, etc.
57 Cf. de la Tourette, *Op. cit.*, 185.
58 Bourru and Burot, *Variations de la Personnalité*, 1888, 139–143.
59 Charpignon, *Physiologie du Magnétique*, 1841, 171.
60 Bourru and Burot, *Op. cit.*, 52.
61 *Ibid.*, 135.

62 Ball, *Morphinomanie*, 1888, 20–38.
63 This increase in the number of sensations and in the quantity of memories that can be recalled during somnambulism does not mean that, from other points of view, there cannot be an intellectual downgrading during this abnormal state. In the following chapter, we will show to what degree, in certain cases, somnambulism is a state much like infancy.
64 See a study on this state of perfect somnambulism produced with a hysteric who was strongly anesthetic in the normal state: Jules Janet, *L'Hystérie et l'Hypnotisme d'après la Théorie de la Double Personnalité*, *Revue scientifique*, 1888, I, 616.
65 Volume 2, Chapter 2.
66 Paulhan, *Review Philosophique*, 1888, II, 126.
67 *Ibid.*, 1888, I, 56.
68 Joly, *L'Imatination*, 1877, 48.
69 Forster, cited by Herzen, *Le Cerveau Organe de la Pensée*, 286.
70 Maury, *Op. cit.*, 76.
71 Teste, *Op. cit.*, 278.
72 Erasme Darwin, *Op. cit.*, I, 376.
73 On the analogies of chloroformic sleep and somnambulism, see: Baragnon, *Op. cit.*, 295; Despine, *Op. cit.*, 81 and 542; Maury, *Op. cit.*, 253.
74 See Erasmus Darwin, *Op. cit.*, IV, 8; and especially Moreau (de Tours).
75 Cf. Delasiauve, *Traité de l'Épilepsie*, 148 ff., and 487.
76 Mirville, *Des Esprits*, 1863, II, 219.
77 *Ibid.*, 237.
78 Myers, *Automatic Writing. Proceedings of the* S. P. R., 1887, 235.
79 Azam, *Op. cit.*; Bourru and Burot, *Op. cit.*
80 Azam, *Op. cit.*, 65.
81 Myers, *Automatic Writing. Proceedings* S. P. R., 1887, 230.
82 Azam, *Op. cit.*, 102.
83 *Ibid.*, 189.
84 Bourru and Burot, *Op. cit.*, 187.
85 Gilles de la Tourette, *Op. cit.*, 220.
86 Grasset, *Histoire d'une Hystérique Hypnotisable*, Arch. De Neurologie, October 1887.
87 Bourru and Burot, *Op. cit.*, 123.
88 Pigeaire, *Op. cit.*, 44.
89 See Gurney, *Proceedings* S. P. R., 1882, 285.
90 Or hystero-epileptic: the assigned diagnosis of epilepsy seems to me rather doubtful since hypnotism is very rare among true epileptics.
91 Dr. Philips (Durand de Gros), *Course de Braidisme*, 1860, 155.
92 See the examples of superior memory in somnambulism: Bertrand, *Op. cit.*, 99 ff.
93 Richet, *Op. cit.*, 167.
94 We will return to this *plasticity* of certain somnambulists when we speak of suggestion in the following chapter. Here we are only pointing it out to help explain the formation of successive personalities.
95 Beaunis, *Op. cit.*, 216.
96 See Gurney, *Proceedings*, 1887, 527.
97 Baragnon, *Op. cit.*, 154.
98 Richet, *Op. cit.*, 177.
99 Gauthier, *Op. cit.*, 358.
100 Liébault, *Le Sommeil et les États Analogues*, 1866, 80 ff.
101 Deleuze, *Op. cit.*, 188.
102 Gauthier, *Op. cit.*, 304.

103 The exact inverse occurred with Félida, for whom "eleven confinements took place in the normal state." Azam, *Op. cit.*, 91.
104 "What do you want me to say about her? She is a madwoman," spontaneously said one somnambulist cited by Charpignon, *Physiologie du Magnétisme*, 388.
105 According to Gilles de la Tourette, *Op. cit.*, *23*.
106 Gauthier, *Op. cit.*, 363.
107 Delatour, in *l'Hermès (journal magnet.)*, August 1826, 116.
108 Baragnon, *Op. cit.*, 1853, 172.
109 Myers, *Proceed.* S. P. R., 1887, 514.
110 According to Lange, *Histoire du Matérialisme*, trans. I, 349.

Chapter 3

Suggestion and the narrowing of the field of consciousness

Every personality, once constituted, thinks and acts. In what way will the diverse personalities that we have seen form and grow almost before our very eyes think and act? We can refer this question to the study of a particular fact that is more important than all the others – obedience to suggestion – because the presence or absence of this docility is the essential trait of their thoughts and actions.

All people act on each other and social relations consist almost entirely of reciprocal actions and reactions. But this influence ordinarily occurs, or seems to occur, through an intermediary: voluntary consent. If you act in a certain way, undoubtedly it is because you are following my advice, but it is also, and especially, because you choose to follow it. It is not important to investigate here whether or not this consent is freely given; undoubtedly one often consents to act because one cannot do otherwise, but this is not important. It suffices to remark at this point that most often there is more or less resigned acceptance and consciousness of that acceptance. Now, it has been shown that in numerous cases, this intermediary of voluntary consent is entirely powerless and even totally disappears: individuals come under an extraneous influence and immediately obey without consenting to obey and without knowing that they obey. To this *influence of one individual over another, which is executed without the intermediary of voluntary consent*, we give the name of *suggestion*.

The phenomena of suggestion were first noted by the magnetizers during certain states of artificial somnambulism, and knowledge of these facts was swept along by the current of naïve misapprehension that for so long has tainted these studies. But for some years now they have been rescued from this unjust oblivion and, in reaction, they have been accorded an importance that is perhaps somewhat exaggerated. Also, they are now so well known that it is not useful to go back over their description. Following a rapid and unavoidably incomplete historical review, which has as its main goal to show how ancient the study of suggestion is, we will content ourselves with recalling, by means of certain examples, the most important facts. Furthermore, in this chapter we will only study one form of suggestion, the simplest of all – one executed by subjects shortly after they receive them, without any change of psychological state in the interval, and one which

DOI: 10.4324/9780429287671-3

the subject understands and executes with full consciousness. We defer to another study the analysis of suggestions executed by the subject after an awakening or a change of state and those which present themselves with the appearance of being unconscious acts. After a description of the facts, there naturally follows the study of the hypotheses, more or less probable, which explains them and the verification of those hypotheses. Following the advice proffered by Paul Janet[1] in the articles he has devoted to this question, we will attempt to confirm our suppositions by the natural acts that present the same characteristics as suggested acts. But in order to examine things that are comparable and produced in the same circumstances, we will choose our examples of natural actions from among those executed by the same persons who have been shown to be suggestible.

3.1 Historical summary of the theory of suggestions

The authors who, in our time, have drawn attention to the phenomena of suggestion are today all very well known and some of them rightly celebrated. It is not necessary to recall the work of Liébeault, Richet, Bernheim, Binet, Feré, and so many others who have linked their names to this study. If one were to produce a history of suggestion in our time, one would have to produce a complete history of hypnotism – something we have no intention of doing. But one might forgive us if we take a tour, unfortunately all too rapid, of the old magnetizers who, as ignorant and mistaken as they were, nevertheless had already discovered and studied nearly all the phenomena, whose description today redounds to the glory of many of these authors. We have the conviction, which we hope is shared, that there were among them true savants who were so devoted to their science that could not think to look for glory or an advantage of any kind. They devoted their lives to tasks that we can hardly imagine, to studying phenomena that are extremely protracted and difficult, of which the diminished hypnotism of today provides no real conception. They brought to this study a patience, a tenacity, and sometimes an intelligence that should have earned them more success. Many charlatans have clothed themselves, and still do clothe themselves, with the name of magnetizer, but this is no reason to direct a general scorn on all those who have been the true precursors of experimental psychology.

The magnetizers of the past were perfectly cognizant of the phenomena of suggestion. The 1784 report on the experiments of Mesmer was already explicit on this point: "All were obedient to those who magnetized them. They were happy to enter into drowsiness; his voice, a look, a sign drew them into it … One cannot help but recognize in these consistent effects a great power which excites the patients, masters them, and of which the magnetizer seems to be the repository." Puységur, one of the first to establish artificial somnambulism, remarked on the phenomenon: "When I judged that his ideas were going to bring about an unpleasant state, I stopped them and tried to inspire him with happier ones. He did not need me to make much effort in this. I then perceived that he was calm, imagining himself to be shooting for a prize, dancing at a festival, etc. I nourished these ideas in him and in that way made him move around a great deal on his chair, etc."[2] Deleuze, one of the first teachers of magnetizers, indicated how it is an essential characteristic of the somnambulist "that he is completely obedient to the influence of the one who magnetizes him."[3] Some pages later, he very nicely describes posthypnotic suggestion, which is executed after awakening, but we will not be speaking about this matter in the present chapter.[4] In the same period, the abbé Faria put suggestion to work "in a scientific fashion,"[5] and his influence was such that all subsequent works always recount many experiments imitating his. All of the authors who have written on magnetism describe actions, hallucinations, and dreams imposed on somnambulists by the words of the magnetizer.

Braid concentrated on, and produced in his own way, the one phenomenon that all the magnetizers were able to teach him, and yet he allowed himself to be deceived in his experiments with phreno-hypnotism when he claimed to stimulate various passions in his subjects by pressing on different bumps on their cranium. Charpignon, a true magnetizer, very clearly reported his phenomena as originating from suggestion,[6] and Dupotet knew very well how to excite these same sentiments of anger or affection without touching the cranium, simply by speaking to the subject.[7] It must not be forgotten that in 1854 Hébert de Garnay presented a public course of lectures with the title "Oral Suggestion,"[8] and that all those who were doing magnetic work learned these lessons. So there should be nothing surprising to find in the works of all the later magnetizers mention of experiments and discussions relative to these phenomena. In regard to all these facts, which have been consistently acknowledged in works of modern hypnotism, nothing would be easier than to find examples in works published between 1850 and 1870.

But, one might say, if the magnetizers recognized these phenomena, they explained them badly and brought in useless references to a mysterious fluid. I believe that almost all the magnetizers distinguished, as Dr. Philips (Durand de Gros) clearly did, between the state of suggestibility in which the subject is placed (the hypotaxic state) and the suggestion itself which is delivered in this state (ideoplastic phenomena). Their whimsical theories of physiology were mostly applied to the first situation, that is to say, to the techniques employed to put a subject into a suggestible state, while they explained suggestion itself in terms of laws that were uniquely psychological. Moreover, I must admit that this manner of separating things does not seem that foolish, and that I am not disposed to believe that suggestion can explain everything, and, in particular, that it can explain itself.

If you prefer extravagant theories in which one relates all possible phenomena to the psychological influence of the magnetizer or to "the force of the imagination," as was said at the time, it is easy to find many examples. That is how Bertrand explains the odd beliefs of somnambulists: the claim to see the fluid, the prevision of illnesses, and even the action of metals. He says, "These are always the ideas of the magnetizers who influence the sensations of the somnambulists … Metals, when magnetizers will it, should not have any control over magnetized persons. It is the idea that renders them noxious."[9] Later, in 1850, Dr. Ordinaire carried on a very interesting discussion opposing the theories of the fluidists of his day.[10] The great argument that he keeps returning to is suggestion in the waking state. He says, "*Without previous magnetization*, I have obtained insensibility ... paralysis, intoxication, delirium – all without the need to put the subject to sleep – by simply saying "I want"... It is sufficient for me to say, "I want you to sleep" in order to put the person to sleep." What could be more ridiculous than to say that suggestion is a discovery of our day?

Not only psychological phenomena, but also the more unusual physiological phenomena were studied in connection with the power of the imagination. Daring experiments with blistering through suggestion and clearly psychological explanations of stigmata of the convulsionaries are fully presented in the works of Charpignon.[11]

But all these works, no doubt rich in exact observations and summaries that are ingenious but often incomplete and obscure, have been almost completely forgotten. It was only around 1875, when Barrett[12] in England and Richet[13] in France demonstrated to the scientific public the existence of irresistible suggestions and illusions imposed through speech, that the attention of psychologists and physiologists were strongly drawn to such original and fecund studies. It should not be forgotten that this work was first identified and begun by the old French magnetizers.

3.2 Description of some psychological phenomena produced by suggestion

It is difficult to summarize all the psychological phenomena that can be produced by suggestion, because on the one hand they are numerous and extremely varied, and on the other we do not find among them the sharp differences that we do with cataleptic phenomena. The best way to classify positive suggestions (the only kind studied in the present chapter) consists, we believe, of arranging them in their order of growing complexity.

(1) *Phenomena of cataleptic appearance.* If one lifts the arm of a suggestible person, during somnambulism or in the waking state, especially if one holds it in the air for some time, almost always the arm will remain in the position in which it was placed. This is a phenomenon totally analogous to what is observed during catalepsy and it sometimes presents with identical characteristics. As a matter of fact, if one takes the precaution of choosing a subject whose arm is totally anesthetic to begin with, one sees the limb remaining in the air for a long time, slowly descending without jerking, and all this with no change in respiration during that period. We know, of course, that this absence of shaking and respiratory disturbance simply indicates the muscular anesthesia of the arm and not the existence of catalepsy.

In the same way, one can establish other phenomena of this kind. A pencil put in the hand of a subject, N, gives her the desire to sketch and she will draw lines or small houses on a piece of paper indefinitely. The sight of a gesture sometimes provokes its imitation and repetition. Blanche, a young woman who is very suggestible in the waking state, will exactly imitate all of my movements when she looks at me. Léonie, at the beginning of a certain somnambulistic state, repeats what I say before responding, and Rose, in an analogous state, sometimes responds to questions and sometimes repeats them. "A young woman," someone writes in the *Journal du magnétisme*,[14] "put in rapport with another person, immediately becomes her double. She reflects the gestures, the attitude, the voice and even the speech of her counterpart. If one sings, laughs, walks – she immediately does the same and the imitation is so perfect and so quick that one can be fooled as to the originator of the action. The identification is such that foreigners – Russians, Poles, Germans – whose idiomatic speech is very difficult to pronounce, have held conversations that she has perfectly reproduced. One of them, who had sung a part of his national hymn for her, indicated in French that he was impressed by her very pronounced German accent. She returned his salute by repeating the compliment in the same tone, at which everyone there burst into laughter."

Why should we consider these phenomena distinct from catalepsy? Because the psychological circumstances that surround them are not the same. The cataleptic individuals do not speak, do not understand what they do, and seem to have no idea of their personality or the acts that they perform. As Maine de Biran says, they have sensations, but no idea of their sensations. The subjects we are talking about here are entirely different. They speak and understand speech. They have a personality and take account of what they do. "I think that my arm is in the air," Blanche will say when one asks what she is thinking about. "I have a desire to make small lines," says N when she takes the pencil. "Why do I want to do what you are doing?" another says when she watches me lift my hand. The physical phenomenon is perhaps the same, but the psychological phenomenon does not seem to me to be identical.

(2) *Actions and hallucinations determined by speech.* The really interesting thing about suggestion is found in the commands which one can give by speaking. As a matter of fact, words that are addressed to these subjects, instead of being repeated without thinking, as occurs with cataleptics, *are understood*, and through their meaning they always determine the actions and hallucinations, *without the consent* of the person. One might say to one of these individuals, "Rise! Sit! Move your arm!" or more simply still: "Watch your arm move!" He understands very well what one wishes to say, but, without consenting, he actually rises, moves his arm, or sits. As soon as the meaning of the words is grasped, the action is executed.

In this way, one can induce a new phenomenon which, no doubt, already exists, but cannot be easily established during catalepsy – the phenomenon of hallucination. Subjects who in this situation can speak, tell us about what they are sensing, and, through words and gestures, show us that, in regard to our words, they experience all kinds of false sensations. In this way we cause subjects to hear the sound of bells, of singing, of fanfares; we make them see flowers or birds, to smell odors, to experience tastes, to lift imaginary burdens, etc. In other words, we induce in the subject's consciousness all the phenomena that ordinarily correspond to real impressions made on the various senses.

These hallucinations are usually powerful and as vivid as the real sensations would be. I have a woman drink some so-called magnetized water, and I foretell for her that this water will create a gentle warmth in her stomach. She begins to feel this sensation and finds it pleasant. Then I make more magnetizing gestures over the glass. She takes it, holds it in her hands, and then violently throws it on the ground, uttering loud cries. She says that this over-magnetized water horribly burned her mouth. Léonie has the ability to reread, in hallucination, entire pages of a book she had read on some previous occasion, and she sees the image with such clarity that she will even note particular marks, such as the numbers of the pages and the numbers of the signatures placed at the bottom of certain pages. In this case, the hallucination is the same thing as a sensation.

On the other hand, sometimes the hallucination will be very weak, analogous to an image that is faded and vague, and then we can distinguish two particular cases. The subject might perceive poorly, putting his hallucination at some distance, so to speak. Marie, who cannot hallucinate hearing very well, always claims that the music is in the corridor or the next room and would never say that it is nearby. "Oh no," she says, "One would hear it better if the music were right here." In another case, the subject seems to distance the hallucination in time and make it a memory. Mi, when I try to suggest a present hallucination, always complains, "It is true! You are right! I have heard this, I have seen this … but it is far away … It must have been a long time ago." It is true that I have only encountered one subject who speaks this way, but nevertheless it should be taken into account. Perhaps we could use these weak hallucinations to explain the illusions of memory spoken of by Taine. He said, "In somnambulism and hypnotism the patient, now made sensitive to suggestion, is subject to apparent illusions of memory. If one tells him that he has committed a crime, his face will express horror and fear."[15] Having observed only one subject of this kind, however, I would not dare to claim that "retroactive hallucinations"[16] are always simply weak hallucinations. Sometimes they are a more complex phenomenon.

We have brought together under this one heading both suggested actions and suggested hallucinations, although these two phenomena seem very different from one another. In reality they have deep connections. Not only are they produced in the same subject and under the same conditions, but they are actually inseparable and one never exists without the other. There are no actions without an image in the mind which, in order to be connected with a movement, must be equally powerful. If I tell a subject to lift her arm, she has in her mind an image (muscular or visual, depending on the situation) which is very clear and the perfect equivalent of a hallucination. Here is proof. I command Marie to lift her arm, but immediately I take hold of her hand and prevent it from moving. Since she does not have any muscular sensibility on that side, she does not realize it has stopped. A few seconds later I ask her where her arm is, and she says it is in the air and that she sees it. I command Rose, who is paraplegic, to move her leg. She seems to make an effort, but her leg does not move. When I insist, she gets angry and says, "But I have already lifted my leg. Do you not see that?" One way or another we have suppressed the act that conceals the image and we have left it isolated. We see that it still exists fully and the same, in the form of a hallucination.

On the other hand, it is easy to show that there is always a movement at the same time as when the hallucination is suggested. Sometimes we can verify this directly. With a *visual* subject, that is, someone who, at this moment, executes movements by means of visual images, it is impossible to produce a *visual* hallucination of movement of the arm when the arm does not really move. After bandaging her eyes, I command Léonie to see her left arm raised and shaking. After some moments she says, "Yes, I see it. The fingers are spread." But at the same time her left arm makes exactly the same movement that she says she sees. Here are some remarks about this simple, small, but very important phenomenon:

(1) This movement takes place without the awareness of the subject when it occurs in an anesthetic limb. But this does not necessarily mean that it would be an unconscious movement in the sense of those that we will study later. The origin of the movement, especially its psychological aspect, is very much in the mind of the subject. It is the visual image that has been suggested. It only lacks *muscular sensation in return*,[17] which ordinarily stops the healthy subject from executing the movement.

(2) This experience only results if one induces the hallucination of the particular image, which, for this subject at this moment, is useful for the movement. Léonie is hemianesthetic on the left side and, as it happens in this case, makes use of visual images to execute movement of the left arm, but, surprisingly, she continues to use muscular (kinaesthetic) images to execute movements of the right arm. The result is that the visual hallucination of the arm in movement induces movement on the left side, but not on the right. To produce movement of the right arm there must be a kinaesthetic hallucination of the displacement of the arm, a hallucination that is, moreover, ineffective or even impossible for the left arm. We will encounter these things when we will speak of paralyses in their connections with anesthesias. Here it is sufficient for us to recall how far these new experiments with oral suggestion go to confirm our hypotheses concerning the imitations of movements in catalepsy and show the intimate connection between even visual images and movements.

Even if there are varied and more complex hallucinations that do not consist uniquely in the image of the limb in movement, there are still certain expressive movements, gestures, or words that always accompany hallucination. At the beginning of my studies of somnambulism, being only half convinced of the power of these commands, I committed the grave blunder of having a somnambulist see a tiger enter the room. Her convulsive movements of terror and her dreadful cries showed me that I had to be more prudent, and from then on I did not cause these people to imagine anything more than beautiful flowers and small birds. But if they no longer produced great displays of terror, they still made movements adapted to gentler spectacles. Some, such as Marie, gently caressed the little birds. Others, like Lucie, energetically took hold of them with both hands to embrace them. Still others, like Léonie, who remembers her rural life, threw grain at them to get them to fly. But none of the women could see a hallucinatory flower without holding it under her nose and then making herself a corsage.

When even these kinds of expressive movements are totally absent, which is quite rare, there are still more simple movements that one might call movements of adaptation. According to the observations of Féré, "the state of the pupil varies with the presumed distance of the hallucination."[18] It is true that this very constant phenomenon is barely visible, but the movements of the eyebrows, the eyelids, and the orb of the eye, the movement of the head during auditive hallucinations, the flaring of the nostrils during hallucinations of smell, the moving of the fingers when the subject senses contact with an imaginary object – these are always very strong and easy to certify. Ribot foresaw what observation has confirmed when he said, "If movement is an essential element in seeing an object, then should it not have the same role when the object seen is imaginary?"[19] In a word, movement is as much a part of the suggestion of hallucination as it is in regard to the suggestion of movement. The two things cannot be separated.

(3) *Actions or hallucinations, with points of reference.* Instead of commanding the immediate execution of an action, one can delay it, as it were, and tie it to an agreed upon signal. We are not here dealing with post-hypnotic suggestions; we are assuming that the subject remains in the same psychological state for both the command and the signal of execution. For example, I say to Marie, "When I clap my hands, you will rise and walk around the room." She has heard my command and remembered it, but does not execute it right away. I clap my hands and then she gets up and walks around the room. It is the same for hallucinations. One can attach them to a certain signal, which can be any kind of visual or auditive sensation. If I say to Marie that she will see a butterfly fly across the room when the hour strikes, or that she will see a bird on the window-ledge, the phenomenon is the same: she only sees the butterfly or the bird on the window-ledge when the clock strikes, and not otherwise.

The last point is most interesting, because the hallucination, being tied to a sensation that is lasting, comes and goes, and is susceptible to modification; it takes on precisely the same qualities – persists, disappears, is modified – just as is the point of reference itself. At any moment in the somnambulism, if Marie looks from beside the window, she will see her bird, and this connection can persist indefinitely. From this arises a host of experiences, the best known of which is this. One shows a somnambulist an imaginary portrait on a card that is totally white and then mixes this card up with many others. The subject nearly always finds the portrait on the same card when shown in the same position. Undoubtedly that is because she recognizes the paper by means of some small characteristic marks. If Marie no longer sees the window ledge, she does not see the bird. All that is needed for her not to see it is that she turn her eyes away. Finally, if the point of reference varies in some way – gets larger, gets smaller, is doubled, etc. – exactly the same will happen to the hallucination. This phenomenon has been thoroughly studied by Binet and Féré in their inventive experiments with opera glasses, mirrors, and prisms. I have repeated their experiments with many subjects, especially with Lucie, and my observations are in complete accord with theirs. If, for example, I show her a serpent wound around a lamp, in the mirror she sees a second serpent, as well as a second lamp. In a word, the suggested action or hallucination can be attached to a certain sensation which serves as a signal or point of reference and depends on it absolutely.

One cannot overemphasize the importance of suggestion with a point of reference, for it provides an explanation for a great many other phenomena. Here are some examples. We have seen in the previous chapter that subjects who have total anesthesia of a sense can no longer have a hallucination involving that sense, but it is not the same with those who have only partial anesthesia. Thus, Maria is blind in her left eye, but sees well with her right and can have visual hallucinations. When she dreams she sees coloured objects, as does everyone else, with her left eye as well as with her right eye, and if one suggests a hallucination of sight to her, without specifying it precisely, but having both her eyes closed, she will see it in colour. This can be easily explained as has been recently demonstrated by Binet, by the fact that when one dreams, "the field of the representation, being more extended than the field of sensation, is formed by a synthesis of visual fields."[20] The imagination of the patient completes the visual field and reconstitutes the integral representation of the object.

But then how should we understand the following? In the case of Marie, if we specify that object is to be at some distance on the left, or if we actually close her right eye and leave her left eye open, it is impossible to produce a visual hallucination. Paul Richer has called this fact one of the most important. He says, "In the waking state, Bar. has color blindness in the right eye. When we suggest that she (having closed her left eye) is seeing Arlequin, she sees him covered in small diamond shapes, gray, black and white. Polichinelle too is dressed in white and gray. 'It is original,' she says, 'but not beautiful.' We have her open her right eye and immediately the idea of color reappears; Arlequin and Polichinelle are splashed with the colors in which they are customarily depicted."[21] Since then, many authors have reported identical facts. I have observed a phenomenon of this kind for the sense of touch. Rose, who is insensible in the rest of her body, has recovered sensation in her lips. Hallucinations of contact, ticklishness, heat, etc., are experienced only in the lips and not in the rest of the body. These phenomena, seemingly so unusual, are simply dependent on the presence or absence of points of reference, which allow the subject to localize the hallucination.

If I produce a hallucination in Marie when she has both eyes open and then have her close her right eye, she cannot see clearly and can no longer distinguish points of reference to which her hallucinations can attach themselves, and she then completely loses the vision of the bird or the flower which I had shown her. If, on the contrary, one gives her a hallucination when her eyes are closed, this image does not attach itself to any point of reference and can persist despite the fact that her eyes are closed. The other experiences and modifications which hallucinations undergo after partial modifications of the senses are explained in the same manner.

I also relate to this theory of hallucination with a point of reference a singular phenomenon which is always present in the somnambulists whom I have studied – one which I cannot explain in any other way. Suggested hallucinations can be produced with Léonie only if she is touched on an exposed part of her body by the person who suggests the hallucination. Although I command that she see flowers, Léonie ceases to see them the moment that I am no longer touching her hand or her face. Others may gently touch her or take hold of her hand, but the hallucination does not reappear. If I once again touch her, even lightly, without her anticipating it, Léonie lets out a cry of joy and shows that she is once more delighted by seeing her bouquet of flowers. It is probable that the hallucination is here associated with the sensation of contact of my hand which serves as a point of reference. But in this experience, as in many of those previously described, the psychological phenomena are only rarely conscious and we cannot now be sure of their details.

For my part I am very disposed to explain in the same way, that is, to consider as simple hallucinations with a point of reference, the interesting phenomena described by various authors, such as Dumontpallier, Magnan, and Bérillon,[22] etc., under the name "bilateral hallucinations that vary according to the side affected." These authors say that it is possible to get a subject to experience two different hallucinations simultaneously, one on the right and one on the left. Thus, they say, "one can get a person to experience the taste of rum on the right side of the tongue and the taste of syrup on the left, or to see a frightening picture with one eye and a farcical rustic scene with the other ."[23] From this fact, these authors draw conclusions that to me appear to be very weighty concerning the independent functioning of the two cerebral hemispheres. Without prejudging the theory itself, I believe it is a mistake to employ this particular fact as a means of verification. Simultaneous hallucinations with this different character are easy to reproduce for those senses that are distributed over a large surface area and that furnish the subject with many simultaneous points of reference. To obtain them it is not necessary to take into account the bilateral division of the body or the brain, and one can easily repeat these experiences on the very same side of the body. On my order, Marie simultaneously had the feeling of heat in the thumb of her right hand

and cold in the little finger of the same hand. Also, on the same side, by means of the same eye, she could see a happy scene alongside a sad scene. Finally, she also experiences two sensations of taste on her tongue, but instead of one on the right side and the other on the left, she tastes jam on the front of her tongue and salt at the back, and she finds this very nasty and disagreeable. In a word, I am disposed to believe that in these bilateral hallucinations, different areas of the body and different objects simply serve as points of reference.

The same considerations stand in opposition to many of the theories which are very complicated and do not take into account so simple a fact. One can habituate a subject to a particular action, such as experiencing a contracture or going to sleep at the touch of a particular metal, to awaken when someone presses on a certain area of the body, etc. The object that one gives them is always recognized in a certain manner – for example, the felt pressure at a particular point on the body serves as a signal and leads to the action or hallucination. The subject does not deceive, as one might believe, because she does not consent to this particular suggestion any more than to any other. It is the operator who deceives himself in not taking psychological laws into account when dealing with psychological phenomena. There is an opposite danger of explaining everything in terms of this kind of suggestion. A very delicate critique is needed to attain a balance and no one should boast of having attained it.

(4) *Complex actions and hallucinations: toward automatic development.* With certain subjects, instead of ordering one movement or hallucination after another, it suffices to indicate an initial idea, which then, apparently spontaneously, develops in their minds and manifests in a long series of actions and diverse hallucinations. If I say to Lucie or to Rose "You are going to write a letter, … you are going to sing a tune," they will make their preparations to write; they will compose a letter or indeed they sing all sorts of musical pieces indefinitely. If I tell Léonie that there is a sheep in front of her, she sees it; but immediately, without my saying anything more, she hears it bleat and imitates its sound, and she caresses it and feels its fleece under her hand. If you apply a piece of real gold to the forehead of this subject, she experiences a general contraction. If you take imaginary gold in your hand and similarly apply it to her forehead, it produces the same result. Her thumbnail is hyperesthetic. If one taps it, the subject has minor convulsions and contractures. The hallucination of a bird on her hand produces the thought that the bird's imaginary beak gives her nail a peck, and she has a small convulsive reaction. In the literature one can find numerous examples of these kinds of hallucinations that complicate themselves and complete themselves spontaneously. This is what produces mimed dreams, which are so amusing when one is dealing with a lively and sufficiently intelligent subject. With Lucie, the hallucination of "a voyage," as she calls it, becomes a veritable comedy, with a thousand unexpected adventures. Not only does she experience seasickness on the boats, as did the subject described by Richet, but she enacts falling into the water, swimming

on the floor, and crawling, shivering, onto a deserted island. Naturally, I have had her make the most interesting expeditions to the moon, the center of the earth, etc. All I have to do is give her a theme and her imagination embellishes it with the most extravagant elaborations. I will not say more about these comical spectacles; they are always wonderful to see, but they are now too well known to describe them further.

Is it necessary to see those phenomena called "transference of attitudes and hallucinations through the action of the magnet" as examples of an association of the same kind as we have been discussing – one between images that spontaneously evoke each other? If one induces a phenomenon on the right side of a subject, a particular positioning or movement of the arm – that is, a hallucination on the right side – one can make it pass to the other side in a perfectly symmetrical way by applying a strong magnet on the left arm or the left side of the head. This fact in itself is pretty well indisputable, and if it is not found in all subjects, at least it exists among some. However, its interpretation seems to me to be a very delicate matter.

Without claiming here to be able to provide a general conclusion – which today is impossible – I will simply state the results of my own observations. First, the transfer is a rather rare phenomenon. I have only ascertained its presence in two subjects, Léonie and N. The other subjects either did not change or reacted totally differently with the application of the magnet. Next, even with those two subjects, the transfer could be affected by means other than a magnet – by the approach of my hand or other inert objects. One day I enjoyed myself by inducing the most marvelous and complex transfers by putting an orange peel on the end of a long stick near Léonie's head. To settle my doubts about the action of the magnet, I carried out some experiments, as one always should do, with an electro-magnet. Rousseaux, a professor of physics, with his usual helpfulness, stood nearby and switched the current on and off without any sound and without my being aware of when he was going to do it, while I myself applied the magnet to the subject without knowing if the current was on or not and noted the results. I have to say that the phenomena produced throughout had no relationship to whether the current was in fact on or off.

In short, it is good to know that a phenomenon completely analogous to transfer can be produced through laws that are uniquely psychological, without there even being any specific suggestion in that regard. Recently, in the *Revue scientifique*, Paulhan[24] investigated the law of contrast which automatically brings to mind totally opposed phenomena, one after the other. One says "Yes," instead of saying "No"; one has the desire to laugh when it is appropriate to cry, etc. Doctors know very well this striking phenomenon that emotion sometimes produces in their patients; they will suddenly turn over on their stomach when they have been asked to turn on their back. At the hospital l'Hôtel-Dieu, with Jules Janet, I have myself seen a hysterical woman who had the strange habit of, despite herself, always doing with her left arm what she had been asked to do with her right, and vice versa. The phenomena of allochiria, in which a person feels in his left hand what is done to the right, are well known. I have noted a case of this kind that I will mention as a curiosity, because I do not understand it very well. While Léonie was in a state of somnambulism, I pricked her with a pin on her right side (the side that has sensation); she let out a cry and, surprisingly, got angry with her left hand. She then began a strange delirium in which she maintained that her hand was no longer hers, that it had been changed. In reality, her left hand, which had been anesthetic, had become sensitive to feeling. There must be a psychological automatism, very little known, it is true, that links images related to the two sides of the body and evokes or modifies one in terms of the other.[25]

On the other hand, it seems to me that the magnet, along with metallic plates and electricity, has a real effect on weak nervous systems. Lucie, who has never been in a hospital, who does not know anything about these matters, who up to this point had lent herself to all experiments without emotion, fell down rigid and contracted from her jaws to her feet upon touching a magnet. By means of a magnet, Rose regained a tactile sensibility that suggestion could not restore. Many other facts, which I am not going to go into here, lead me to believe in this action.[26] So here, with due reserve, is the view of the situation that seems to me to be most probable. The action of the magnet is a kind of indefinite excitation, analogous to that produced by an electric current, the plates of Burq, or even passes, and the particular form in which this excitation manifests – return of sensibility, contractions, transfer – depend on laws that are more psychological than physical. Furthermore, this is very nearly the same conclusion that Féré came to through his studies: "The first effect of the magnet or specific metal on the subject is to set up a dynamogeny on the side on which it is applied; the transfer comes only afterwards. Every type of sensory excitation produces the transfer by the same mechanism."[27]

I will not speak about the experiments of Binet and Féré on the polarization of sensations and feelings, because I have not myself come across anything like that. I draw your attention to complementary hallucinations, which I have little studied, only to show what an important role the association of ideas can sometimes play. The hallucination of one colour, when prolonged, is followed, it is said, by the hallucination of the complementary colour. Perhaps I have performed the experiments poorly; perhaps I have not come across subjects who have very strong visual hallucinations. In any case it does not seem to me that colours reported by subjects following a coloured hallucination demonstrate any very clear law.

After hallucinating red, Léonie declares that she sees white; after green, red; after blue, white; after red, green; after yellow, blue; after violet, white; after orange, green; after green, blue. Although some of these coloured hallucinations are the same as those indicated by the theory of complementary colours, there is no very consistent law there. I have not had better luck with other subjects. The colours that Lucie and Marie report seeing are totally random.

Perhaps another experiment might show us how an apparently complementary image is formed. I suggest a hallucination of taste to Léonie and, after some time, I cause it to suddenly disappear. Often she no longer senses anything, but sometimes, as after a visual hallucination, she acknowledges a different following sensation. Thus, the taste of sugar is followed by the taste of pepper, the taste of vinegar by the taste of salt, the taste of chicory by the taste of coffee, and finally the taste of coffee brings in its wake the taste of cognac. This succession of tastes, especially the last two, are, perhaps, very logical, but I do not think they are harbingers of a brand new physical law. These observations in no way undermine the law of complementary hallucinations, because a negative finding does not suppress a positive one. They simply show that this law is not one that can be generally applied and depends on very complex conditions.

This automatic development of ideas in the mind of a subject produces, as does the preceding phenomenon, one of the great difficulties involved in experimental psychology. It is all the more dangerous in that, once produced in one sense, it will repeat itself indefinitely in the same manner. The experimenter is constantly exposed to taking an association of ideas of his subject for a general law of psychology.

(5) *General hallucinations: Modification of the whole personality by suggestion.* This final very interesting phenomenon, which summarizes those preceding, can present itself in two forms. The first has been very well described in the work of Bourru and Burot on the variations of the personality. If one tells a subject that he is reliving a past period of his life and is no longer of that age, or if one simply has him assume a posture, have a contracture, or experience a state of sensibility that he had at such or such an age, one will see him take on all the physical and emotional characteristics that he possessed at that time and, as it were, completely relive a bygone period of his life. The subject senses, thinks, and speaks as he did at that time. He imagines that he sees and hears what existed then, and his only memories are those that he had at that particular period. "When one restores a hysterical woman to the state of illness that she previously experienced (paralysis of the left side and cutaneous hyperesthesia on the left), she believes that she is at the Salpêtrière at the service of Charcot."[28] "It is not the contracture that brings the infantile way of thinking and expression; the contracture leads this patient back to her infancy, because it was in her infancy that it first existed."[29] It is very easy, and also very interesting, to verify this phenomenon. One can bring into play for the subject all the scenes of her life and ascertain, as if carried back to that time, details that she thought she had forgotten and was unable to recall. For two hours Léonie was transformed into a little ten-year-old girl and lived anew her life with a vivacity and joy that was strange, crying out, running, calling for her doll, speaking to people she could no longer remember, as if this poor woman had really returned to age ten. Although at that time she was always anesthetic on the left side, she regained all her sensations to play this role.

Sometimes these changes in sensibility and nervous phenomena through suggestion of this kind bring unusual phenomena with them. Here is an observation that may seem a joke but is nevertheless true and actually very easy to explain. I suggest to Rose that it is no longer 1888, but 1886, in the month of April, simply to see what changes in sensibility would be produced. But a strange thing occurred: she wept and complained of being tired and unable to walk. "What is happening with you?" "Oh, nothing, but in my situation…" "What situation?" She answered with a gesture – her abdomen was suddenly extended and overtaken by a sudden onset of hysterical tympanitic distention. Without realizing it, I had returned her to a period of her life during which she was pregnant. It was necessary to suppress the suggestion to end this unpleasant joke. More interesting experiments of this kind were made with Marie. By taking her to successive periods of her life, I was able to ascertain the various states of sensibility through which she passed and the causes of all the changes involved. Thus, she is now completely blind in her left eye and claims to have been this way since her birth. If one takes her to the age of seven, one sees that she was still anesthetic in her left eye. But if one suggests that she is only six, one see that she has two good eyes and one can establish the period and the very strange circumstances in which she lost sensibility in her left eye. Memory is automatically able to bring about a state of health of which the subject believes she has no recollection.

In the second form of this phenomenon, the same general changes of the whole personality can still be obtained without appeal to memory, but simply through the subject's imagination. This fact has long been known and one recognizes it here and there in the very strange descriptions in the old works. In experiments in the self-described "magnetic magic" of Dupotet, these transformations were frequent and the celebrated master describes them in his familiar bombastic style: "We try to bring decrepitude to birth in a virile subject, to have old age take hold of the lively, frisky young man and present itself, with its indelible characteristic, in a way that none could mistake. It was necessary that the years mark with their seal what nature had positioned in the first quarter of the road of life, so that, without transition, he would become a centenarian. Behold! *At my word*, his spine becomes curved, his limbs tremble, his speech is weak – it has lost its silvery tone. His face wrinkles, his eyes lose their twinkle. He supports himself on a cane that I give him. He is no longer a robust young man. The years have worked their damage. There is nothing left of the flower of youth; his language is that of a brisk old man. His mouth gapes; from his nose hangs a clinging drop. He spits a phlegm-like substance. He smirks maliciously, and he grabs hold and walks with measured step. He is old age itself, a man almost in the grave. But what am I saying? He believes himself young. He casts a provocative glance toward young women, and his eyes seem to say: I am still capable! A vain and boastful old man – I cannot leave you in your innocent demented state. Return, return quickly to your springtime. What is an entertainment to the audience, is a sadness for my heart. A living image of the decline of life, you give us too much to think about, and those moments in which I held you in a trance, my young man, weigh heavily on me as a crime."[30] I cite this segment in its entirety because it gives some idea of the style of Dupotet. I abridge other quotations that I have drawn from a great number of other works: "I said to Miss N: "You are a preacher." Immediately the hands were folded and the knees were slightly flexed; then, with head bowed forward and eyes raised to heaven, bearing an expression of fervent piety, she slowly pronounced, in moving tones, some words of exhortation."[31] We know that, in his articles first presented in the *Revue philosophique*[32] and then collected in his *L'homme et l'intelligence*,[33] Charles Richet evoked these types of experiences, which were subsequently forgotten, and, under the name of *the objectification of types*, presented descriptions of changes of personality through suggestion which have, for five years, been cited in all the works of psychology.

This phenomenon is both very intriguing and very easy to reproduce. Most of my somnambulists are subject to alterations of this kind, but not all of them have been that interesting. Lucie, having changed into an army general, a young girl, a sailor, and an archbishop, is someone who plays out these comedies with great ease. Furthermore, her own character is reflected in these alterations, and, since she is very irreligious, she plays an archbishop who hears the confession of penitents in such an unorthodox way that I am not able to give an adequate description of it. Léonie is only remarkable in certain scenes. Changed into an army general, she rises, draws her sabre and cries out, "Forward! Be brave! ... those who have risen from the ranks do not stand up well ... where is the colonel and his men? ... come on, you have to keep in line better than that ... Oh! The machine gun – what a sound ... our enemies are many, but not as well organized as we; they are not minding their business; ah!, but..." (she points to her chest) "but yes ... I have been decorated on the field of battle for the good conduct of my regiment ." In this scene we do not see a lot of imagination. It is the equivalent of my changing into an old woman of eighty, and not doing much more than coughing and whimpering. "Look here!" she says, pointing at her limbs, "there is nothing left ... I am very tired. I am going to leave you right now." On the other hand, there is one hallucination that fits her very well – changing her into a "grand dame" or princess. She majestically spreads her robe on the sofa, flutters an imaginary fan, and, in an affected manner, speaks of court, of her estate, and of insolent marquis. I am astonished at the perfection of this comedic presentation, even though, as I discover in conversation with her, that this is not the first time and that twenty years previously her first magnetizer had already changed her into a princess. She remembers having had a beautiful velvet robe "entirely similar" and having been received into the grand salon of Dr. Perrier. This physician is one of those who formerly did frequent magnetizations – around 1865. Here we find the proof, if that is needed, of the superior knowledge of all these phenomena of suggestion that the magnetizers possessed.

In regard to the subject of alterations of personality through suggestion, we need to return to a question already studied in the preceding chapter. Are the changes of memory and personality that we have identified in various somnambulists identical with the complex hallucinations produced by suggestion? Without being able to make any definitive assertions – because all these psychological states are very much alike – we will content ourselves with providing some reasons which prevent us from holding these two phenomena as completely identical. The state of memory, which we have consistently seen as very important in these matters, is not the same. During alterations of personality obtained by suggestion during the first somnambulism, the subject did not retain any memory of other alterations. Thus, when playing the role of the great princess, she did not understand what I was saying when I spoke about the costume of the general worn immediately before that, and she did not remember her waking state. While the princess, she did not know who Léonie was and did not even want to believe that such a poor peasant would be living on her estate. She no longer remembered the state of ordinary somnambulism and the personage of Léonie 2. I need hardly add that she no longer remembered the second somnambulism and the personage of Léonie 3. She had totally forgotten what she knew in these states. For example, she no longer knew my name; she spoke with me, incorporated me into her fantasy and gave me a whimsical name. As the princess, she called me the "Marquis de Lauzun" and spoke with me in an affected manner. As the general, she took me for a colonel and offered me … absinth. In these states of hallucination, she retained only very general memories – of speech, habits, ideas of the world – which for this subject form a common foundation for all her states. Furthermore, in these alterations, she retained the memory of the exact same alteration as it had occurred before. She is once more the princess. She says to me, "Look here, Marquis de Lauzun, I saw you some time ago and you spoke of a peasant in whom you were interested and whom I did not know at all." She even remembers people whom she had seen twenty years earlier, when Perrier, already carrying out this experiment, had made her a princess. But it is important to note that she only remembers the *same* fantasy and that she has no memory of any of the others.

When the hallucination is brought to an end, when she is no longer the princess, Léonie returns to her ordinary somnambulism without passing through any intermediary state – whether lethargy or catalepsy. Most often, although not invariably, Léonie 2 on returning retains the memory of the alteration of personality: "What an unusual dream I have had! … I had a velvet robe and was conversing in a beautiful room with a marquis … You were not there." If, as sometimes happens, this memory is completely lacking in the somnambulism of Léonie 2, we are certain to find it in the second somnambulism. Léonie 3, who remembers all the rest of her life and also remembers these hallucinations: "Isn't she naïve, this poor Léonie?" she says. "She thought that she was a princess and it is you who made her believe this."

It is now easy to see that the state of the memory is entirely different during the second somnambulism that we have studied. Instead of being restricted to the state itself, the memory is of her whole life and of all the alterations that have taken place. Upon awakening, the memory of this somnambulism cannot be found in any other state. Here the characteristics are precisely opposite. The state of the memory is of great importance in these phenomena and can, I believe, through their differences, help me distinguish these two alterations in personality without disregarding the likeness. These two alterations are due to that law of the mind according to which an ensemble of complex phenomena automatically develops following an initial simple action: in the one instance, the somnambulism begins with a real alteration of the state of sensibility and memory, while in the other, the alteration of personality depends originally on an idea and a hallucination, and produces alteration of sensibility and of memory only secondarily and in an incomplete manner.

Despite these restrictions, one could imagine it possible to use suggestions on susceptible persons to construct states that would be very analogous to somnambulisms. If I should bring back to a subject's mind those characters portrayed in a previous somnambulism, he would go to sleep again because the suggestion would cause him to initiate the series of psychological phenomena that constitute the second state. Perhaps one might even in this way put to sleep subjects who are not accustomed to somnambulism. But we believe that in this case the hypnotic state would be less straightforward and less clear, and would leave memories, just as simple alterations of personality in our subjects leave memories as of a dream. True somnambulism takes its point of departure from an alteration in the sensitive-sensorial state. Somnambulism by suggestion is only a more or less perfect reproduction of this.

All the preceding suggestions, although more and more complicated, were nonetheless very easily understood. Now we are going to deal with more curious facts, which, in the present state of psychological knowledge, are much more difficult to fathom. We must, at the very least, call attention to them.[34] I want to deal with suggestions that act not on the thoughts of the somnambulist, but on her body. All the magnetizers and physicians have given us examples of this influence of thought on the body. It would take a whole volume of citations in itself to recall the miraculous healings of the saints and apostles[35] and the cures from bread-crumb pills endowed with lofty names.[36] We have only one point to make. Charpignon has already written, "A magnetizer can cause a fictive injury to produce a bit of a bruise or an imagined mustard plaster to redden the skin."[37] "At the will of the magnetizer, bleeding can be brought to a halt and also started up again."[38] We are aware of the more recent decisive experiments of Focachon at Nancy and Bouru and Burot at Rochefort. I have reproduced some of these experiments – for example, using suggestion to produce burns on Léonie and Rose. In one case it produced a distinct redness and swelling of the skin; in the other a true burning with a white blister accompanied by scabs forming in the following days. But the phenomenon that really interests me and is very easy to produce is simply mustard plaster by suggestion. With Léonie it comes on slowly, but with Rose, rapidly, right before your eyes. In a few hours the skin notably reddens in the designated area; it swells and gives the strongly marked appearance of a true mustard plaster, the residue of which persists longer than usual.

This swelling of the skin is directly related to the thoughts of the somnambulist. First, it is produced precisely in the designated area and not elsewhere. Next, it takes the shape that the subject ascribes to it. One day I said to Rose, who suffers from hysterical contractions of the stomach, that I would put a mustard plaster on the affected area to heal it. Some hours later, I noted a raised mark of dull red colour, having the shape of an elongated rectangle, but, surprisingly, with no clearly defined corners because they seemed to be clearly cut off. I remarked that her mustard plaster seemed to have a strange shape. She said to me, "I guess you do not know that one always cuts off the corners of Rigollot's mustard papers so that they do not do any harm." The preconceived idea of the shape of the mustard plaster determined the size and form of the redness. Another day (these kinds of mustard plasters had the effect of very easily relieving her stomach cramps at the points where they occurred) I attempted to suggest to her that I had cut the mustard plaster in the shape of a six-pointed star; the red mark turned out to take exactly the shape I had described. I suggested that Léonie have a mustard plaster on the left side of her chest in the form of an "S" to get relief from her nervous asthma. My suggestion healed the illness completely and produced a very clear mark in the shape of a large "S" on her chest. We cannot now give more examples of the influence of thought on the body. That would go beyond the boundaries we had set for this chapter, because here we are speaking only of suggestions that are consciously put in play during the course of a single psychological state.

The other phenomena produced by suggestion – therapeutic actions, contractions, and those phenomena that can be called negative such as anesthesias, amnesias, and paralyses – all require a special discussion and should be examined separately. The phenomena that we are now going to describe, although very different from one another, nevertheless form a group that have common characteristics and can be explained in the same way.

3.3 Various psychological theories of suggestion

The old magnetizers explained the submission of the somnambulist to the person who put them to sleep as due to the blending of nervous fluids. Some physicians and even some philosophers today do not hesitate to explain all the details of the physiology of the central nervous system that occurs in hypnosis. I admire this courage, because I am not able to do the same, and I limit myself to uniquely psychological studies that have been made of this curious phenomenon.

All these psychological assumptions present a very clear picture. They show very few differences and evidently converge, one on the other. In that is the proof of their validity and, without claiming to completely change them, we will simply try to constrain certain exaggerations and delineate the doctrines that pertain to all. A scientific explanation can never be complete. It consists simply of tying one phenomenon to another and changing the terms of the problem. On what other phenomenon does docility to suggestions depend? This is what we are going to investigate, and we are going to undertake this investigation through ordinary methods, observing the psychological facts that accompany the phenomenon of suggestion, disappear with it, and always remain proportional to the power of the suggestion itself.

(1) *Suggestion considered as a normal psychological fact.* Many authors have tried to equate the phenomena produced by suggestion with those which normally

occur among healthy people. In a very interesting chapter, Bernheim gathered together all the automatic actions that occur during normal life in order, gradually and without our realizing it, to lead us to the phenomena of suggestion. Paul Janet recommends this kind of method and compares suggested acts to contagious laughter, and to yawning that spreads from one person to another, and to similar things, in order, he says, to reduce any sense of the marvelous.

No doubt there is a real truth in these approaches, which we have already noted. There can be no reality that is absolutely and completely abnormal, and, from a certain point of view, it will simply be a development of an ordinary reality. But this is a proposition that should not be exaggerated, at least not to the point of confusing every sort of illness with perfect health. Without speaking about different properties which seem to exist and make normal automatic phenomena less conscious than those produced by suggestion, I see a difference between the two groups that is so significantly important and complex, that it does not seem to me there is any way to get rid of it. The authors who carefully study these facts in normal life are always citing examples of walking in step, blushing of the shy, contagious laughter among young girls and contagious yawning. But there is a yawning gap between these facts, as real as they may be, and complex hallucinations or alterations of personality produced through suggestion. In a word, if I calmly ask the person next to me to look on the other side of the room for a bouquet that does not exist, he will laugh in my face. If I say this to Marie, she runs to look, brings it back, and even finds that it smells very nice. What is the psychological difference between these two people? Herein lies the problem of suggestion.

This doctrine that strongly likens the phenomenon of suggestion to normal automatism has another very grave difficulty. It disposes us to think that suggestion is a primitive reality, existing naturally, independent of every other phenomenon, and, in fact, capable of explaining all the others. Anesthesia, amnesia, alterations of personality, somnambulism, etc. – all become the result of suggestion. As to this suggestion itself which explains all, no one seeks its origin because it is a naturally given fact.

Without specifying the authors to whom people attribute this doctrine and of whom, I believe, people have an exaggerated opinion, I can neither share nor understand this way of seeing things. In truth, a normal individual is not suggestible, or they are extremely suggestible for only two or three insignificant acts. To say that one is going to put an individual to sleep by suggestion, and then profit from this suggested sleep by giving all kinds of suggestions, is to say that one is going to use suggestion to make suggestible a person who is not. This is something I do not accept. Suggestion can neither create itself nor destroy itself. It is not logical to believe that one can suggest to an individual to become suggestible when they are not. Neither can one say that one is going to suggest to a patient to be no longer suggestible when they are. This would be to use automatic obedience to make one seem to disobey you. They have no more regained their lost voluntary consent than they have lost it in the first place.

Suggestion is like education: it makes use of pre-existing dispositions; it does not create them. In the same way that there are animals and even people who rebel against education and cannot be transformed by it, so also there are people, happily the majority, who rebel against suggestion and who submit to it only after an accidental and unusual modification of their psychological organism. Restating ideas that he had so well expressed in his *Cour de braidisme*, Durand (de Gros) says, "This pretension to explain everything by suggestion is obviously overdone. In fact, to make a suggestion to someone, it is not necessary to have first rendered him suggestible, that is, made him disposed, whether through mesmeric passes, or the visual method of Braid, to undergo the influence of the suggested idea. Therefore, there is before suggestion – or above it – something that is not suggestion – the magnetic or braidian procedure which creates the pre-existing state of suggestibility in the individual."[39] Although there might be some reservations to be made concerning this opinion, since it seems to link suggestion uniquely to somnambulism, it seems to us to be generally correct. There remains the question as to what the state may be, on whose abnormal quality the phenomena we have enumerated above depends.

(2) *Suggestion explained by the state of somnambulism.* The passage from Durand (de Gros) that we cited gives us the best known version of the hypothesis according to which the phenomena of suggestion depend on the state of somnambulism. On the one hand, this state would be most uniquely defined in terms of the aptitude for receiving suggestions. On the other, suggestion would be the more powerful the deeper the state of somnambulism. Thus, the problem of suggestion leads to the problem of somnambulism, and the explanation of somnambulism would then apply also to suggestion. Richet said, "The principal feature of somnambulism derives from automatism, which takes on different forms according to the procedures and persons involved ... automatism or aboulia characterizes somnambulism from the psychic as well as the somatic point of view."[40] "Somnambulism," says Despine, "is characterized by automatic activity of the brain during the paralysis of its conscious activity which manifests as the 'self.'" Beaunis says, "in somnambulism automatism is absolute and the subject retains no spontaneity of the will except what his hypnotizer allows him. He realizes in the celebrated ideal; he is like the staff in the hand of the traveller."[41] Finally, Bernheim, whose thinking we do not want to force, since he is one of those who is most insistent on the importance of suggestion outside somnambulism, also seems to favour this opinion when he writes in several places that "the hypnotic state exaggerates normal suggestibility,"[42] and that "in somnambulism suggestion attains its greatest effect."[43] No doubt, one cannot deny that in this hypothesis, which connects suggestion to the state of somnambulism, there is a certain degree of truth. Suggestibility is often encountered during hypnotic sleep, especially at the beginning, and it is even during this state that one typically first discovers and studies it. From a practical point of view, it is sometimes useful to hypnotize a person in order to give suggestions. But from a theoretical point of view, this

equating of the two phenomena seems to me to present problems and lead to an incorrect interpretation of somnambulism. We have explained this state in the preceding chapter without dealing with the phenomena of suggestion. Now we must show that they are actually independent. Suggestibility can be very complete outside artificial somnambulism. It can be totally absent in a state of complete somnambulism. In other words, it does not vary with somnambulism at the same time and in the same sense.

Natural somnambulism presents some characteristics that distinguish it from hypnotic somnambulism. Nevertheless, one sees very clear phenomena of suggestion in this state. In this matter the most decisive observations are those of Mesnet. He placed various objects between the hands of individuals during their crises of natural somnambulism and suggested the idea of a gun battle, of writing a letter, or of singing in a café concert.[44] In another account, he reports that he could speak with a woman during a crisis of natural somnambulism and that he told her to walk around the garden five times. She responded mechanically, "Yes", and departed as one shot from a spring.[45] We also know about the effects of suggestion upon dreams of people who are asleep, and the curious experiences of Maury.[46] But these states are ordinarily considered to be the same as hypnotic sleep, and the existence of suggestions while dreaming does not seem to be anything new. Now this is not actually fair, because there are very striking differences between dreams and somnambulism, and I really cannot understand this habit of many authors to equate the state of a hypnotized subject with true sleep. If one claims that Lucie is asleep when she is agitated, then we are all sleeping all the time, because we are never more awake than she is. But it is easy to verify suggestibility in states that are totally different.

We find this especially in intoxication and, in its final stage, alcoholic delirium. An individual, P, entered a hospital in the state of subacute alcoholic delirium. He cried out all night, seeing filthy animals running around on his bed and witnessing a massacre scene in which someone cut off the heads of everyone in the hospital. That evening, he was calm, saw the room as it was, recognized people and spoke quite sensibly. If one said to him, "Look! Can this be? A rat on your bed! Chase it! Catch it!" he would spring up, throw off his bedclothes, get on his feet and run after the imaginary rat. Say, "Look! There is a key. Go and open the armoire and bring me a towel," and he would take the imaginary key, run to a wall where there was no armoire and return holding nothing in his hands, saying to us, "Here is the towel." I showed him some flowers in a vase; I paralysed him, rendered him blind – all with only a word. Was this individual somnambulistic? Not at all. Throughout he remained in a completely normal state, retaining a complete memory for all that he had said (although the memory of his actions dissipated quickly).[47] Suggestion occurred here without any attempt to hypnotize him.

It is the same with hashish intoxication. I will not talk about my own observations because I have only seen this kind of intoxication a few times and in poor circumstances. However, the descriptions of Moreau (de Tours) are very good and very precise and so I will use them here. "Left to himself, the hashish user experiences its influence on all he sees and hears. A word, a gesture, a sound, the least noise will give his illusions a particular stamp. A few words can cause him to go from joy to sadness, and all the very happy thoughts he had just been enjoying become gloomy."[48] A young man who takes hashish may become convinced that he is dying; if you show him a cross-beam hanging on the wall and say to him, "It is you who are hanging there," he will say to you, "I know; it is horrible to die so young."[49] This is a clear example of suggestion. But it is only produced when the delirium is very pronounced; otherwise the ideas merely pass through the mind and do not become fixed.

There is no need to say a great deal about other pathological states, such as certain crises of hysteria or catalepsy in which the subjects, for instance, repeat the words they hear or take on and mirror the postures they see in pictures. We have already described some of these phenomena. What is important to highlight is that suggestibility sometimes occurs in a very clear form in states that have every appearance of being regular and normal.

We know that some people are suggestible in the waking state without having undergone any change in their consciousness. This fact, which was already recognized by some magnetizers, has been the subject of recent studies by Richet, Bernheim, and many others. Its importance cannot be exaggerated. Take Marie, who is twenty years old, intelligent, and who seems to have, like everyone else, that liberty of which we are so proud. Without touching her, and without putting her to sleep, I draw near her, saying, in a calm voice, "Look! In the corner on the left of the room is a large bouquet of roses. Marie, find it for me." She runs to the back of the room, bends down, appears to bring back a large object in her hands, seeming to lower her face to smell them several times, and comes over to me. She says, "This bouquet is for you, with my congratulations, for it has a beautiful smell." I answer, "I have brought you a beautiful peach. Here it is, on the table. Give half to X and eat your half." "Oh! How big it is. I cannot eat the whole thing." She takes a knife, cuts through the air, and offers a quarter to X (who is astounded), and eats with an expression of great satisfaction. These experiments produce the same results with Rose, M, and many others, perhaps with a little less vivacity. The results are not the same with Lucie, Léonie, or N, who, as we have seen, execute these kinds of suggestions unconsciously. But, one might say to me, Marie is somebody whom you have often hypnotized, and that is the reason she is subject to suggestion.

Very well. I can cite three other observations that to me seem extraordinary. One is of a thirty-year-old woman, Be., who had been hypnotized ten years ago, but not since; another is of a young woman of twenty-two who has never been put to sleep by anyone; the third is of a young woman of sixteen, whom I have already mentioned using the name of Blanche, who no longer undergoes hypnotism. In the waking state all three are veritable automatons. No sooner does the idea of some action enter their heads, in any way whatsoever, than they immediately execute it. They will keep their limbs in the position in which they are placed indefinitely, imitate movements made in front of them, and immediately experience any kind of hallucination. Be. sees me leave the room and return through the window. She believes she can hear me speaking on the other side of the wall, although I am standing next to her. I tell Blanche that an elephant has entered the room; she steps aside to make room and amuses herself by offering it some bread so it can take it in its trunk. In other words, they are more suggestible than the most docile somnambulists. I repeat, they are absolutely not in a somnambulistic state. Somnambulism is a second state of being that interrupts the normal course of life and leaves no memory. These women experience no change of state of being. They are always in the same state and have no memory loss. Two hours later, Be asked me how I have been able to come back into the room through the window without breaking anything.

I am inclined to believe that this suggestibility in the waking state – in the interval between somnambulisms, or even where there has been no somnambulism – is very frequent, especially among neuropaths, to use the general term. For my part, I have carried out a study of about twenty people, and if one seriously looks into this matter, one will find it in nearly all patients. This is what helps me understand the production of sleep by simple verbal affirmation that recent works have so often mentioned. Since these individuals, without any special preparation, execute everything that is said to them, in hearing talk about sleeping, they see themselves as someone who is sleeping, maintaining that attitude and sometimes actually going to sleep. As we have said, this is not true somnambulism. Ordinarily, excluding special training, there are neither variations of sensibility nor characteristic problems with memory. We always have the same individual in front of us, even if they keep their eyes closed and take on a stupefied attitude, because now they are enacting sleep, just as before they enacted laughing and tears. The subject is neither more nor less suggestible than before; and will dream anything you want, just as before they clearly saw elephants. At a word, they wake up, that is, change their attitude, just as they lift their arm if someone tells them to do so.

One may very often be deceived into believing that you have put an individual into a somnambulistic state, when in fact you have not changed that person in the least – one has simply established a docility, a passivity that is attributed to imagined somnambulism because one has not investigated whether or not these exact same qualities had existed before the sleep. This is precisely what happened with Blanche; instead of suggesting that she walk or say a prayer, I told her to sleep, and she fell backwards with the look of a person who was profoundly asleep. On the surface, this phenomenon seems to prove two things: first, production of somnambulism by simple suggestion, because she spoke and acted like a somnambulist; and second, the identity of somnambulism with ordinary sleep. In reality Blanche was neither in a state of somnambulism, nor even in a state of true sleep. Her existence was not interrupted by a new life, and her thought was not suppressed. She remained in the same identical state. I do not know if she was susceptible to true somnambulism or not, but to verify that it would have been necessary to submit that state to other procedures capable of producing a more real modification of consciousness.

Now let us consider the matter from another angle and ask ourselves if somnambulism, when it exists and can be verified by other features, is always accompanied by a high degree of suggestibility. If suggestion often acts outside of somnambulism, is it at least always more potent when applied to somnambulists? First, we must recognize that there are individuals who are very suggestible during their hypnotic sleep, especially at the beginning. If subjects are put to sleep rapidly, for long intervals, and if they are awakened shortly after they have entered into somnambulism, in a word, if one does not give the secondary existence time to develop and complete itself, then only the initial phase of somnambulism will be observed in which suggestion is very powerful. But if it is decided to set aside more time to the study of somnambulism, one will do well – that is at least what seems best to me – not to hurry things, not to pressure the subjects, and to keep them in somnambulism for a long period of time; then some very interesting modifications will be noted. Most authors[50] insist that their subjects remain inert, incapable of making a spontaneous movement and unable to think anything on their own. In their studies they have not gone past this first period of somnambulism, that near-cataleptic state in which certain subjects remain for a very long time. When the second state of being is complete, the subject is far from inert. The subject moves, wants to get up and walk, thinks of doing a thousand foolish things, and is often, as is the case of Léonie or Lucie, very difficult to keep in bounds.

In this situation, suggestions are far from being all-powerful and can provoke every kind of resistance. Charcot says,[51] "The awakening of ideas is not nearly as incomplete as in catalepsy. There is a tendency toward the reconstruction of the self and there can be resistance on the part of the subject." Indeed, a self is reconstituted. It is more or less different from that of waking, but it exists: "He has whims which are sometimes impossible to disrupt,"[52] he discusses the ideas one is trying to impose on him,[53] and at one moment he evades things in ingenious ways[54] and at another he resolutely rejects the orders we are trying to give him. This resistance varies with the actions which are used to try to command. It is negligible if the act is insignificant, great if the command is arduous or simply disagreeable to the subject. I have never been able to make Léonie kneel during somnambulism by conscious suggestion. I have never been able to get Lucie to get up from her bed when she is lying down. "This resistance also depends on the moral force of each individual, which is not the same in everyone."[55] Neither is it among somnambulists, one should add. Also, I am not very frightened about the great social danger that some claim to find in hypnotic suggestion. I am in complete agreement with the opinion on this matter expressed by Gilles de la Tourette, after a thorough study of this resistance of somnambulists: "All these crimes that one might suggest seem simple, only a laboratory where the daggers are in the box and the pistols go off only in the imagination of the subject."[56] As soon as the action becomes a bit serious, as soon as the subject no longer has absolute confidence in her magnetizer, she resists, refuses to carry out the task, and, if all else fails, enters a grand crisis of convulsions, which excitable women always do when they are troubled.

If subjects in the somnambulistic state are capable of this kind of resistance, they are also capable of voluntary consent. Very often the somnambulist does what is said by a sort of compliance which is inspired by various motives. First, she nearly always has some sympathy for her magnetizer and does not want to argue with him. Then too, she is very lazy and does not want to attempt useless resistances. Finally, she is entertained by the experiments and often takes their success to heart. In general, somnambulists have a positive attitude about executing what is asked of them. But an action executed from voluntary consent, through compliance, is not a suggestion; also, very often one takes as a suggestion what is not, or what is only partly so. As soon as somnambulism becomes somewhat developed, we encounter resistance, and voluntary consent comes in to modify the acts executed by suggestion.

But a much more important remark is provided to us through the study of certain subjects in certain specific somnambulisms that can be reproduced at will. There are certain somnambulisms, totally genuine from every point of view, in which every kind of suggestibility has completely disappeared, even for subjects who are very suggestible in the waking state. Many authors have already pointed out that some somnambulists in certain states possess a great freedom. Puységur already noted the relative independence of his somnambulist.[57] Liébault remarked that it was necessary for him to pick his moment for making suggestions, and added that if you mistakenly choose a time when the somnambulist is not focused, he will engage in conversation with everybody and the attempt will most often fail.[58] Dr. Philips,[59] who loved to coin words, clearly distinguished a first somnambulism with allonomy (obedience to another) and a second somnambulism with autonomy (spontaneity and independence). He called the second somnambulism "hyperphysiological" (why I do not know), although in my view this state is the most physiological or normal. Bernheim, who has shown very clearly that the somnambulist is not a pure physical automaton,[60] also remarked, with regard to the thesis of Dr. Chambard, that the degree of suggestibility is not always connected with the apparent depth of the somnambulism.[61] Finally, Azam expressed the same truth in a very full manner – and at a time when treatises on the subject were not common – when he said about Félida: "She is a total somnambulist."[62] "There are degrees of somnambulism that are more and more complete," with a perfect sense of a world that is exterior and independent. But these experiments remain isolated; they have not been spontaneously reproduced and do not seem to have changed the opinion of authors about the relation between somnambulism and suggestion.

We believe that one can find, and even reproduce at will, somnambulisms that are totally identical to that of Félida. In fact, we have described in many subjects a series of somnambulisms, more and more profound, which are sometimes very prolonged and very difficult to produce, but in which the subject little by little recovers all sensibilities and all memories which had seemed lost. In the last of these states, the subject, so ill and so diminished in the waking state, becomes totally identical to the individual at her healthiest and most normal, in regard to sensation and memory. When I observed this state for the first time in Lucie, I wanted to repeat the usual experiments with suggestion that was used with somnambulists. Lucie seemed surprised. At first, she did not move, but then she burst out: "You must take me for a fool if you believe I am going to see a bird in my room and run around after it." It should be remarked that she had done precisely that in her first somnambulism, but now all suggestibility had disappeared. It is the same, although it shows a little less clearly, with Léonie. She is very suggestible in her first somnambulism, but as one progressively deepens her second somnambulism she becomes less and less so. This phenomenon is especially curious in regard to Marie and Rose. First, because the passage from one state to another does not occur as it does with Lucie (a twenty-minute sleep followed by a sudden awakening), but happens slowly and by degrees. Second, because they are totally suggestible in the waking state. One sees these women, so subject to hallucination and so passive when awake, recover, not only their sensations and memories, but also their spontaneity and independence, more and more as they enter into this state of so-called sleep. Their catalepsy of the limbs and their immobility in positions in which they have been placed – which always come into play as soon as the person is even slightly suggestible – also disappear completely. However, these characteristics and all suggestibility reappear when this particular somnambulism is removed and the subject is returned to the waking state.

Jules Janet has tried to reproduce these experiments relating to this superior somnambulism in a celebrated subject, Witt. Following my instructions, he has continued the passes after the first somnambulism and even after the state of lethargy of the subject, and he has obtained the same results, which he had not foreseen.[63] This woman, whose somnambulisms have made it possible to study every aspect of suggestion, had a somnambulism that was easy to produce but totally unknown, during which it was impossible to make any suggestion whatsoever.

These phenomena seem to me very important. They show that if somnambulism is a second existence, it is not necessarily a feeble one, without spontaneity and without will. The elements that make a personality weak and subject to suggestive influences may or may not be found in the state of somnambulism. Therefore, we must expect to find the explanation of suggestion and its unique power neither in the definition of somnambulism nor in the causes that produce it.

(3) *Psychic hyper-excitability.* Another hypothesis has been proposed which is interesting and clearly approved by many authors, but only within certain limits by Binet and Féré. They say, "We believe that it is necessary to look to a second phenomenon, psychic hyper-excitability, for the cause of susceptibility to suggestions. In our opinion, if the suggested idea exerts an absolute power of a hypnotic over intelligence, sensation, and movement, it is above all through its intensity."[64]

Binet returns to this supposition with more detail in an article, more curious than convincing, on the intensity of mental images.[65] It seems to me that the facts cited in this article should be acknowledged, but interpreted in other ways.

To begin with, I have some reservations that some perhaps might find too abstract or too metaphysical concerning this expression "the intensity of psychological phenomena." In a very remarkable discussion concerning psycho-physiology, an anonymous physician, who is also a philosopher,[66] made the comment that sensations can be neither given a size nor added up, that, in a word, two sensations, even if they are both *minima*, are not subject to comparison, in the way mathematical units are. No doubt the external causes of our sensations – sound, temperature, etc. – and even the effects of our sensation in the external world – movements, muscular contractions, etc. – are measurable and can have different intensities. But are the sensations themselves, considered internal, which is their only reality, subject to quantification? To me it does not seem so. The temperature moves from $0°$ to $15°$ and from $15°$ to $30°$, and my sensation moves from cold to tepid and from tepid to hot. Can one say that my sensation of heat is a multiple of my sensation of cold? No doubt there is a corresponding difference of quality, which we relate to how we scientifically represent a difference of quantity in the external world, but it is not itself a quantity. Instead of maintaining that one image is more intense or less intense than another, it would be good for us to show that two images are really identical as far as their nature is concerned, and that one should not mistake a difference in quality for a difference in quantity.

In my opinion that is precisely what is happening in most of the examples cited by Binet. He tells us that a subject can have ideas in mind that are not experienced as hallucinations and that are not translated into action: one can think of a dog without seeing one or intend to speak about an action without executing it. But if one stays with it, focusing on it for some time, the idea becomes a hallucination or an action. At the start it was very weak and then it became stronger.[67] I, on the contrary, believe that this difference in the outcome is due to the fact that the idea has become totally different. Psychological theories that hold, rightly, that the image and the sensation are the same are true only for simple phenomena. The image of the colour blue (when we are not just talking about the word) is identical in nature to the sensation of blue. But this does not mean that the idea of a dog is the same as actually seeing a dog, and that the difference between the two is only a matter of degree. Here we are dealing with two groupings that have enormous differences in the quality and complexity of the images associated with them. The idea of a dog can be simply an abstract connection between various images or characteristics, it can be a simple word used in various ways by various people, or it can be merely a very vague one-colour image – in other words, a very simple thing. The real sensation of hallucination of a dog is a collection of a great variety of visual, tactile, and auditive images. To go from one to the other it is a matter not of intensifying the image, but completing it. It would be a blunder, with a subject who has difficulty seeing hallucinations, to keep on repeating or shouting loudly, "You see a dog! You see a dog!" – this would accomplish nothing. What is needed is to clarify and complete the image: "You see its ears, you see its tail, you see its long yellow fur, you hear it barking." Or, if you are dealing with subjects who can do so, you could even allow time for them to develop their own image. If, during a quick conversation with Léonie, I say to her that there are sheep in the meadow, on the river bank, etc., with each phrase I evoke a vague image which will not amount to a hallucination. But if after saying to her, "There is a sheep in front of you," I suddenly stop and do not say anything else, the idea develops little by little, she sees more detail, she feels the fleece, hears its cry, and finally says, "It is a real sheep," which means a complete sheep, not a more intense image of a sheep. The complexity of the image gives birth to its objectivity.[68] It will be the same with actions which either do or do not take place, depending on whether the motor image does or does not have the chance to become sufficiently complete.

Binet also tries to find proof for the theory of the intensity of mental images in research on hypnotic suggestions, although we cannot go into that subject now. He says something that is very true – that the mere communication of the idea of an act to a subject in the waking state is not enough to bring about its execution. It is necessary that the act has been actually suggested to the subject during somnambulism and that this suggestion has not been erased by a crisis or some other incident. And he concludes from this that the idea suggested during somnambulism is more intense than if it has been merely communicated during somnambulism and forgotten on awakening, with the memory of the idea still persisting – and one can make a case for the opposite opinion. Actually, the idea suggested during somnambulism is not represented in the same way, nor by the same images, nor is it associated with the same memory, neither is it a part of the same consciousness as an idea communicated during the waking state. It is entirely different, not more intense.

Finally, Binet cites and interprets an observation which I have myself previously made.[69] Having remarked that Lucie would obey only me and wanting to elucidate this electivity, I asked another person, M, to make a suggestion in my name to Lucie during the day: "Mr. Janet," he said, "wants you to lift both arms into the air." This command was immediately executed, although when M spoke in his own name, absolutely nothing happened. In recounting this event, Binet said that the command made in my name had been very intense. I was very surprised to hear this explanation, because Binet, it seemed to me, forgot one of the most ingenious and truest theories that he himself had contributed to establishing – that of suggestions with a reference point. When one suggests to a subject that there is a portrait on a piece of paper, why is it seen on this piece of paper and none other? Is it because the image of this particular piece of paper is more intense? No, the author very rightly tells us that the portrait is associated with a particular feature of the piece of paper and is evoked only by that feature. Why would one not in the same way say here that, by habit and training, Lucie's suggestibility has been, so to speak, dammed up, and her obedience is attached to a point of reference which is always the same – my name and my person. It is because of this quality, and not because of intensity, that my name produces the action. In obeying a stranger who gives her a command in my name, Lucie is deceived (unconsciously, it is true, but we see this as unimportant), like a somnambulist who sees the portrait on a card other than the designated one. Furthermore, in the somnambulism that follows this experience, she was furious about her automatic error and promised herself that it would never happen again. She kept her word, and this experience was never repeated. Errors of this kind are not rare among somnambulists. I have ordered N to go to sleep when I raise my arm. She goes to sleep when another person raises his arm. This is an unconscious foolishness that Lucie and Léonie were quite incapable of. Is it that the image of the raised arm of a stranger is more intense for N than for Lucie? On the contrary, this is less than clear, seeing that his arm was mistaken for mine.

I pass over the paralyses and anesthesias which Binet explains as a weakening of images, and which seem to me due to a totally different cause.[70] But I want to pause at a particular expression of this author. He says that suggestible individuals are overtaken by a *psychic hyper-excitability* which gives birth to hallucinations and impulses. The expression is important because one finds it used by various authors. This same idea is found in the abnormal psychology of Moreau (de Tours) when he attributes impulsions to a *psychic excitation.* This expression – totally incorrect, as we shall demonstrate – has contributed greatly to engaging the author in his celebrated paradox of genius and folly, "so easily do we allow ourselves to be lured by words." Without talking about the consequences, let us examine the expression itself. Can one say that suggestible individuals would be, from a psychological point of view, hyper-excited? But these are people who are overcome by anesthesias, amnesias, and paralyses of all kinds – things never indicating excitation. Lucie is totally anesthetic; Rose is anesthetic and paraplegic; Marie is hemi-anesthetic and blind in one eye and deaf in one ear; Blanche has all of her senses reduced to a minimum, etc. How can one say that if Lucie obeys my voice, it is that the psychological phenomenon – here the auditive image – is more intense in a hyper-excited consciousness. In that case she would hear my voice like the booming of a cannon. But no, she is half deaf and hears little. Can one say that Marie imitates my movements because the visual phenomenon is more intense for her than for another? But she is nearly blind and can read only the largest letters written on a blackboard. These are stunning manifestations of hyper-excitability! One might say that this excitation is not in the senses, but in the mind. So be it! But what about the example of Blanche, the most suggestible person I have ever seen, who is almost mentally challenged and who remains inert all day long, only becoming stirred at meal times?

In a word, if you consider the category of suggestible people as a whole, you will find the weak, the hypo-excited, if one can say so, and not the hyper-excited. But now let us demonstrate the opposite. Let us actually excite these individuals by using agents that create this effect. I often make use of magnetic passes for this purpose, not because I assign them any particular importance, but because in practice they are excellent for exciting the sensibilities of hysterics. But if this procedure offends, let us employ another. No doubt the best would be an electric bath applied by a static machine, but psychologists do not yet have well-equipped laboratories at their disposal. So let us be content to make passes on the arms, the legs, and the trunk of an anesthetic subject, such as Rose, using currents of moderate intensity. Or, more simply, let us place some plates of lead or tin, which have an effect on her, around her forehead. After a certain time has passed, sometimes fairly long, and if nothing interferes, she will recover all her sensibility. In fact, now she possesses a psychological hyper-excitability, being sensitive to the least impressions and recovering all the memories of her whole life. Well now! As we have already said, she is certainly no more suggestible. Her hearing, which has become hyper-excited, since she hears the slightest sound, produces neither hallucination nor impulse. Her sight, which has become very acute, produces no imitative movements. The subject has become normal in regard to her will, as well as her sensibility and memories. The same thing happens with Lucie and Marie. This allows us to declare that suggestibility is an indication of the weakness, rather than the intensity, of psychological phenomena.

3.4 Amnesia and distraction

The theory which seems to us to be closest to the truth, and which our experiences urge us to support, is the one that Richet has put forward on several occasions. When he described some examples of very curious changes of personality through suggestion, Richet said that there are two basic phenomena: first, an amnesia for all the notions that constitute the old personality, and second, the formation of a new idea of the personality: "First of all, they have lost every notion of their old state of being, since they live, speak, and think absolutely as the personality that has been presented to them."[71] Later, taking up the same question in a more general way, he says that suggestibility or abolition of personal will is undoubtedly explained as a kind of amnesia. "To stop a thought, another is needed to serve as an obstacle. To hinder a feeling, another, stronger one needs to be brought into existence. One can suppose *that it is the simultaneous memory of two feelings or of two thoughts that fails to occur*."[72] This view seems to me to still hold true, despite all the new observations that have been made.

Indeed, it is easy to see that at the moment when subjects are taken over by a suggestion, they forget everything and cannot recall any memory opposed to the ideas that invade their consciousness. When Be. saw me enter by the window, she forgot that the window was closed, that the curtains were drawn, that they cannot be opened from the outside, etc. When Blanche saw the elephant that I spoke about, she forgot that we were in a study, that the door into the room was small, that there was a stairway, a corridor that elephants could not get through, etc. When Rose joined me in climbing to the top of the Eiffel tower, she forgot that the tower was not finished, something that she spoke about a moment before. On the other hand, when subjects are no longer suggestible, they experience, as a prime characteristic, a striking return of antagonistic memories. One might recall what

Lucie said when, in her second somnambulism, she laughed at the suggestions: "Do you think that I am so stupid that you could get me to see a bird *in my room*?" So she then was remembering that she was in her room and that birds do not enter it, etc. Finally, we can artificially establish one final thing: when we ourselves restore to the subject those memories which have been lost, we halt a suggestion which, had this not been done, was about to take hold. At my order, Blanche puts out her tongue; I remark to her that she is in the presence of her father; she stops doing it. She thumbs her nose at me; I tell her this is not nice, and she drops her hands. But sometimes it is necessary that a great number of these antagonistic images be injected and especially at the beginning of the suggestion in order to halt it. These different experiences prove that a *notable amnesia always accompanies actions performed through suggestion.*

So it is that amnesia is the principal cause of suggestion, just as it is the basic foundation for somnambulism, showing how large a role memory plays in our psychic life. Amnesia alone, as memory itself, cannot be a primitive phenomenon. We have already remarked, with regard to the alterations of memory during the various somnambulistic states, that we ought to return to it here. Just as memory depends on sensation, amnesia depends on anesthesia, and this is because one is able to experience a certain sensation only if the image can be retrieved. If our subjects have losses of memory at the moment when they execute a suggestion, they must have corresponding anesthesias.

This seems easy to verify for some of them, because they constantly exhibit notable, well-known anesthesias. For that reason, I do not think this moves us forward very much in each case, and I will simply summarize my observations by saying that strongly suggestible people, at least of the kind we are now talking about, for the most past have notable anesthesias. Most of the surface of the skin of alcoholics is insensible. The natural somnambulists of Mesnet have lost much of their sensation. Hysterics that I have studied have great gaps in their sensibility. On the other hand, the healing of their illness is characterized above all by the return of lost sensation, and from this point of view, it should be possible to say very easily that *suggestion is tied to anesthesia,* which takes away from the subject not only particular sensations, but also all memories which are expressed in terms of images of the same kind.

Nevertheless, a demonstration of this kind would be insufficient. On the one hand there are indeed very suggestible individuals who have little or no hysterical anesthesia. Be. would be an excellent example of this category; although suggestible to the degree that I have described, she has all her sensibilities intact. On the other hand, constant hysterical anesthesia does not explain the kind of amnesia that accompanies and produces suggestibility. Loss of the sense of touch or of colour produces consistent loss of certain kinds of memories which are tied to tactile sensations or sensations of colour, but does not explain the particular and momentary loss of such and such a particular memory which can be expressed by means of various images. Thus, when I say to Léonie that she is a princess, she at once forgets that she is a peasant – a necessary condition for the hallucination to develop. This is indisputable; but Léonie's anesthesia explains only that she now forgets this quality of being a peasant, the memory of which she had a moment ago, even when her insensibility remains the same.

So it is necessary to recognize the existence of a second species of anesthesia, one which is less known, but whose psychological importance is very great. An individual with normal sensibility is able to not only exercise all her senses successively, but also, to a certain degree, to appreciate diverse sensations simultaneously. Placed in a group of many people, one can follow a particular conversation, and yet hear a question addressed from behind oneself, and see a new person come and act accordingly. These are very simple things of which persons of a suggestible temperament are completely incapable. If they look at someone and converse with that person, they no longer hear or even see other people. Lucie has an unusual response in this regard. As soon as she is no longer speaking directly to someone, she is no longer able to hear that person. Someone can come up behind her and call to her, or shout insults in her ear,[73] and she does not turn around. A person can stand in front of her, show her objects, touch her, etc., without her noticing. She can knit or read, and it is also with the same apparent close attention. One can open the door, touch her arm or face, or speak to her, and she does not perceive it. Even more unusual, below her breasts and on her thumbnail she has hyperesthetic and hysterogenic points where the slightest touch provokes cries of pain or even convulsions. When she is occupied with a task of the kind mentioned or in a simple conversation, I can strike her chest or her thumb without her saying a word. An anesthesia of this kind has often been noted during somnambulism. Such a somnambulist hears only the voice of her magnetizer and of no other person. Another might see only the light their magnetizer has kindled and not those that might have been kindled by others. We will have to come back to these matters, if not to explain them, at least to describe them.[74] At this moment we are content to point out that this anesthesia is not peculiar to elective somnambulism, but exists in a high degree among all suggestible individuals. It is an exaggerated state of *distraction* which is not temporary and does not result from voluntarily directing the attention on one single sense. It is *a natural and perpetual state of distraction which prevents these individuals from appreciating any sensation outside that which actually occupies their mind.* Finally, let us remark that when these individuals, in diverse circumstances that are now known, cease to be suggestible, this distraction disappears, and we can say that it plays a large role in all the phenomena that we study.

Indeed, this anesthesia by distraction brings with it a particular amnesia that is precisely what we need to understand suggestion. Here is an instructive example. Lucie, who ceases to see and hear people as soon as she stops speaking with them, is also oblivious of their presence, as one can see by the way she conducts herself. She imagines that they left when she stopped conversing with them, and when one makes the effort to bring them back to her attention, she says, "Well, you have returned?" What is most striking is that she no longer is aware of their presence and speaks loudly of their secrets, not being restrained by the thought of the presence of these persons. Léonie is the same, during her somnambulism, at least – because she is not, like Lucie, consciously suggestible in the waking state. With me, she begins by saying that she does not want to speak with anyone but me and will not leave me. If I get her to speak with someone else and I stop speaking with her, she completely forgets about me, and when this person departs, she wants to go with her, as if there were no one else around. Now it is not very difficult to understand why Léonie, when I address her as a princess, has forgotten that she is a peasant. She is so distracted that at that moment she no longer has the sensation of her dress, her apron, her cap – the only things that can actually recall her previous life to her.

The same distraction explains why Marie, no longer seeing the room, the walls, the floor, forgets that we are in a hospital room and that no one has brought a bouquet of flowers here. Just as general tactile anesthesia takes away all memories tied to tactile sensation, so this variable and temporary anesthesia for certain objects caused by the distraction temporarily takes away all memories which are tied to the sensation of these objects.

Since, in the phenomena studied so far, this anesthesia and this amnesia caused by distraction only bear upon the images opposed to the suggested act. They allow the consciousness of this act itself to continue to exist in a more isolated and, consequently, more developed, state. We all know the stupidities we can perpetrate in an instant of distraction. Indeed, if one takes into account the conditions of its production, a suggested act executed by the subject is the ideal of distraction.

3.5 The narrowing of the field of consciousness

In our studies up to now, we have taken under consideration the quality of the phenomena that occupy the conscious awareness. However, it is likely that psychological existences can manifest other differences beyond those that result from the nature of auditive, visual, and tactile images. Without speaking about the intensity proper to each image, which seems to us to be an issue that is far from clear, is it not possible that, on the one hand, there are differences in quantity, in the number of the psychological phenomena that occupy various consciousnesses, and, on the other hand, that all people are not equally endowed in this matter and experience in any given period a number of very different ideas. Here we have a proposition that it seems to us very apt for explaining the character of the anesthesias that we have talked about. Let us undertake first to examine the proposition in itself and to show that it is intelligible and credible; then we will see how it can explain the phenomena that we are studying.

Herbert Spencer wrote: "The phenomena that make up the object of physiology are presented under the form of an immense number of series which are joined together. Those that make up the object of psychology are presented only under the form of a simple series."[75] Indeed, it is a very widespread opinion that the conscious awareness of a person at one moment is but a single phenomenon, and that, consequently, psychological life is made up of a succession of phenomena coming one after the other, forming a long series, which stretches out for the whole of the life of the individual, but remaining isolated, unaccompanied by other simultaneous events. No doubt, we have a good idea of coexistence and even a notion of objects spread out in space. But this notion, far from being primitive, is derived from the notion of succession and the idea of time. We know that Spencer attempted to form the relation of coexistence through the union of two relations of sequence, and how, since Stuart Mill, the English school is fond of demonstrating that "time is father to space." If one completely accepts this opinion, as Taine seems to, who regards consciousness as a centre without extension, a sort of mathematical point, one will perhaps find it strange to still speak of a number of psychological phenomena in consciousness at any given moment, since, at every moment, this quantity ought to be a unity. Nevertheless, we can still pose certain reservations. As the fine work of Wundt and his students on the duration of psychic phenomena has shown, these phenomena do not always succeed one another with the same rapidity, and two individuals can even, in a given length of time, present a very different quantity of mental images.

We do not believe that one can adopt unreservedly the hypothesis of Stuart Mill and of Spencer and reduce the scope of consciousness in that way. Despite the curious demonstration produced by the English psychologists, it does not seem to us that it is possible to derive the notion of space from the notion of time and the relation of coexistence from the relation of succession. The idea of space, which is an original idea, in reality derives from the sensation of extension that the actual coexistence of a great number of visual or tactile sensations gives us.[76] On the other hand, our own observations have not revealed to us that consciousness is reducible to a unity. As I write this page and think of the opinions of philosophers about the extent of consciousness, I see my paper, my light, my room, and at the same time I hear muffled sounds of a concert in a house nearby, which leaves me with a pleasant impression. All of these things exist at the same time in my mind. I am not saying that my work is enhanced by all this; no doubt it would be better if I were not thinking about them. But in the last analysis, such as it is, it moves forward despite the buzzing of sensations and images that at this moment run up against each other in my conscious awareness. Besides, could it possibly be otherwise? The simple act of writing requires many conscious phenomena – the view of the paper, the pen, the dark markings, the sonorous or muscular image of the words, the expression of the ideas thought, etc. If I have a single image in my head, no doubt I will express it perfectly, because it will be translated by my whole body; I cease to move, to think – I have become a statue, like the cataleptics that I have studied.

In fact, in catalepsy there exists a nearly absolute unity of consciousness – specifically, right at the beginning of the return of consciousness, at the appearance of a kind of annihilation, when the nearly exhausted mind is incapable of conceiving many sensations at the same time. Only one sensation remains: it is of its own proper existence and gives the subject the appearance of a human automaton. Perhaps also, at the other extreme of intellectual development, when a perfect intellectual life allows a mind to include all images in a vast synthesis, to unite in one single idea those of a general relation, all the sensation that it experiences or of which memory gives the subject a recall – perhaps then, if this state is possible, we find the intellectual unity reached at moments by the great exemplars of genius in exalted thought. But the ordinary life of thought does not fall so low or rise so high. It maintains itself at a medium level to which the images presented to the mind are numerous and where their systematization is far from complete. Dumont understood this very well when he wrote: "For us at each instant there is a group of numerous coexisting sensations ... The self is at the same time both a series and a group; it is a series of groups."[77] Similarly, a very psychological magnetizer has more recently said "In the waking state, despite the apparent monoideism that has seduced many psychologists, our thought is always very complicated. Simultaneously, we have a crowd of sensations that war among themselves and a crowd of memories that seek to become disentangled from the pressure of dominant ideas."[78]

In addition, we must keep in mind that there is the opinion that Spencer espouses in practice whenever it is a matter of explaining any real phenomenon: "Dream consciousness is like that of an old or indolent man: the elements are less coherent and *less abundant* ... The contraction of *the area of consciousness* betrays itself by the absence of these *innumerable collateral thoughts* that successive scenes of action ordinarily bring into play."[79] And elsewhere: "Although the phenomena of consciousness form a series, there are *simultaneous changes*: the visual field is not absolutely reduced to a point, there is a vague consciousness of nearby points.... In the fabric of consciousness there are many threads; the outside ones are loose and do not adhere well; but on the inside there are a series of changes that tighten the cloth and form that which we can call consciousness properly speaking.[80] This latter reservation is very apt. This small group of phenomena, better known than others, is the result of attention, of apperception (as Wundt calls it, following Leibniz), which does not extend as far as does consciousness itself. But the author is less aware that human consciousness, clear or not, ordinarily extends itself sufficiently far as to include a great number of collateral and coexisting images.

Spencer even gives us an excellent term, very precise and useful, that we are keeping: the area or field of consciousness. Indeed, we know what is meant by the visual field: "It is that expanse of space from which we can receive a luminous impression, when the eye is immobile and the stare fixed."[81] Could not one similarly call the *field of consciousness* or maximum extent of consciousness, the largest number of simple or relatively simple phenomena which can be present at once in the same consciousness, reserving, as Wundt proposes,[82] the term "internal point of focus" for that part of the phenomena of consciousness towards which attention is directed? It would, I believe, be of the greatest importance for experimental psychology to be able to determine – albeit in an approximate way – the field of consciousness as one measures the visual field with a campimeter or a perimeter. As far as we know, Wundt is the only one who has attempted an experimental determination of this kind.[83] Unfortunately, he uses procedures and reasonings that seem to us neither very clear nor very precise, and quickly passes over this difficult question. His conclusion is that "we would be justified in accepting twelve simple representations as the maximum expanse of consciousness." At first glance, and perhaps wrongly, I find this number to be far too small. The binocular visual field, which is only a small part of the total field of consciousness, clearly contains much more than twelve simultaneous visual phenomena. Consciousness, which also includes other sensations and their images, should contain many more. But here there arises a host of questions pertaining to the sense of the words being used and to the very idea of a simple representation. That makes this problem one of the most difficult – as well as, in my view, one of the most important in all of experimental psychology.

Despite these difficulties, and despite the impossibility we unfortunately encounter in trying to carry out precise measurements, it seems that there is one thing quite easy to establish. The field of consciousness, like the visual field, can vary; it is not the same for all individuals, nor for every moment in the life of the same individual. Between the cataleptic person who, as we have shown, has only one image at a time, and an orchestra leader who simultaneously hears all the instruments, sees the actors, and follows, from memory and by sight-reading, the operatic score, there are many possible degrees. At this moment, the lower degrees interest us the most, because it is very easy to show that suggestible individuals possess a very narrowed field of consciousness, and that this characteristic plays a large role in the modifications of their will.

Taking into account that we cannot measure it directly, the narrowing of the field of consciousness ought to manifest itself in a manner that is perhaps somewhat indirect but nonetheless very certain in the anesthesias. Let us consider two individuals who, at some given moment, have different fields of consciousness: where one senses ten phenomena, the other only senses five. Should we conclude that there are five phenomena that the second individual does not sense, at least at the moment, and is therefore to a certain degree momentarily anesthetic? Also, when a person like Lucie can only hear one person at a time, I naturally suppose that her field of consciousness is small, like a vessel already filled with liquid, to which one cannot add another drop. This is only a supposition, but it does make sense of the facts.

But, one might say, anesthesia is not a proof of a narrowing of the field of consciousness, because the images produced by the remaining senses can themselves be very numerous and compensate for the loss of the other senses. Indeed this sometimes happens: for those blind from birth, for example, the remaining senses become sharper and more developed, and can sometimes fill the void left by the visual sensations. Someone who pays attention to one object, can no longer see the others, but in regard to this object, they will have very vivid and numerous sensations which prevent their field of consciousness from being truly narrowed. All this is true, but things do not happen this way in hysterical anesthesia. The loss of one sense does not lead to the heightening of acuity in other senses – quite the contrary. The concentration of consciousness on an object does not make sensations related to this object more numerous, than attention does. A hysteric thinks very little about things; but the little she does think does not, for all that, make her know more, because the senses which remain are diminished in every way, and she has only very confused notions of the objects she looks at. For her, anesthesia, even when momentary and due to distraction, is a loss without compensation.

Another proof of the narrowing of the field of consciousness with suggestible individuals can be derived from phenomena produced by them when one shuts out their remaining senses. All the authors refer to the stupefaction and obliteration of intelligence and memory which quickly follows for an anesthetic hysteric when one closes her eyes or places cotton in her ears.[84] It seems that the visual or auditive images that might remain are not enough to allow the formation of a psychological life. The little remaining light seems to be extinguished and all consciousness disappears into a complete sleep. It is true that there is, in this a matter, a great difference between a hysteric and a person of limited intelligenet or even an epileptic. Whereas, in the latter case, if one suppresses their feeble resources for thinking, they remain stupefied, as I have shown in the case of R. In the former case, a quick decision is reached, and, because her ordinary psychological life has been destroyed, she begins a second. This is perhaps the reason hypnotization is so easily accomplished with hysterics by simply closing their eyes. Let us put to one side the second existence which may be identical or superior to the first, this sleep, this destruction of the ordinary state which develops quickly with the closure of the eyes – does it not show that the field of consciousness was very small and composed almost entirely of those phenomena that one takes away? Who are those who satisfy this condition, who have the kind of consciousness which will accordingly be suggestible? It would be necessary to answer this question by means of data and statistics that I cannot provide. I can only indicate what to me appears likely. It seems to me that individuals whose field of consciousness is restricted in an abnormal way are divided into two groups: the ill and children. In the one case, it seems that a kind of fatigue or weakness restrict the number of phenomena that can enter into the one consciousness because, for most of those who suffer from a debilitating illness, one encounters the following psychological symptoms: distraction, concentration of thought on one point, obliviousness of bystanders, and the suggestibility that is so characteristic of certain forms of typhoid fever. In the other case, consciousness is little developed in all the senses and is as restricted in its extent as it is in its nature and variety. The impetuous acts of children, their naïve beliefs, their anger and sudden tears – all show this to be true. But this does not show, at least in my view, that children are hypnotizable; this is not the same thing. Suggestion reflexively activates a mechanism of consciousness that already exists and that daily operates spontaneously and at random. Hypnotism, if it is to produce the somnambulistic state, must interrupt the ordinary orientation of thought in order to substitute another. Fortunately, children do not usually experience the mental instability and anesthesias that produce this upheaval. It seems to me that if a true somnambulism is easily produced in a child, it is a sign of hereditary defect and inchoate nervous disorder. Also, one should not use the often repeated and unfortunate phrase, "the mother is the first hypnotizer." Rather, the mother is the first to influence the beliefs and actions of the child, which is completely natural, since she provides the judgement and will the child does not have.

Now, why is it that individuals placed in somnambulism sometimes, in this new existence, exhibit a severely constricted field of consciousness and great suggestibility? Because this second existence often resembles that of the ill and children. Somnambulistic subjects sometimes lose sensation, at least in the beginning. Richet says they exhibit excitability of the muscles, in which they resemble hysterics.[85] Since my subjects were already quite hysterical and ill in a waking state they could hardly become more so. I was especially struck by the second characteristic: *the similarity between somnambulism and childhood*. This fact has been noted for some time. One magnetizer, the Count of Rédern, has remarked, "the beginning of mensambulance (somnambulism), is a sort of childhood that requires some understanding."[86] Among modern thinkers, Fontan and Ségard have quite rightly emphasized this characteristic.[87] Indeed, nothing is more curious than to see thirty-year-old women, who when in a wakeful state are serious and cool, in somnambulism take on the mannerisms of a child, gesticulating, playing, laughing at everything and speaking with a childish lisp, reverting to nicknames like Nichette or Lili, and in essence completely taking on the attitude of a very young child. Perhaps, as I have observed, the return of the motor sense, which predominates in childhood, is characteristic for such people. But at its core, it seems to me, is the formation of a new kind of existence, one with few memories or experiences which are its own. The somnambulist can, if we ask them, have memories of waking, but they do not come spontaneously; they are like memories recounted in a strange language, one that is comprehended only with some effort. Or else, they can recall the memories but do not identify with them, as if they were the memories of another. "That would bother someone else a great deal," Léonie has said, "but as for me I do not care one way or another." These comparisons may be hypothetical, but there is one fact for certain: true somnambulism begins with an end to normal consciousness, *la petite mort* of Félida, as Azam calls it, after which consciousness is reborn little by little. It begins in the form of catalepsy, which is a fixed idea that is almost complete. This then naturally exhibits a fairly narrow range, until in its perfect development it extends so far that no suggestibility remains.

Consciousness can, therefore, at any moment in life, expand to a fairly extensive field. Each time we see in someone this *obedience to suggestion*, or better yet the forgetfulness and distraction to which this disposition has led, we also note a *narrowing of the field of consciousness* and a marked decrease in the number of phenomena which can occupy the mind at any given time.

3.6 Interpretation of the phenomena of suggestion: the dominance of perceptions

A doctor from the 18th century, who predates Biran and Régis in certain points, stated that movement of the limbs can be determined by three things: by will, *by thought*, and by passion. "This principle, which is determined by the driving faculty of thought, without the intercession of will, is one which sets Régis apart from Maine de Biran and agrees with present day English psychology."[88] "To think is to withhold speech and action," said Bain.[89] This, however, applies to those of us who are able to withhold them, but for the individuals that we are describing, to think is to speak and to act. One can never study with more ease this influence of thought upon movement than by witnessing the actions, whether through suggestive influence or by themselves, of those individuals whose consciousness is restricted and who have as a consequence numerous anesthesias and consecutive amnesias.

When the field of consciousness has narrowed as much as possible, and the mind is only able to hold on to one phenomena at a time, it is presented as a sensation or an image. When observing the actions of individuals in catalepsy we are only able to see the automatisms of images. However, as soon as the field of consciousness begins to expand, each sense no longer functions in isolation, but is accompanied by many accessory and interpretive images which facilitate the creation of an idea of the self, an idea of the external world, and of language. In a word, phenomena are presented under the form of *perception*. Thus, when observing these individuals, we are able to explain the *automatism of perceptions*.

A perception, like an emotion but with far more complexity, is a synthesis, an integration of a large number of images. These systems were originally created when each of us *understood*, for the first time, the nature of an object, the use of a tool, or the meaning of a word. We know already, from our studies of emotions and memories, that such systems are durable and tend to be retained for a long time. Here, as previously, one of the elements of a given group evokes the others.

Therefore, without reviewing the preceding studies, it suffices to show (1) how ths automatism of perceptions resembles the mechanism of sensations and emotions, and (2) in which ways, given its greater complexity, it differs.

(1) This new automatism is, in certain respects, identical to the first, but simply more complicated. When a mind of this kind hears this phrase, "Walk around the room!" she is capable of understanding it, that is to say, that she will develop an awareness of images (muscular or visual, as the case may be) of the movement of her legs, visual images of the appearance of the room as she begins walking, and then other motor images and other visual images as her perspective of the room changes. Thus, there is a long succession of varied representations of the room until, at last, returning to her point of departure, a final image which will reproduce her initial image of the room. But she stops there, the field of consciousness

is too narrow to receive other images; the subject will not hear the amused comments made about her path, will not see the people present, and therefore will not recall what made her actions ridiculous or pointless. She will not make judgments that require the comparison of several perceptions, or at least will make only very simple comparisons between the two or three perceptions of her limbs and of the aspects of the room that she sees, and can speak only to say, "I walk around the room." We have stated that images presenting themselves in similar conditions, without encountering contradiction or revision, were not only associated with a real movement, but were themselves (from another point of view), a true movement. So it is not surprising that this person, thinking in the way we describe, actually moves and, as we observe, walks around the room.

The automatic development of perceptions leads to a new phenomenon, that of hallucination, which seems to require a particular explanation. The product of this phenomenon seems to be something different, something happening in the mind instead of manifesting in a movement of the body. In reality, this difference is, as we have seen, only very superficial for, in any suggested act there is already present a hallucination, and any suggested hallucination is, in some way, an act, a movement of the body that we command. But, it may be said, hallucination presents a new and essential character. Instead of remaining internal, appearing to the subjective subject as the image of a movement, it seems to belong to the external world and become objective. However, this difference is not absolute. Rose, on the order to move her leg, sees it in the air and has an objective image of an act. Léonie, who feels a vague discomfort, of either hot or cold, has many subjective, albeit hallucinatory, images. We could say that the notion of objectivity is added to the hallucination when it is sufficiently complex, as has been already explained. It is the degree of complexity that determines our distinction between internal images and objective perceptions. "Our ordinary representations seem to us internal because they are much less complex than real perceptions."[90] The subjects we study have, thanks to the automatic development of images, very complex representations and confuse them with external objects. In most cases, however, the question is much simpler, for a hallucination associated inseparably with a real perception, naturally takes on the same appearance and the same nature. When Marie sees a bird perched on the window sill, she does not believe that the bird is *in* her and the window sill is *outside* her. So in this there is no new problem. Undoubtedly, suggestion-induced hallucinations raise many particular and interesting problems, which have already been studied in other notable works. But when one in a general way considers the automatism of the mind, one sees no reason to separate the suggested hallucination and the suggested act.

With regard to more complicated suggestions, with regard to hallucinations with a point of reference, and with regard to changes of personality, we understand that they are the consequence of more complex perceptions. In the mind of the subject, at some point a certain idea of a princess or an archbishop has been formed. Evoked by a word, then left to itself, this idea subsists and shows us, in the form of acts and hallucinations, the elements it contains, because, in this restricted mind, no perception is formed at the moment to obstruct the suggested idea.

(2) These characteristics are very similar to the automatism of isolated images during catalepsy that we have already discussed. Let us now take a look at new features which belong to the automatism of perceptions. The acts we are studying now are, in many respects, superior to cataleptic attitudes by reason of their number, their varieties, their adaptation to circumstances, and sometimes even their independence.

Since consciousness during catalepsy is too restricted to permit the understanding of signs and language, actions can only be provoked through a small number of emotions that can be brought into being. Among these emotions, only those which form part of a system develop and provoke associated acts, an ensemble already frequently established: a scene of anger, the religious scenes of communion and salvation, etc. That is what Léonie's complicated actions during catalepsy are reduced to. This cannot be compared with the infinite diversity of acts and hallucinations that a word can bring about in subjects who are simply suggestible. Cataleptic acts are perfect, without hesitation, lacking any characteristics which do not concur with the general expression. The suggested acts are less perfect, and the facial expressions never acquire the same unity or the same intensity.

While the former are invariable, as we have shown elsewhere, suggestions are not always executed in the same way. The former do not adapt themselves to circumstances and proceed without concern for obstacles, or stop when the obstacle is insurmountable.

Let us focus on this last point. Léonie, when she plays the communion scene, walks a few meters forward and a little to the right. If she lacks space, if she runs into a wall, she does not think to move over, she stops against this wall, head down and hands clasped, pressing on the wall until the end of catalepsy. However, I will now refer to another person, one who behaves very differently. If I tell Marie to walk and go to a designated place, she does not stop in front of walls but knows how to find the doors and avoid obstacles. She changes and corrects her actions according to circumstances. I told her one day to sweep the room. She went to a corner where she expected to find a broom, but not finding it, and without waiting for me to add anything, she looked in another place where it is commonly kept, found it, and began to sweep. Lucie, when I tell her to write, takes a pencil if she is in bed, and finds a pen and ink if she is up. In conclusion, the cataleptic sees nothing, hears nothing outside the action with which her very restricted consciousness is entirely occupied. The somnambulist who acts on a suggestion is also very focused and unaffected by many impressions; but she can, to a certain extent, hear words and see objects, so long as they fit with her dominant perception, and she can adapt to these new impressions.

This difference is understandable. It corresponds to the difference which exists between a sensation and a perception: the one invariable, because it is unique and can exist only in a single way and only produce a series of images having the same characteristics, and the other variable, because it contains multiple elements that can change, depending on the circumstances, without the overall perception disappearing. Richet was kind enough to share an experiment with me in which he removed the brains from ducks. The behaviour of these laboratory specimens reminded me of cataleptics. At first sight, the ducks without brains could not be distinguished from the other ducks, they fled, quacking and spreading their wings like their comrades. But when the whole flock came up against a wall, their difference was evident. While ducks with intact brains scattered to the right and to the left, ducks without their brain bumped against the wall and did not move. This comparison may seem absurd, because it compares a cataleptic's behaviour with animal behaviour, that is to say, the acts operated under suggestion to the acts of intact ducks. This similarity does not seem to me too absurd, because intelligent animals also behave according to complex perceptions that allow them to vary their actions and adapt them appropriately.

Here is another difference relating to the previous one. The cataleptic performs few acts, does not modify them, and never resists. The mind, reduced to a single idea, bars any alien elements. The more extensive the perception of the suggestible, the more resistance can be present. Not that the subject can resist freely and by an act of the will; they have none in reality. But among the constituent elements of a perception or among the images which it evokes, it can encounter those that are opposed, or better yet, it can encounter images that are part of another perception, of another synthesis different from the one which evoked it. If I tell Léonie to kneel, she does not do it, because her first magnetizer made her kneel to punish her. She cries out, "But I did not do anything wrong, I do not want to be punished." One time I wanted (it is true that the idea was unfortunate) to transform her into her own husband to see how she would play the role of a person she hated. The hallucination had barely begun, and the instant she saw herself in a man's clothes she began hitting herself indignantly. The opposing images were more numerous than the suggested images. Another day I suggested that she steal tickets from a safe. She paused, appalled, before carrying out the act. I tell Lucie to say her prayers, she responds with irreverent gestures and taunts against religion. The idea of prayer awakens that which is contained in the subject's mind, that is, images quite opposed to its realization. The more the subject's field of consciousness expands, the more the revival of these ideas become probable, and the power of suggestion is lessened.

However, in the subjects we studied whose field of consciousness is still very limited, this resistance is quite rare and does not seem to me to be a true freedom. It is simply one image opposing another whose force is equal to that of the first. The mind is like a scale that oscillates and leans towards the side with the greatest weight. Nothing has changed the mechanism of action and belief, which is always only determined by perception. Since catalepsy is the dominion of sensations and emotions, the states we have studied fall into the realm of perception.

3.7 The characteristics of suggestible individuals

These and previous conclusions are fraught with difficulty and raise a serious objection that must be verified by our hypotheses. If a suggestion has no power of its own and acts solely as a perception placed within a suggestible subject, it cannot by itself provoke automatic actions in these subjects. All ideas, all perceptions must find a favourable environment for their development in order to impart to these individuals a very specific quality of conduct.

Indeed, we believe that this is really so and that our theory of the dominance of perceptions applies to both the natural and suggested acts of these weak individuals. Nothing is more curious, in fact, than the character and conduct of these people whose consciousness undergoes the most singular changes that result from its narrowing. We understand that this subject has tempted many novelists who, following the taste of the day, include in their works a portrait of a hysteric or of a somnambulist. Unfortunately, in my opinion, most are content with some scientific terms collected at random and believe they have thereby adequately represented a four-phase nerve crisis or a hemi-anesthetic heroine. This portrait of hysterics has also tempted those who deal with mental illnesses, the descriptions of Legrand du Saulle, Moreau (de Tours),[91] Ball,[92] Ribot,[93] are among the most interesting. Fortunately, we are not trying to do anything of that sort. Rather we gather, from a single point of view, the observations that we have made which confirm the general idea that we have put forth on the nature of consciousness among these patients.

An observation I made one day by chance (they are often the best) illustrated for me better than any research the nature of the intelligence of the enfeebled persons of whom we speak. I arrived one day to see Lucie, with the intention of continuing research on the phenomena of anesthesia. She pretended to be too tired to answer any questions. In reality, she had been bored by my experiments the day before and did not want to start again. "Well," I say, "we will be lazy today. But so that I have not come for nothing, you will tell me a story." "How silly! I do not know any stories. Surely you do not want me to tell you the story of Ali-baba?" "Well, if I do, why not? I am listening." Then, half laughing, half irritated, she begins the story of Ali-baba. At first, she falters and stops frequently to see if I am listening. Little by little, she no longer pays any attention to me and becomes excited … Suddenly she screams and stops, her eyes fixed on a corner of the wall. Then she speaks quietly to herself: "Here they are, all of the thieves … hidden in large pots …." She is not telling me a story anymore, she is seeing, she follows the whole scene as it unfolds before her eyes and, from time to time makes comments to herself as children do at a show. "They'll all be killed … that's good." As for me, the story of Ali-baba had never seemed so interesting and I took care not to interrupt. What I saw being played out before me was the manner in which hysterics and somnambulists think. Rather than the dull and abstract way that most of us think, their thought is colourful and alive, it is image and almost always hallucination. Richet once asked a somnambulist what time something had happened:

"Wait," she said, "I do not see." Then she said, "I know now." She saw in front of her a dial whose needles marked the time. A thought which presents itself with such vividness can hardly be compared to the hesitant and variable thoughts we have. "I saw it with my own eyes," we say when we are certain, but these types of minds see everything with the same clarity and detail, it is not surprising that they are convinced by it all! "Every internal fantom contains an affirmative conception," said Taine.[94] No doubt, but the affirmation will be all the stronger and the fantom all the more colourful and appear more real if our imagination is accompanied by a certain degree of conviction that the object exists. How much stronger is the conviction in people whose every thought is equivalent to a sensation. When we dream, the most absurd ideas seem to us realities, because they take form and stand before us. Minds like these are always in a dream and everything is before them as a real object. St. Teresa described, in a very precise way, this state of mind that she must have been familiar with: "I know," she says, "people whose mind is so weak that they imagine they see everything they think. This state is quite dangerous."[95] Whatever the idea that currently fills their minds, nothing else can stand up to their convictions. It is not in the power of any reasoning, any objection, however well founded, to shake it, because it is more than a conviction, it is the impossibility of thinking otherwise. Do not debate with suggestibles; it is useless. When I want to modify a conviction of Léonie, I always get this answer, which, in essence, is full of common sense: "I see that this is real, why do you want me not to believe that it is? You believe what you see... you do not see the same thing as me... what do you want me to do? You do not know how to see, too bad for you." Is this not similar to the way believers in religion speak: "You do not understand therefore you lack faith. But I understand, I feel, I see … so I believe." This conviction can become the origin of devotion and of fanaticism.

We find in the same people another characteristic that, at first glance, seems quite opposite to the previous one and difficult to reconcile with it. It is an extraordinary credulity. When they are told stories, instead of simply listening to them, they take them as reality. I am not talking here about hallucinations that one intentionally communicates to a somnambulist. I am talking about daily occurrences within the normal life of these enfeebled minds. Lucie, in passing on the street, heard a few words about someone she knew. The meaning that she relayed to me was absurd and probably was not said in the way she heard it. She remained completely convinced, however, and it was impossible for me to change her mind. The most incredible example I have seen of this credulity is the following. A hysteric heard, in her youth, that women with her disease died at menopause. Twenty years later, at the first manifestation of menopause, she prepared to die. She began choking, and she might be dead if we had not discovered her belief and, not without difficulty, modified it. She made up her mind to live, and since then has done quite well. Rose was sick and paralyzed. No cure, physical or mental, seemed to have any effect on her. During the delirium of a hysterical crisis, I heard her say, "They cannot cure me, it is not an illness that I have, I am bewitched by that old wizard who is angry with me. There is nothing that can be done." I made her confess this

remarkable story and managed, with great difficulty, to remove this truly delirious conviction; I had no further difficulty suppressing the paraplegia. But let us
put aside these extreme cases, where credulity has dramatic consequences. Let us
accept, in a general way, that hysterics, awake or asleep, are like little children
and do not need hypnotic practices to be convinced. They believe everything that
enters their mind.

Their activity naturally has the same characteristics as their thought. The
thought is at first extremely quick, instantaneous. As soon as an idea is formed, it
must be carried out, and the movement is accomplished as though by a convulsive
discharge. Lucie thinks of leaving the room, and here she is, barely dressed, running and gesticulating in the street. Léonie, in a somnambulistic state, wants to go
down to the garden, the door resists a little. Suddenly, there she is at the window,
and I hardly have time to restrain her. If she is interested in someone, she always
rushes to find or follow them as soon as she hears them mentioned. More examples are unnecessary. One would have to describe their whole life and all their
actions, for this same characteristic of irrational precipitation is always found.
Finding a motive for their actions, even the most serious, is therefore futile. A
somnambulist told Bertrand[96] that "she was going on the rooftops to look for a pin
or a nail that she thought she had seen there." Lucie went out one day and bought
a lot of furniture that she could not afford. "I felt like seeing the effect," she
said, "of having my room a little fuller." The reasoning behind these acts are all
determined by the desires or sensations of the moment. They give no thought to a
future happiness or a distant misfortune. The recklessness of hysterical women is
incredible and it is found equally in the conduct of all weak or degraded people.

These sudden and absent-minded acts, however, are sometimes violent and
long lasting. They sometimes resemble convulsions, sometimes contractures.
Rose is thinking of crocheting something, a vestment for a priest, I believe. She
is constantly working on it, always talking about it, even in a somnambulistic
state and during her crises. For eight days she could not think of anything else.
Then, after a sudden remark, an expression of disgust, she did not want to touch
it anymore. When she starts to yawn, it continues for hours without her being
able to stop. After having been paralyzed for seven months, she was cured by a
prolonged somnambulism. But then it seemed as though she wanted to injure her
legs, because she would run all day without stopping, until she was exhausted.
Marie, usually very sweet and good-tempered, became angry with a servant and
suddenly decided not to say another word to any of the people at the hospital. She
would talk to me when I arrived, but she remained silent with everyone else. This
lasted more than a fortnight until it stopped suddenly. She did not want anyone to
refer to the episode and said that it was nothing. It would be very easy to add here
many examples of the single-mindedness that these enfeebled minds show in acts
that they undertake, quite at random, and then end, equally at random.

Their activity demonstrates another characteristic parallel to the one we already
have seen with this type of intelligence. Though random and tenacious, their

conduct is nevertheless liable to modification by any sort of external influence. These people, seemingly spontaneous and enterprising, are the most oddly docile when we know how to direct them. Just as one can change a dream by a few words addressed to the sleeper, so can one modify the acts and the whole conduct of an enfeebled individual by a word, an allusion, a small sign, which she obeys blindly, but which she would resist furiously if we seemed to command her. A word can evoke laughter or crying or blushing, and a word can make them calm or violent.

This modification of their actions by the influence of others is demonstrated in a remarkable manner in their habits of imitation. We are all more or less influenced by the people we spend time with, but in enfeebled minds, this modification produces a complete and rapid transformation. Even the most serious acts may have no other origin than that of imitation. "A first suicide acts like a chemical match, and who could keep count of the similar cases of death that follow? An unfortunate man imagines he will throw himself under the wheels of a locomotive. The sudden inspiration of this new kind of suicide immediately awakens the desire of those who aspire to leave this life, and the imitators smear the wheels of this heavy machine with their blood."[97] Very often crime, like suicide, will be the result of this kind of contagious imitation. For a certain period of time, murders will be of the same kind and corpses will be mutilated in the same way. Imitation can even become an illness and induce certain individuals to continually imitate the acts they see.[98] Nervous diseases can be acquired by imitation. Natural somnambulism can be produced by reading the story of the somnambulist Caselli. Demonopathic epidemics, the Andous disease in Belgium, the possessions at the monasteries of Kérndrep, of Loudun, of Morzine – these are facts too well known for me to have to emphasize them.

To understand this behaviour, let us look to the conditions that seem to make it most likely to occur. These sudden and absurd impulses, these irresistible imitations will be more pronounced the greater the state of psychological weakness. "Is not one of the most extraordinary effects of drunkenness to make us give way to impulses which we had previously resisted?"[99] Moreau (de Tours) gives a curious example. An unfortunate man who wished to put an end to his life could not resolve to kill himself, yet when drunk was able to carry out his suicide.[100] Somnambulism, which can sometimes be considered as an inferior existence to that of the waking state, also presents us with examples of this kind. "An individual, a natural somnambulist, is struck by a number of verses he has read that end in '*ique*' and jokes about it. That evening he falls asleep, thinking no more about it. The next day, he wakes to find his notebook, in which he had written during the night, filled with 75 verses ending in '*ique*'[101]:

> *Oh! toi qui sais chanter sur ton luth poétique*
> *La gloire du prélat et la vertu civique,*
> *Permets, fils d'Apollon, que ma mure pudique*
> *Se revête pour toi de sa blanche tunique ...* etc."

Another patient, a hystero-epileptic, reproduces in her natural sleep all the sounds she has heard throughout the day.[102] Just as the unleashing of passions is complete during a dream,[103] just as an inclination, long dormant during the waking state, regains its power during the dreaming state,[104] so also weak impulses in one state can become all powerful in another. Three hysteric patients were in the same ward of the hospital and, as often happens, did not get along with each other. In their normal state, they each presented uniquely, but when they were in crisis, they copied each other so well that they shared the same delirium and pronounced exactly the same words. For at least one of the patients, whom I had seen in another room, her form of crisis and type of delirium, which she had not previously demonstrated, was a pure imitation. Hashish creates a similar disposition, "It produces in the will and in the instincts such laxity that we become the plaything of the most diverse impressions. By a word or a gesture our thoughts can be diverted to a host of topics."[105] Moreover, says Richet, "The intoxication of hashish resembles the hysterical state, there is the same exaggeration of feeling and the same impotence of will. All ideas are realized without us being able to stop them."[106]

As in catalepsy, the automatism of ideas is sometimes revealed, not only by their duration, but also by their associations. We see some acts explained by the involuntary connections between ideas. "We know the story of the poor young man from the house of Mailly, of whom his feudal lord speaks in his memoires. A sachet had been given to him by Mademoiselle de la Forge. Bewitched by the magical power of this sachet, he begged his family to consent to their marriage. Their refusal caused him the deepest despair and he resolved to drown himself. But he had scarcely taken off the sachet when the charm lost its hold over him and the coldest indifference replaced his former passion."[107] How many foolishnesses, how many crimes committed under some influence, occurring as the consequence of a fixed idea, could be explained in the same manner. One loses, as in the dream state, the power to direct one's thoughts. They develop in their own way, and one follows after the other, until the sequence is fully realized. In this case, the action seems all the more irresistible, because it does not come up against the other ideas present in consciousness, it develops from them naturally. Just as we are not surprised by our own dreams, hysterics and somnambulists are rarely surprised by their own absurd actions, because they do not have in mind any opposing images with which to compare them. This association of ideas still has, especially in these persons, a singular effect which it is necessary to understand. The association often operates by contrast, and the thought of one thing rapidly brings about the idea and then the realization of something absolutely contrary, "They want to laugh when they see crying, say inappropriate words while thinking modest thoughts, etc."[108] This association, in contrast to what we have already reported, exists in normal interaction, even before being observed in communication experiments. In a word, there is not a single characteristic of suggested acts that does not find its analogy in the natural conduct of these extremely suggestible individuals.

Let us now undertake the same study on the feelings and passions of these same enfeebled persons, always in the same states that we have described, when, either by disease or by hypnotizing processes, the field of their consciousness has been restricted and cannot simultaneously contain more than a number of images, which is less than it should typically be able to contain.

It is a commonplace observation that people of this kind are extraordinarily emotional and that, under the slightest pretense, they seem to experience, with an unheard-of violence, all the jolts of joy, sorrow, love, terror, etc. Examples of this excitability abound. It is enough to say in front of Lucie (awake or in first somnambulism) some absurd story of a crushed dog or a husband who beat his wife, and her expression will immediately change, and she will retire to a corner, crying uncontrollably. The joy of catching sight of me again upsets Léonie. For a few minutes there will be shaking, sobs, inarticulate screams – almost a nervous breakdown. It is with a veritable nervous crisis that all of Rose's emotions conclude. I once saw her have, for forty-eight hours, a series of almost uninterrupted crises, following a disappointment because someone she was waiting for had not come to see her.

What can we make of this suddenness and this violence of emotion? Let us first notice that the expression of emotion is, if I am not mistaken, much more violent than the emotion itself. These great upheavals of their whole being, if they have not actually brought on the crisis (because then the nature of the phenomena changes), can calm down as quickly as they were provoked. We must not seek to console hysterics as one would an ordinary person, talking to them about the purpose of their sorrow and showing them it is futility. No, for if we talk about the subject which caused them anger or despair, however we talk about it, we increase their cries and their tears. It is simply necessary, without any tactful transition, to abruptly change the subject. For a moment they are taken aback, they hesitate, and then, in a few seconds, give themselves completely to the new subject and laugh with gaiety, while still having tears in their eyes. Léonie had lost a child, a few years ago, under the saddest of circumstances, and it was, for the poor woman, a legitimate cause of grief. The most trivial incidents – a feeling of sympathy, a date, the black colour of a piece of paper – when she was in a state of somnambulism reminded her of her grief. There were tears and cries, followed by interminable contractures. These things did not occur when she was in a waking state. I tried at first to console her, but in vain. It was not until later on that I thought of a way to stop this sorrow. As soon as her face became sad and she began to shout, "Oh! my poor little girl," I immediately changed the subject to something pleasant, she laughed and it was over. Better still, if we get them to express what they are feeling, we then see that in reality they feel very little. One day, Lucie, who was a complete anesthetic and who did not even feel a severe burn, had a cut to her hand which caused a lot of bleeding. She screamed and shouted as if she were enduring a real martyrdom. I was a bit surprised, because at this stage she did not even feel a pin pressed into her hand, and I asked her if she really was in pain. "Well, … no, not exactly," she said, "but you see, I am bleeding. *I must be in a great deal of pain*; it is only natural that I scream ... ah! ..." I find this remark that she let slip very significant. She does not scream because she is really suffering (I think she felt nothing at that moment), but because she should be suffering. A more or less vague idea of suffering, perhaps a very weak hallucinatory image of an old pain, that was all there was below these loud cries and this despair.

In certain cases, it can be said that emotions are very real: the sorrow of Léonie in thinking of her child, and Lucie's terror during her crisis are true feelings. Agreed, but that does not mean that the expression of emotion still plays a large role, because I am willing to believe that the real emotion comes after the outward expression. An American psychologist whose name is well known, William James, has proposed a very seductive theory on the origin of emotions.[109] According to him, it is contrary to common sense to say, when we lose our fortune, we are sad and we cry. "This order is not correct, the second mental state is not immediately introduced by the first, the physical manifestations must be interposed between them. The rational order is that we feel sad because we cry, angry because we strike, etc." All our thoughts produce in us physical modifications, movements, changes to the circulation, to breathing, the condition of the skin, glands, bladder, etc. By a kind of shock, sensitivity brings to consciousness the awareness of these changes and we have an emotional reaction which is precisely the more or less confused sensation of all these changes. The author concluded that a person who was totally without sensation would not be aware of these organic changes and therefore would no longer experience emotions. He wrote to me about it when, in my early studies, I had reported Lucie as a total anesthetic. I told him that hysterics seemed to me a poor choice to verify this theory, first of all because their anesthesia was not very real,[110] secondly because they are indeed very emotional. It has since seemed to me that these observations were in fact more supportive of William James' theory, but in a different way than he had put forth. Emotion is not suppressed for the hysteric by her anesthesia; although she does not feel the changes in her skin, she sees her own movements and hears her own cries. But in her case it seems to be produced and maintained by the very exaggeration of the manifestations. Like those who make big movements and scream loudly to get angry, hysterics gesticulate a lot for the smallest things and react to their own grimaces. "Oh! Listen to how well I scream," Lucie might say. "I must be angry, so I am." Even in the case of real emotion, it is the power and nature of the physical manifestation, always determined by the same laws, that bring the force of emotion.

These few observations on the conduct of suggestible persons find their corroboration and confirmation in some fairly well-known and celebrated phenomena. It is now widely accepted that hysterics and people of a similar type lie continuously. Many have repeated this axiom, based on a few famous cases, without having sought to verify its accuracy. I am not trying to rehabilitate their reputation, but I think it is fair to say that they do not lie much more than ordinary people. Of approximately fifteen people that I studied, who certainly were not perfect, I have scarcely met one with whom the habit of lying was truly remarkable. When this characteristic is encountered, one must not be indignant, which would be perfectly out of place; it is better to try to explain it.

Many psychologists who reasoned more than they observed hold that veracity, the habit of loving and telling the truth, was natural to humanity, and was found consistently when the human mind was observed in all its primitive ingenuousness in children and in primitive peoples. I will not talk about primitive peoples, with whom I am unfamiliar, but I will point out that children, unless they are little prodigies, are far from being scrupulous tellers of the truth. They embellish their stories, and they know how to lie as soon as they know how to speak. Moreover, that fact seems to me quite natural and simple. The idea of truth is actually quite an abstract idea, the result of a series of complex judgments that we are not capable of making as children. I even believe that we have no clear understanding of truth and its importance until we become interested in the sciences. The spirit of truth and the scientific spirit are two analogous things, and one who does not have an interest in knowing the truth of things does not recognize the importance of being able to state how things are. Also, every simple, rudimentary mind, which makes few abstract connections, does not direct its speech by the abstract idea of truth, but by the dominant images in the mind. Thus, the mind of the hysteric, precisely because of the loss of many senses and the narrowing of the field of consciousness, is a rudimentary mind; she does not understand anything about science and cannot imagine that one could be interested in it; she says what comes to her mind without any other concerns. If one thinks of the hallucinatory character of all their ideas and the lack of control that characterizes their thinking, instead of being scandalized by their lies (that are otherwise very naïve), one should rather be surprised that so many of them are still such honest people.

One might make a similar remark about their conduct. Morality is no more a natural thing than is truth. It is not depreciating it to consider morality the most beautiful result of the work of human intelligence. The idea of good and the idea of duty are abstract connections, judgments, real discoveries. To conceive of them, it is necessary to bring together in the same thought a very large number of ideas which seem quite unrelated: the idea of the present act, its future consequences (even distant), the regard for others, their similarity to ourselves, their rights, etc. It is no wonder that an enfeebled mind, at a moment when it can only hold one image, cannot gather and compare all these ideas. If the actions of such a person are moral, it is because chance circumstances or habits of thought happily bring back into her mind images of honest or harmless actions. But the same chance may lead to images of dishonest actions, which will be carried out without meeting any obstacles. We are very surprised that some authors speak at every turn of moral responsibility and allow for its existence even in dreams. "Mr. Fodéré is of the opinion that a man who committed an immoral act during his sleep would not be entirely excusable ... He would merely have executed the actions which preoccupied his mind when he was awake."[111] Doubtless a waking thought is sometimes repeated in a dream; but, in the waking state, it is challenged by other simultaneous ideas; in the dream state, it is isolated and dominates. Has a person not done what he can by resisting as much as he can, exercising his will as much as he can? How can he be responsible for thoughts and actions that develop automatically? It is the same for suggestible individuals; they have no responsibility because they have no will. They are selfish, vain, jealous, for these are their principal vices, but they cannot be otherwise. The strength of their minds became sufficient to form the idea of personality and to direct conduct according to this idea, but it cannot rise beyond and give actions more general motives. Morality is like science: it requires complete minds. It is unsupportable for these impoverished intelligences in which the separate elements of thought are more alive than the whole.

3.8 Conclusion

The studies we have carried out recently on all these phenomena are so numerous and complicated that they have made us aware of a new form of psychological automatism. In some respects they are similar to the phenomena already studied in the preceding chapters, while in others, they differ considerably. Among the authors who in our time have studied the phenomenon of suggestion, there are some who, driven by the discussion, seem to have expanded the meaning of this word inordinately. For them, all action, all human thought which is determined and regular, seems to be suggestion. No doubt, they use this expression above all to make it clear that all these regular states, all these determined actions, are due above all to psychological factors and not to physical ones. In this they are completely correct, and they have helped to promote awareness of the importance which it ought to have in explaining the human person. But, once this is admitted, it is necessary to note that not all psychological phenomena are identical and that there is no advantage in replacing the old known words of memory, emotion, and association of ideas, by this new word "suggestion," as if all these phenomena had just been discovered. For us, suggestion means an automatism of a particular kind, that which gives rise to language, and in general, to perceptions. This automatism is in part analogous to the previous ones. Just as an emotion or a memory is constituted by a union of partial phenomena which have been aggregated or synthesized by consciousness in the past, in the same way the intelligence of language and of one perception in general are a complex set of phenomena, which have been once gathered at the moment when language was learned, or when perception was formed for the first time. This synthesis, once made (in this work we do not have to occupy ourselves with the activity which presided over its formation), is preserved; when one of its terms is presented, the total perception which has been initiated is completed, and the other images that constitute it follow. By laws which we do not need to revisit, these successive images form hallucinations, beliefs, and actions. This was already the case in the automatism of sensations and in that of memory. It is quite natural that this same characteristic is found in the automatism of perceptions.

Language can express anything. It can happen that, in its simplest form, suggestion leads to very simple actions, analogous to those which determine the simplest sensations. At its higher degrees, it brings about more complex changes, analogous to those which bring about the modifications of memory. But these suggestions can only have power because there was already an automatism of images and memories which they bring into play in a more complicated fashion.

In studying, in the preceding chapter, the automatism of memory, we had already encountered a new fact which seemed quite foreign to the automatic phenomena that we had described but which had come to intermingle there. It pertains to the judgments that the subject made from time to time about their own personal phenomena and about the states in which they found themselves. The phenomena – sensations, images, or memories – which filled their consciousness, were brought about automatically. But, from time to time, they were compared and synthesized into a new and complex idea, that of a new personality. This was the current unifying and synthesizing activity of consciousness, manifesting itself amidst the automatism of images and memories. This phenomenon took on a much greater significance in the study that we had recently conducted. When our subjects became capable of making many of these new syntheses, of coordinating and comparing a quantity of sensations and perceptions, they ceased to be suggestible. This teaches us that the automatism of perceptions, which is the foundation of suggestion, is the result of a past activity that continues to act in the same way, but is in opposition to the activity of the current thought. The more it develops, the more it is able to make new connections with the more numerous elements that are brought to consciousness, and the more the automatism is reduced. The more the psychological state was simple and the field of consciousness restricted, the more automatic activity manifested itself. We cannot push our study further in the direction we have followed up until now. By moving from the simplest conscious phenomena to the more complex, we have seen automatism decrease more and more. We must now move on to another point of view and see whether this regular and determined activity does not hide itself and exist in another form, when it seems to have disappeared from consciousness.

Notes

1 Paul Janet, *Les Suggestions Hypnotiques*. Rev. litt., 1884, II, 101.
2 *Lettre de Puységur* from the 8th of May 1784 for the Société de l'Harmonie presided over by Mesmer, reproduced in Aubin Gauthier, *Hist. du Somn.*, II, 251.
3 Deleuze, *Instruction Pratique sur le Magnet. Anim.*, 1853, p. 85 (the 1st ed. is from 1825).
4 *Ibid.*, 118.
5 On the *Abbé Faria*, see de la Tourette, *Hypnotisme*, 1887, 22.
6 Charpignon, *Physiologie du Magnétisme*, 1848, 374.
7 Dupotet, *Journal du Magnétisme*, 1849, 396.
8 *Journal du Magnétisme*, 1855, 541.
9 Bertrand, *Traité du Somnambulisme*, 1823, 323.

10 *Journal du Magnétisme*, 1850, 120, 207. See a discussion of the same kind with the title: *Opinion de M. Delatour sur l'action magnétique et sur celle de l'imagination*, in *l'Hermès*, 1826, p. 265.

11 Charpignon, *Op. cit.*, 361, 366 and *Journal du Magnétisme*, 1849, 550.

12 Cf. *Proceedings S. P. R.*, 1882, 338.

13 Cf. Richet, *Du Somnambulisme Provoqué, Journal d'Anatomie et de Physiologie of Robin*, 1875, 348.

14 *Journal du Magnétisme*, 1849, 66.

15 Taine, *Intelligence*, 3rd edition, 1878, II, 222.

16 Bernheim, *De la Suggestion*, 1886, 183.

17 Cf. Figure 1.3 in Chapter 1 of this volume.

18 Richer, *Hystéro-épilepsy*, 1885, 705.

19 Ribot, *Le Rôle des Mouvements, Revue Philosophique*, 1879, II, 380, and *Psych. de l'Attention, passim*.

20 Binet, *Sur les rapports entre l'Hémianopsie et la Mémoire Visuelle, Revue Philosophique*, 1888, II, 486.

21 Richer, *Op. cit.*, 707.

22 Bérillon, *La Dualité Cérébrale*, 1884, 109 ff.

23 *Ibid.*, 179.

24 Paulhan, *L'Association par Contraste. Revue Scientifique*, 1888, 263.

25 See similar reflections in regard to psychic polarization in a work by Bianchi and Sommer, *Revue Philosophique*, 1887, I, 148.

26 Cf. *Proceed. S. P. R.* 1882, 236.

27 Féré, *Sensation et Mouvement*, 75.

28 Bourru and Burot, *Variations de la Personnalité*, 1888, 145.

29 *Ibid.*, 130.

30 *Journal du Magnétisme*, 1849, 591.

31 Dr. Philips (Durand de Gros), *Cours de Braidisme*, 1860, 116.

32 1883, I, 225.

33 Richet, *L'Homme et l'Intelligence*, 1883, 233.

34 For a more complete treatment, see *The Production of Somnambulism by Suggestion*, in Volume 2, Chapter 4.

35 *Journal Magnétique*, 1849, 524. – Grellety, *Du Merveilleux, des Miracles et des Pèlerinages au point de vue Médical*, 1876, 38.

36 Ellis, *Aliénation Mentale*, 1840, 155.

37 Charpignon, *Physiologie du Magnétique*, 364.

38 *Journal de Magnétisme.*, 1852, 446.

39 Dr. Philips (Durand de Gros), *Revue Hypnotique*, I, 351.

40 Richet, *L'Homme et l'Intelligence*, 530.

41 Beaunis, *Revue Philosophique*, 1885, II, 116.

42 Bernheim, *Op. cit.*, 1886, 166.

43 *Ibid.*, 227.

44 Mesnet, *Automatism*, 1874, 16.

45 Mesnet, according to Gilles de la Tourette, *Op. cit.*, 239. – Cf. Taine, *Op. cit.*, II, 18.

46 Maury, *Le Sommeil et les Rêves*, 124, 128, 394. Joly, *Imagination*, 58, 120.

47 Cf. Volume 2, Chapter 1.

48 Moreau (de Tours), *Du Haschich*, 1845,156.

49 *Ibid.*, 93.

50 Cf. Richer, *Op. cit.*, 711.

51 Charcot, *Maladies du Système Nerveux*, 1887, III, 339.

52 Demarquay and Giraud-Teulon, *Recherches sur l'Hypnotisme*, 1860, 21.

53 Cf. Fontan and Ségard, *Médecine Suggestive*, 29, 192. – Ribot, *Maladie de la Volonté*, 1883, 137.

54 Fontan and Ségard, *ibid.*, 178. – Cullerre, *Magnétisme et Hypnotisme*, 1886, 268.
55 Binet and Féré, *Magnétisme Animal*, 1887, 73 and 214.
56 de la Tourette, *Op. cit.*, 375.
57 Cf. *Ibid*, 144.
58 Liébault, *Le sommeil et les États Analogues*, 1886, 350.
59 Dr. Philips (Durand de Gros), *Cours sur le Braidisme*, 1860, 97.
60 Bernheim, *Op. cit.*, 149.
61 *Ibid.*, 10. Cf. 71.
62 Azam, *Double Conscience*, 1887, 133, 135.
63 Jules Janet, *Hystérie et Somnambulism d'après la Théorie de la Double Personnalité*, *Revue Scientifique*, 1888, I, 616.
64 Binet and Féré, *Op. cit.*
65 Binet, *L'Intensité des Images Mentales*, *Revue Philosophique*, 1887, I, 473.
66 Cf. Revue Scientifique, 1875, I, 876.
67 Binet, *Op. cit.*, 1887, 475.
68 Cf. Souriau, *Sensations et Perceptions*, *Revue Philosophique*, 1883, II, 75.
69 Binet, *Op. cit.*, 1887, 476.
70 Cf. Volume 2, Chapter 2.
71 Richet, *L'Homme et l'Intelligence*, 236.
72 *Ibid.*, 529.
73 We reserve for Volume 2 everything that relates to latent or subconscious actions or acts of hearing.
74 See cf. Volume 2 Chapter2, the passage on elective sensibility.
75 Spencer, *Principes de Psychologie*, Trad., I, 419. – See Ribot, *Psychologie Anglaise*, 1875, 207.
76 See Rabier, *Leçons de Philosophie*, I. 227.
77 Dumont, *Théorie Scientifique de la Sensibilité*, 1875, 85, 87.
78 Ochorowicz, *Suggestion Mentale*, 1889, 502.
79 Spencer, *Op. cit.*, I, 645.
80 *Ibid.*, I, 426.
81 Chauvel, *Précis Théorique et Pratique de l'Examen de l'Oeil et de la Vision*, 1883, 69.
82 Wundt, *Eléments de Psychologie Physiologique*, Trad. [AC561], 1886, II, 231.
83 *Ibid.*, II, 241.
84 Binet and Féré, *Archives de Physiologie*, 1887, II, 373.
85 Richet, *L'Homme et L'Intelligence*, 512.
86 Cited by Perrier, *Journal du Magnétisme*, 1854, 69.
87 Fontan and Ségard, *Op. cit.*, 55.
88 Paul Janet, *Un Précurseur de Maine de Biran*, Revue Philosophique, 1882, II, 374.
89 Bain, *Les Sens et l'Intelligence*. Trans., 1874, 298.
90 Souriau, *Op. cit.*, 75.
91 Moreau (de Tours), *Psychologie Morbide*, 1859, 76.
92 Ball, *Maladies Mentales*, 1880, 519.
93 Ribot, *Maladies de la Volonté*, 1883, 111.
94 Taine, *Op. cit.*, II, 76. Cf. *Ibid.*, I, 89.
95 Hack Tuke, *Le Corps et L'Esprit*, 1886, 14.
96 Bertrand, *Op. cit.*, 87.
97 Legrand du Saulle, *La Folie devant les Tribunaux*, 1864, 537.
98 Cf. Saury, *Etude Clinique sur la Folie Héréditaire (les Dégénérés)*, 1886, 96. – Cullerre, *Op. cit.*, 253.
99 Moreau (de Tours), *Le Haschich.*, 137.
100 Id., *Psychologie Morbide*, 404.
101 *Le Révélateur du Magnétisme*, April, 1838.
102 *Journal du Magnétisme*, 1855, 487.

103 Maury, *Op. cit.*, 87.
104 Charma, *Du Sommeil*, 1852, 19.
105 Moreau (de Tours), *Le Haschich*, 1845, 66.
106 Richet, *L'Homme et l'Intelligence*, 124.
107 De Gasparin, *Les Tables Tournantes*, 1855, I, 427.
108 Liébault, *Op. cit.*, 235.
109 William James, *What is an Emotion*, from Mind, n° XXXIV.
110 See Volume 2, Chapter 2.
111 Georget, *Maladies Mentales*, 1827, 126.

Index

Taylor & Francis Group
an **informa** business

Taylor & Francis eBooks

www.taylorfrancis.com

A single destination for eBooks from Taylor & Francis
with increased functionality and an improved user
experience to meet the needs of our customers.

90,000+ eBooks of award-winning academic content in
Humanities, Social Science, Science, Technology, Engineering,
and Medical written by a global network of editors and authors.

TAYLOR & FRANCIS EBOOKS OFFERS:

A streamlined
experience for
our library
customers

A single point
of discovery
for all of our
eBook content

Improved
search and
discovery of
content at both
book and
chapter level

REQUEST A FREE TRIAL
support@taylorfrancis.com

Routledge
Taylor & Francis Group

CRC Press
Taylor & Francis Group

For Product Safety Concerns and Information please contact our EU
representative GPSR@taylorandfrancis.com
Taylor & Francis Verlag GmbH, Kaufingerstraße 24, 80331 München, Germany

www.ingramcontent.com/pod-product-compliance
Lightning Source LLC
Chambersburg PA
CBHW070343270326
41926CB00017B/3968